Praise for _Raising Expectations (An_

"_Raising Expectations_ is a breathtaking   MW01062466
of America in the twenty-first century. In the battles McAlevey recounts, hardly
anyone comes out standing tall. But her story, along with those of so many
brave health care workers, fills me with hope."

Barbara Ehrenreich

"This book renews my faith that organizing works. It calls for a new kind of
unionism and makes a compelling case for a new vision for the American labor
movement. In the whole-worker theory that McAlevey tested and retested
in real-life campaigns, all the issues negatively impacting the poor, working
and middle class become the cause of unions, not simply wages and narrowly
defined workplace conditions ... _Raising Expectations_ is so refreshing because
it aspires to tell us how we can rebuild a movement that can win."

Van Jones

"A veteran labor organizer whose tactics have earned her admiration—and
condemnation—McAlevey pulls no punches ... This memoir/manifesto ...
calls for putting the 'movement' back into the labor movement. McAlevey
argues that unions must make connections to communities and social justice
campaigns if they're going to renew themselves and transform the economy ...
McAlevey's prescription is right: raise expectations, and then raise some hell."

John Nichols, Progressive Honor Roll of 2012: Most Valuable Book, _Nation_

"The signal strength of Jane McAlevey's bracing, provocative, fantastic-read
of a book is that in the act of reading it you begin to feel the kick-ass power
that strong organizing can help create ... For union members (and those
aspiring to union membership), _Raising Expectations (and Raising Hell)_ does
just that: raises expectations of what good organizing can do, and what good
unions can be ... Many sections read as pithy how-to guides: what you need to
do a sticker-up; how to identify leaders in the workplace; what to do to keep
momentum going in a campaign. In reading this comprehensive and gripping
narrative of the blow-by-blow, you can imagine how tight the corners you are
forced into can become, and she gives you many escape routes."

Penny Lewis, _New Labor Forum_

"Jane McAlevey gives us an on-the-ground account of the obstacles the union
hierarchy throws in the path of a bold and energetic organizing effort that
scored a string of brilliant successes before the hierarchy cracked down. We
need to read this book and learn its lessons partly for what it tells us is wrong
about unions, but also because it demonstrates that good organizers can in
fact succeed. That message is heartening because the simple truth is that we
can't rebuild a democratic left in the United States without a revived labor
movement."

Frances Fox Piven

"This book is gripping, funny, sad, and very thought-provoking. Jane McAlevey uses her own experiences in a movement that has been undergoing dramatic changes within a workforce that has undergone even greater changes to suggest to the reader the necessity and potential for a transformation of the union movement into a real labor movement. Once I started reading it, there was no stopping."

Bill Fletcher Jr.

"This rousing memoir of McAlevey's decade-long experience as a union organizer spares neither the companies nor the union bosses … McAlevey is not afraid to name names, offering millionaire CEOs with government contacts their fair dose of scorn. But her strongest fury is with the union leadership who seem to thwart her at every turn. Politics and turf wars are a recurrent theme in this book, which result in the destruction of the health care workers union in Nevada and McAlevey's departure from union work. This is a passionate defense of her efforts and a plea for others to pick up the gauntlet for workers."

Publishers Weekly

"The most readable and fun account I know of what it means to build a militant and participatory labor movement, even if the account ends in double-dealing, disaster, and expulsion."

Dan Clawson, *Contemporary Sociology*

"Full of moxie, McAlevey names names and puts it to you straight. You'll cheer, you'll boo, you'll probably throw it out the window more than once, but you'll count to ten and pick up where you left off with a book that has something to teach everyone who thinks—and especially those who doubt—that meaningful, lasting change is indeed possible."

Season Butler, *CounterFire*

"A breath of fresh air for anyone who's longed to get a glimpse of what a labor movement with a pulse looks like."

Lucy Herschel, *Socialist Worker*

"*Raising Expectations* is both uplifting and depressing—a great encapsulation of the labor movement—told through the lens of McAlevey's experience as a labor organizer with the Service Employees International Union. McAlevey's personal story is indicative of the experience of many activists who become labor organizers."

Bennett Baumer, *Indypendent*

RAISING EXPECTATIONS (AND RAISING HELL)

My Decade Fighting for
the Labor Movement

Jane McAlevey with
Bob Ostertag

VERSO
London • New York

This book is dedicated to the thousands of working people with whom I worked, whose courage and sacrifice and hopes and fears are, in the end, the only reason this story matters.

This paperback edition first published by Verso 2014
First published by Verso 2012
© Jane McAlevey and Bob Ostertag 2012, 2014

Parts of Chapter 1 originally appeared in *New Labor Forum* 12(1): 2332, Spring 2003

5 7 9 10 8 6 4

Verso
UK: 6 Meard Street, London W1F 0EG
US: 20 Jay Street, Suite 1010, Brooklyn, NY 11201
www.versobooks.com

Verso is the imprint of New Left Books

ISBN-13: 978-1-78168-315-6
eISBN-13: 978-1-84467-922-5 (US)
eISBN-13: 978-1-78168-450-4 (UK)

British Library Cataloguing in Publication Data
A catalogue record for this book is available from the British Library

Library of Congress Has Cataloged the Hardback Edition as Follows:

McAlevey, Jane.
 Raising expectations (and raising hell) : my decade fighting for the
labor movement / by Jane McAlevey, Bob Ostertag. — 1st Edition.
    pages cm
 Includes index.
 ISBN 978-1-84467-885-3 (hardback : alk. paper) — ISBN (invalid)
978-1-84467-922-5 (ebook)
 1. Labor movement—United States—History—21st century. I.
Ostertag, Bob, 1957- II. Title.
 HD8072.5.M385 2012
 331.880973—dc23
                      2012033619

Typeset in Minion Pro by MJ&N Gavan, Truro, Cornwall
Printed in the US by Maple Press

Contents

Prologue: Florida, November 2000

The message hit my pager about midnight. I was watching the 2000 presidential election returns on my neighbor's TV. (I didn't own a TV; I hate those things.) The men with the weird toupees who feed television "news" to the nation had called Florida for Al Gore. Then for George Bush. That's when my pager went off.

> don't call DC, don't call headquarters, get next plane to Palm Beach airport. immediately. don't call us. rent car, go to Hilton.

I had never seen a page quite like that and don't believe I ever will again. I looked at the pager, then at the TV, where confounded anchors were stammering about Florida, then back at the pager. Then I put the pager down, picked up the phone, and booked the next flight to Palm Beach. Before the sun was up I was on my way.

The place I was leaving was Stamford, Connecticut, where I was running a pilot organizing project for the AFL-CIO. When you work as national staff for either the AFL-CIO or one of its member unions, you can expect to periodically get "pulled" from whatever merely urgent thing you are doing to some other thing that is actually dire. The practice can be overused by people buried in Washington offices who are convinced that everything on their desk is of utmost importance and who have forgotten how disruptive it is to real organizing of flesh-and-blood workers. But in this case, there wasn't anything more important anywhere; the presidential election was on the line.

The West Palm Beach Hilton was all hustle and bustle, jacked-up adrenaline, and frayed nerves. All the senior organizers from the AFL-CIO were converging on the place, which became the union command center in the battle for Florida. We were the Special Ops: people who knew how to hit the ground running, how to turn on a dime from one task to another, how to press the pedal to the metal and also how to wait—to "zig and zag," in organizer shop talk. The first person I saw there was Kirk Adams, head of the AFL-CIO National Organizing Department.

"Hey, McAlevey, no, I don't know the assignment yet, don't talk to me, I am too busy trying to figure it out, be ready to roll when I do."

Palm Beach County was the land of the butterfly ballot and the hanging chad. Butterfly ballots were punch card ballots with the candidates and issues displayed on both sides of a single line of numbered voting marks—an arrangement especially liable to misinterpretation by people with poor vision, such as the elderly. Hanging chads were tiny bits of paper that should have fallen out of the ballots when voters punched in their choice of candidate but hadn't, leaving a trail of ambiguity that could be used to obscure the intent of the voter. Thousands of ballots were being discounted or contested due to this rather archaic paper voting system.

Finally, our plan took shape. Each of the senior staff would be given a team of organizers and we would start knocking on doors and collecting affidavits from people who would swear under oath that they had meant to vote for Gore but, confused by the butterfly ballot, had accidentally voted for Bush or Pat Buchanan.* Other teams were dispatched to grocery stores, and some were sent to a candlelight "protest" vigil. I was given a team of organizers, an attorney or two, a van, and a stack of maps indicating our assigned condominium complexes, mostly inhabited by senior citizens, and we raced off to collect affidavits.

It was like shooting fish in a barrel. From the first complex we hit until we were pulled off the assignment a few days later, it was hard to

---

* Pat Buchanan was an ultraconservative third-party candidate running for president on the Reform Party ballot line. For years he had been widely accused of being an anti-Semite, which made it particularly painful for the county's elderly Jews to realize they had just inadvertently punched the button that corresponded to his name.

find an elderly voter who hadn't screwed up the ballot or didn't want to make a sworn statement. These places were full of funny, highly educated, cranky New York Jews. I was a New Yorker myself, with a partly Jewish upbringing,† and these people felt like home to me. I adored them. And they were really pissed off, especially the ones who thought they had accidentally voted for Pat Buchanan ("the SS guard," they called him). There were holocaust survivors, and sons and daughters of holocaust survivors. What's more, many of these folks had been union members in the Northeast before retiring. You would knock on their door and it was as if they had been sitting there impatiently wondering when the union would finally show up. Soon there were long lines in the community rooms, because we hadn't anticipated such an outpouring. These folks could hardly stand up, there were walkers all around, but no one was leaving until they'd all met the lawyer, told their stories, and filled in the affidavits. And they were ready to do much more than that. Affidavits? Lawyers? Hell, these people were furious.

I reported this every morning and evening at the debrief meetings for lead organizers. "So when can we actually mobilize them, put these wonderful angry senior citizens into the streets and on camera?" I would ask. But we didn't do anything of the sort. Instead, we did a candlelight vigil, which was an awful, badly organized affair, just the kind of event that makes me crazy. First, because it could have been huge, and second, because everyone who came was bored—a good recipe for how to get motivated, angry people to stay home the next time they get a flyer. But it got worse. Big-shot politicians from across the land were starting to show up, and they all came to the vigil to calm people down. It was a mind-blowing thing to watch. Were these guys idiots, did they want to lose, or what?

I heard someone from the press mention that Jesse Jackson was coming in two days to do his own rally and march. Hmm. Why hadn't we heard of that? Then, later that night, during the regular debriefing on legal updates on the recount and the next day's assignments, a higher-up said, "Jesse Jackson is coming to do a big march. We won't be participating in it."

---

† My father married several times. The woman he married when I was eleven was a Reform Jew, and I was raised with all-Jewish traditions from then until I was sixteen, when I left home.

I thought I had heard him wrong: "Um, sorry, can you repeat that?"

"The Gore campaign has made the decision that this is not the image they want. They don't want to protest. They don't want to rock the boat. They don't want to seem like they don't have faith in the legal system. And they definitely don't want to possibly alienate the Jews—you know, it's Jackson—so we are not mobilizing for it."

While my heart was sinking my head was exploding. The American electoral process is breaking up like the *Titanic* and we don't want to rock the boat?

"I'm sorry, something doesn't seem quite right here. As the person leading a field team in largely Jewish senior complexes, and, frankly, as someone raised by Jews, I can tell you that we need to take people into the streets. We need to let them express their anger. Republicans are starting to hold little rallies demanding that Democrats not be allowed to 'steal' the election. We need to either support this rally or do our own or both."

I also knew that to turn them out would require some resources, beginning with transportation from each condo complex. Most of these people didn't drive or didn't like to drive, which was why they lived in the condos, but that also meant they were generally home where we could find them. We had an instant mobilization in waiting; we could have 30,000 people in the streets in two days. I knew that the only outfit in Florida with the money, staff and experience to make this happen was organized labor.

What was on the table here was more than a rally. It was a question of what sort of power was going to be brought to bear on a defining national crisis. The Gore people not only wanted to project a nice image, they wanted to *be* nice. They wanted everyone to go home and hand everything over to something called "the legal process." This was ridiculous, because when and how and where this went to court was deeply political. Al Gore himself appeared to actually believe that if he could politely demonstrate that more Floridians had voted for him than for Bush, the "democratic system" would award him the election. Gore was right in the sense that he had won the state. There were other Democratic Party honchos who were not so naïve, but they lived in a world where you deal with these things behind closed doors. They were completely unprepared for the hypercharged political street theater exploding in Florida, and couldn't understand the difference between a narrowly conceived legal strategy and a mass mobilization direct action strategy. They thought there was no difference.

OK. That was the Democratic Party. We were organized labor. We didn't represent the candidate. We represented thousands of union workers whose votes were being stolen, and millions more who would suffer if the whole damn election was stolen. We knew how to mobilize and we had the resources to do it. We had the Florida voter lists. We had the computers. We had an army of smart people on the ground, ready to go. And we had a base of literally millions of really angry people. We could have had buses of senior citizens chasing Katherine Harris, Florida's secretary of state and the Bush campaign's hatchet woman, all over the state—a Seniors Truth Commission of lovely, smart, appealing, telegenic elders lined up with their walkers outside every single meeting Harris was in and camped outside her house at night while she slept. Don't Let the Republicans Steal Votes from Your Grandparents. All they needed was a top-notch lead organizer and an experienced field team, a lawyer, a communications team: in short, exactly the big support we had on hand. They could have operated 24/7, like in a strike. Unions know how to do strikes, don't they?

That moment, when we could have supported the Jesse Jackson rally and didn't, could have organized something big of our own and didn't, was the turning point, the moment when the Gore campaign and their unquestioning AFL-CIO cohort snatched defeat from the jaws of victory. And by the way, it wasn't like I was a big fan of the contemporary Jesse Jackson. But Jackson could turn people out and give a good speech—the same one he'd been giving for thirty years. The fact that our choice was between joining a rally led by Jesse Jackson and not doing anything at all was beyond pathetic.

Oh, well. All that was at stake was an endless war in Afghanistan, an unprovoked war on Iraq, American torture, warrantless wiretapping, eight years of doing nothing on global warming, not to mention a relentless class war against workers and their unions, all building up to a second Great Depression. No big deal.

The rally was the next day. We were *prohibited* from mobilizing or from showing up in any union identifiable clothing, and we were discouraged from attending at all. Only 2,000 people attended, which was not the momentum we needed (or could have generated). What made it even worse was that this was the *biggest* event in the entire debacle of what would always be referred to as "Bush v. Gore"—a legal dispute. All we were there to do was collect affidavits for lawyers. It was perhaps excusable that Gore's political team, mired in the limitations of electoral politics, would think like that. But I was with the *unions*. The working people who go toe-to-toe with the bosses using every tool in the shed: strikes, pickets, boycotts, blockades, sit-ins, workplace actions of all kinds, expressions of international solidarity, and more. A presidential election was being stolen. General strikes have been called for less.

Karl Rove and the Republicans were not nearly as naïve. They were bringing their people into the street in an escalating series of demonstrations. They actually understood what was happening. I remember vainly pointing this out at a nightly debrief, but was reminded, as I was reminded several times a day, that Gore "didn't want that image."

Meanwhile, our legal game plan was sputtering along. Enough affidavits and irregularities had been found to trigger what were called "manual one percent precinct tests" in Palm Beach and soon after in Broward counties. Elections officers would randomly pull a sample of one percent of the ballots. Teams from both the Democratic and Republican parties would review each ballot and challenge the vote if they felt there was evidence that the vote had not been counted as the voter intended. If the number of challenges crossed a certain threshold, the county would move to a full recount.

When it was announced that that Palm Beach County was going to a full recount, half of the labor organizers were sent to Broward County to replicate the affidavit operation we had honed in Palm Beach, and the other half was assigned to be at the Palm Beach tables actually recounting the votes in Palm Beach. I was among the latter.

Most of my colleagues on the first Democratic counting team felt as if they were right at the wellspring of history. But counting ballots by hand was the last thing I wanted to do. I wanted to mobilize the base. Naïvely, for a minute I'd actually believed that we, the national AFL-CIO, might break with the Democratic Party and run our own field operation in Florida. Once I realized how ridiculous that was, that our field operation would have to operate in a vacuum of Democratic Party strategy, and that counting was where the action was, counting I would go.

We arrived for the first day of counting in Palm Beach to a mob of TV cameras—filming a Republican rally. Angry white men, mostly, and some white women, with flags and placards that said "Gore is a Sore Loser" and "Don't Let Them Steal the Election." Their plan was to be as intimidating as possible to those of us walking in to begin the recount, and of course to grab media headlines on their message of Gore stealing the election. It was like walking the gauntlet of Operation Rescue, the violent anti-choice group that blocks entrances to family planning clinics and harasses the women trying to get in. This was high political theater.

"The whole world is watching" is of course a cliché, but for us it was a true one. We worked in teams: two counters and one observer to a team, two teams to a table. The Democratic counters sat opposite the Republicans, with the observers on either end. The allegedly neutral observer would hold up a ballot which we counters were prohibited from touching. We were supposed to call out "Gore" or "Bush" or "Neither." Otherwise, there was absolutely no talking in the room, and we had to maintain poker faces.

During the breaks, I tried to size up the opposition. The Bush counters were overwhelmingly young white men with crew cuts. I am blue-eyed and blond, and a crowd of white people is not something that *automatically* gives me the creeps, but these guys did. The word that came to mind was *Aryan*. In my mind I was in a world war; these were the friggin' Nazis. Our side was quite the opposite. New Labor was as much a rainbow then as it is today. On the AFL-CIO's Democratic team, people who looked like me were a minority.

We didn't get to talk until lunchtime. Back at the counting tables, as we waited for someone to bring more ballots, out of the blue the Aryan across from me whipped out a camera and aimed it at me. Didn't say a word, just snapped my photo. It took me a minute to realize that the Republicans had had a lunch meeting, too. This picture taking must have been the upshot, because a bunch of them now had small cameras, and when they thought no officials were looking they'd whip them out and start snapping close-ups of us.

At the end of the day—one of those days when you hardly breathe, when you thank God that at some point your body will just take over for you and breathe on its own—the same young Aryan came up to me just outside the counting room and started laughing and pointing with his friends, and taking more photos. I left as quickly as I could for the evening debriefing. Somewhere in the blur of events that night we heard that Broward County was close to winning a manual recount, too. We thought Miami-Dade still had a long way to go.

The next day the Republican Operation Rescue-esque crowd in front of the counting facility was even bigger. I kept pointing this out to my higher-ups, but really I had given in to the fact that all we were going to do was count ballots, and thus ultimately we would lose. The whole carnival was surreal enough, but knowing this in my bones added a ghostly sheen to it.

As we walked in to take our seats for day two of the count, I saw the same gaggle of Aryan boys. They were staring, trying to be intimidating, but I ignored them. When I sat down, one at the table behind mine called for my attention, and when I turned he snapped a close-up of my face. I shot my hand up to get the attention of the Democratic floor leader and said, "This guy needs to stop taking pictures." But then I stopped protesting. Clearly, the crew-cut gang would do anything they could think of to stop or slow the counting. We thought Gore had actually won, so we wanted to continue, and they didn't. This room was the only place in the nation where votes were being hand-counted, and in every stack of ballots, Gore was winning. We knew it, and our opponents knew it.

After the lunch break, I noticed that each of the Aryans had a book sticking out of his back pocket. I strained to catch the title: *The Christian Militant's Bible*. That night I began to freak out about the whole thing—the stupid Democratic Party, the stupid AFL-CIO, the Aryan cult, the whole package. I was feeling very alone and needed to talk. I called my dear friend Valerie and her boyfriend up in New York City. When I mentioned the Aryans and their weird Bibles, they said James Ridgeway at the *Village Voice* wrote a lot about the religious Right and promised to get me hooked up with him the next day.

Next, Broward County hit the magic number in the one-percent precinct test, triggering a full recount there too. Miami-Dade County was beginning to look like recount number three. Shit was starting to fly in Florida; it was increasingly obvious that Al Gore had actually won the state, although no one was saying this in public. You knew it if you were on the counting teams, going to evening debrief and reviewing everything you could remember from every hanging chad you had examined that day. The Republicans clearly understood that if enough ballots were recounted in Florida, Al Gore would be president. We were about one week into counting and two weeks past the election. We'd just had the "no one is going home for Thanksgiving" meeting. Tensions were definitely rising.

Meanwhile, the Republicans were executing all the plays the Democrats should have used. They had rallies every day in Palm Beach, Broward and Miami-Dade, angry marches demanding that the "Gore-Loser" team stop trying to "steal the elections." They had a message, they stayed on it, and they were driving it.

The next morning, James Ridgeway called to inform me that the Christian Militants were indeed a right-wing cult, a sort of softer version of the Aryan Nation. Great. I headed for the recount. Security was super tight. All the counters had to wear security badges and wait in a holding area until allegedly neutral staff were at their stations on the floor and the cops opened the sealed counting room. Just before they let us in, the Christian Militant who had been taking all the pictures of me got right in my face and said, "We know who you are. You have a horse and your father is retired and lives in upstate New York. Can't wait to photograph you today." You have to remember that this was 2000, that Timothy McVeigh had blown up the Oklahoma Federal Building just five years before. I was rattled, but I put it out of my head and walked to my table.

With Broward and Palm Beach in full recount,‡ our sights were fixed on Miami-Dade County, where, our evening debriefs told us, a one-percent precinct test would soon begin. The Democrats and Republicans were supposed to each assign a team of two counters to the decisive one-percent precinct test in Miami-Dade. That night I got a call from Joe Alvarez, a Cuban American in the top echelon of the AFL-CIO.

"Jane, we have decided to make you one of our counters for the one percent precinct test in Miami-Dade. Hey, Jane, fucking win it. Check out of your hotel in Palm Beach, get in your car, there's a room at a hotel in Miami for you. Get there tomorrow and take everything. You are not coming back to Palm Beach, you are going to Miami with me and we are going to win."

When I got to Miami that night, I felt like I was on steroids. I sat up in the hotel alone, knowing I needed a good night's sleep and wasn't going to get it. I turned on the TV and immediately got sick of watching news.

‡ The counting was on-again-off-again-on-again, and so on. It's impossible to list all the stops and starts. There were many.

Gladiator was on the pay-per-view movie channel. I watched it. I even watched it a few more times while I was stuck in Miami. To this day, *Gladiator* is the only blood-and-guts action movie I have ever seen.

In the morning we traveled in a van with darkened windows. We turned the corner to the courthouse and there were more TV cameras, more cops and security, and more sheer chaos than I had ever seen. But there was total silence in the counting room, under a bank of who knows how many TV cameras. It felt like those famous chess tournaments with one little table in a big room, a tense silence, and a crowd behind red ropes staring at your every twitch. We won the one-percent precinct count test.

The Republicans had clearly never considered counting ballots the be-all and end-all of their strategy, and now they launched the blitzkrieg they had prepared. They were staging actions across Florida, driving the same, well-honed message about the "Gore-Loser ticket stealing the election." I was spending the first day of the count as a Democratic floor team leader.

As we returned from lunch, the Republicans suddenly launched their coup de grâce. We heard loud shouting and noises outside the counting room, and then a bunch of guys rampaged in, throwing tables and chairs, making it impossible to continue. Counting was indefinitely suspended. The media could talk of nothing but the "chaos" in Florida. The US Supreme Court stepped in and took the case out of the hands of the Florida court.

The Gore people were flipping out because, guess what, they hadn't planned it this way. They'd imagined they were involved in a civilized legal proceeding, that they were going to "win the case" methodically by recounting the votes, that the law was going to keep the matter local, away from the Supreme Court where things didn't look so good. But oh wait, the Republicans have this whole direct action thing, working in perfect sync with their legal action.

I got another call; I can't even remember who it was.

"Hey Jane, you get to do what you wanted to all along! We need a *big* rally in Miami *fast,* because this legal thing isn't working."

"Um, you can't actually make a big rally happen now. We blew it. Mass mobilizations can't be turned on and off like that. When we landed in Florida, we could have done it, raised people's expectations that we could win, built the momentum, the whole bit. Not now, it's too late, the right wing has the momentum."

And then, the only coup in the history of the United States was complete.

Once you have been organizing for enough years, and seen enough efforts succeed and fail, you realize that there are "movement moments." These happen when large numbers of people are willing to drop what they are doing, forget that the utility bill won't be paid on time or that they will miss their favorite TV shows or their daughter's soccer games or their gym session or whatever, forget about how many hours of sleep they think they need every night, and go do some stuff they would never have imagined they could, like facing down cops or bosses or Aryan Republicans carrying *The Christian Militant's Bible*, or talking to TV cameras, or approaching total strangers about their concerns, or rounding up their neighbors to go to an event with something real at stake instead of the weekly bridge game. People get in this unusual state either because they are truly pissed off and there is no other option, or because for some reason the horizon of what they think they are capable of achieving suddenly expands—or, most likely, a combination of both.

Florida in early November 2000 was a such a moment: People were willing to leave their daily grind and step into history to defend their democracy, on a scale that could be called massive without exaggeration. And what a wonderful and unlikely crazy quilt of people they were.

But movement moments don't last forever, and it is much easier to snuff them out than to keep them lit. Everything depends on optimism: the optimism organizers call "raised expectations." And one key to keeping expectations raised is to respect the passions and desires of people who are not full-time organizers and political junkies, who have complicated and overwhelming lives they are trying to hold together, full of obligations they are putting aside for a moment for the sake of a collective goal.

The Democratic Party and the AFL-CIO leadership smothered the movement moment in Florida, snuffed it right out. The state was Gore's to lose, and the absolute determination with which the labor elite and the Democratic Party leadership crushed their own constituents' desire to express their political passions cost us the election.

Introduction: Organizing Is About Raising Expectations

Raising Expectations. Who in the world would give such a name to a book? An organizer, that's who. At its core, this is a book about organizing. And organizing, at its core, is about raising expectations: about what people should expect from their jobs; the quality of life they should aspire to; how they ought to be treated when they are old; and what they should be able to offer their children. About what they have a right to expect from their employer, their government, their community, and their union. Expectations about what they themselves are capable of, about the power they could exercise if they worked together, and what they might use that collective power to accomplish. Ultimately, expectations about where they will find meaning in their lives, and the kinds of relationships they can build with those around them.

Of course, there is much more to organizing, but everything else flows from raising expectations. In the normal course of human events, workers don't expect much from their jobs, government, or unions, because the reality is they don't *get* much. The job of the organizer is to fundamentally change this.

So first and foremost, this book is about organizing. Why? Because if there is any one message I hope to convey, it is that present-day American service workers can militantly confront corporations and government and win. I have seen it with my own eyes, contributed to it with my own hands, and felt it in my own bones. Yes, it is true that unions have been knocked back on their heels and nearly out of the ring as the United

States has got rid of the unionized jobs of the industrial era and transitioned into a globalized hi-tech service and finance economy. But this is why the story that fills this book is worth telling, because the organizing I have been involved in for the last ten years has *won*. As a result, there are thousands of workers who now expect to have a greater say in what goes on at their workplace, expect their jobs to be more productive and effective, and anticipate a better quality of life when they are old and that they will have more money for their children's education. Their relationship with their coworkers has become richer, they feel less intimidated by their superiors, and when they face a collective problem they have a realistic chance of finding a collective solution.

By organizing I mean something very particular, for which I have no simple shorthand description. One could look at this entire book as an explanation of what organizing means to me and how this differs from other activities that commonly go under the same name. I call it whole-worker organizing. The good news is that whole-worker organizing is all about methods that must be applied systematically, and that effective ways to do this can be taught. Whole-worker organizing is not mysterious or magical. It's not rocket science. But it's not an inborn talent, either. It is a skill set that can be studied and practiced like any other. As with any other skill, some people will have an instinctive flair for it. But there are plenty of others who could do it well if they were trained and given the opportunity to put their knowledge into practice.

This brings us to the second theme of the book: the incessant turf wars in which labor leaders engage on the upper floors of the house of labor that consistently undermine the organizing done on the ground floor. These internecine struggles have everything to do with the power and ambition of particular leaders, and nothing to do with strategies that actually work. They demonstrate total disrespect for the efforts and desires of the workers these squabbling leaders supposedly represent. You will see this dynamic unfold again and again throughout this book. It forms a background noise that is sometimes a dull roar and sometimes a deafening din, but is always present. A turf war was literally the first thing I encountered when I signed up with the labor movement and the organizing project I had been recruited to direct was nearly shut down before it even began. Ten years later, another turf war drove me out of a local that I had helped build into one of the most successful in the nation.

Whole-worker organizing begins with the recognition that real people do not live two separate lives, one beginning when they arrive at work and punch the clock and another when they punch out at the end of their shift. The pressing concerns that bear down on them every day are not divided into two neat piles, only one of which is of concern to unions. At the end of each shift workers go home, through streets that are sometimes violent, past their kids' crumbling schools, to their often substandard housing, where the tap water is likely unsafe.

Whole-worker organizing seeks to engage "whole workers" in the betterment of their lives. To keep them consistently acting in their self interest, while constantly expanding their vision of who that self interest includes, from their immediate peers in their unit, to their shift, their workplace, their street, their kids' school, their community, their watershed, their nation and their world.

Whole-worker organizing is always a face-to-face endeavor, with no intermediary shortcuts: no email, no social networking, no tweeting. It's not negotiated deals between national unions and giant corporations, and it is certainly not workers waking up one day to find themselves dealt into a thing called a union that sends them glossy mailers telling them how to vote.

Whole-worker organizing is a continuous process. Unions and other social movement organizations are always fascinated by the power of organized religion, a power they often try to "borrow" through mostly opportunistic alliances with religious leaders. They mistakenly think that the reason people show up at a place of worship week after week to donate their hard-earned money is because of their religious faith. But the reason that regular participation in organized religion strengthens their faith is that it offers a structure in which they can deal with all their tangled and complicated concerns, continuously, year in and year out. Because of this, organized religion raises their expectation of what kind of life they can aspire to.

The fragmented organizational turf of social justice movements is the opposite. Each organization addresses its own set of concerns and no others. At the most pragmatic level, this ignores the rather obvious fact that real people don't actually have time to go to a union meeting, an environmental issues meeting, a community meeting, and a school meeting; attend their church or temple or synagogue; go to work; and take care of themselves and their families. But even if there were magical people whose time expanded like a balloon to accommodate all the meetings of all the organizations dealing with issues that touched their lives, the fragmented structure of their efforts would not add up to any real collective power. Not to mention that spending so much time in meetings would drive them crazy.

Whole-worker organizing contrasts sharply with the more common approach known as labor-community alliance building. The term itself reinforces the idea that shop floor issues of wages and working conditions are the proper domain of unions and that when unions move beyond this narrowly defined terrain they are in the foreign land of "community," where they must exercise a sort of diplomacy. It is not an overstatement to assert that when unions buy into this labor/community dichotomy it is the end of organized labor as a progressive force. The point is not to build an alliance between "labor" and "community" but to bring community organizing techniques right into the shop floor while moving labor organizing techniques out into the community. We actually developed methods for doing this, beginning with a power structure analysis that enables workers to systematically pool their knowledge of their communities and integrate this knowledge with conventional research done by union professionals. The power structure analysis gives workers a map of the resources available to them and of the weak points in the power structure where their resources could be most effectively applied. This technique became the basis for a cycle of expanding returns: new skills and understandings spread broadly among our members, leading to meaningful victories that deepened the ties among our members and between them and others in their communities—which fed back into yet more skills and understanding, eventually enabling the workers to challenge the political and economic power structure that dominated their lives.

These ideas are similar to what is sometimes referred to as social movement unionism, and there are journalists and scholars who advocate social movement unionism who have written up some of the work described in this book as case studies of what they are talking about.* I

---

* Some of these include: Dan Clawson, The *Next Upsurge: Labor and the New Social Movements*, ILR Press, 2003; Janice Fine, "Building Community Unions," *The Nation*, December 14, 2000; Robin Finn, "Public Lives; In 15 Mug Shots, a Model

have no problem with "social movement unionism," but those of us who actually did this work prefer "whole-worker organizing." Our term puts organizing at the core, and names the workers as the ones deciding when and where to take on "non-workplace issues," instead of some community liaison staffer from a union or union front group.

M ost of labor's leaders believe that the kind of deep organizing I am talking about is not a viable option in the United States today; they cling instead to whatever shred of power they retain from the organizing work done by generations before them. Deep organizing, they say, requires too many resources and too much time in an era of union decline and instant electronic communications, and it can't win you anything meaningful anyway, given the weakened power of American workers in the age of global outsourcing. They argue that workers must compensate for the economic power they have lost in the workplace by building political power through electoral politics, and electoral power comes from broad rather than deep organizing. What labor must do now, these leaders conclude, is not organize but grow—rope in as many new members as possible, as fast as possible, so that these same leaders can be the brokers for their expanded base in political campaigns. Not deep organizing but shallow mobilizing.

The most immediate problem with the shallow approach is that workers who are grown instead of organized have only the most tenuous relationship with their union. The political endorsements their unions give to candidates or ballot initiatives mean little more to them than the endorsements of their bosses or Fox News. And even in cases where grown workers do propel a candidate into office, what then? Workers who are not deeply organized have little leverage once the candidates they helped elect are deluged by lobbyists from corporate interests that actually *are* highly organized, and even less power to create a political environment in which the few politicians who are principled enough to take on corporate power would have the political room to do so.

of Disobedience," *The New York Times*. November 9, 2000; Dan Hosang, "All the Issues in Workers' Lives: Labor Confronts Race in Stamford," *Colorlines,* Summer, 2000; Jane McAlevey, "It Takes a Community: Organizing Unions from the Outside In," *New Labor Forum*, Spring 2003.

For the past decade, the most prominent exponent of "growth, not organizing" was Andy Stern, the national president of the Service Employees International Union (SEIU), the union I worked for during much of the period covered in this book. In 2010 Stern stepped down, and his long-time protégé Mary Kay Henry took his place. I would like to present the stories in this book as Exhibit A in the case against Stern, SEIU, and the "shallow mobilizing" vision for American labor that they have come to personify.

One of the many ironies in this story is that unions did train many exceptionally skilled organizers during my ten years in the labor movement. Unions invested truckloads of money in developing these organizers. The AFL-CIO even created a new National Organizing Department. What happened? The answer leads us right back to the two main themes of this book.

Many of the newly trained organizers were not committed to deep organizing. They were ordered to take shortcuts of all kinds, because organizing is too slow—a refrain they heard often from Tom Woodruff, the organizing czar at SEIU and, later, Change to Win. Often a national union would send a team of talented and trained young organizers to help a group of workers win the vote to form a union, then put them on planes to another election the next day. Meanwhile, the new union members, full of raised expectations about the changes their hard-won union would bring to their lives, would show up at their first meeting and ask, "Wow, where did everyone go?" This practice of "air dropping" organizers in for intense, time-limited campaigns is the very opposite of deep organizing.

Even when a few organizers are left behind, they are often the least impressive, the ones the national union doesn't trust to handle an organizing drive. A cycle of diminishing returns begins. There is a tremendous drop in energy, turnout diminishes at each successive meeting, and the organization that took so much effort to build begins to crumble. All of this happens during the crucial period when the new union is negotiating its first contract with the boss. The contract, if it is won at all (often the whole effort collapses without even one contract) is disappointing, and the last wisps of the energy charged by the organizing drive evaporate. To the workers, the union becomes nothing more than the contract, and the contract is only engaged when a worker files a grievance. The union becomes an insurance plan, like car insurance, to which workers pay dues "in case you need it." Staff talk to workers like Geico claims adjustors after an accident.

The workers lose their organization, and the national unions lose their organizers. There are only so many times those energized, idealistic young people can watch their hard work go down the drain before they are outta there. If they came from the rank and file, they return to their old jobs. If they arrived at organizing from college, they move on to some other kind of social justice work. At best, they stay in the labor movement, but often shift from organizing to policy or research or politics. In all cases, when they leave, all the precious organizing skills that the union taught them and the workers need so desperately leave with them.

The few organizers who do make it through this stage eventually find themselves caught up in some ugly turf war between rival union leaders, and this drives them out of labor with an even more bitter taste in their mouths than those who departed in the slowly unwinding cycle of diminishing returns. That cycle moves at a snail's pace compared to the damage done by leadership turf wars, which can wreck years of work in just a few weeks or months. Organizers see all their gains vanish before their very eyes, and they have only the vaguest idea of what issues triggered the destruction, an imposed ignorance labor leaders justify with the tired old song about not wanting to air their dirty laundry in public.

Another theme that runs through this story is the pervasive sexism among the men who are most in control of the resources in unions today. It plays out in ways that go far beyond obvious issues, such as the lack of women in leadership positions. In fact, there were more women leaders at the end of my decade in labor than when I began, but the culture hasn't caught up to those numbers. And during those ten years I constantly confronted hostility from men who sensed that I was not willing to play the games with them that their male prerogative had led them to expect. I experienced straight-up sexual harassment too, both emotional and physical. And there was also hostility from women who had been around for a long time and survived even worse sexist behavior, and who took my unwillingness to tolerate what they had put up with as an affront, a threat, or both.

The sexism in labor was and is so constant and pervasive that if I discussed every instance when it had a negative impact on the work I was trying to do, there would be no room to talk about anything else. And I want to write a book about organizing and how American workers can win, not about sexism. So I try not to dwell on it. But it is there, every day.

This book is about organizing, not about me, but the story that follows will make more sense if I describe how I came to work with unions. The people who generously gave me their time and wisdom during the writing were unanimous in their opinion that my first draft suffered because I'd begun the story at the point where I entered the labor movement with a developed set of ideas on organizing often at odds with "the way things are done in labor," but with no back story about where these ideas had come from. They convinced me that a brief synopsis of the experiences that have shaped my understanding of organizing and of power—what power is, where it comes from, how to accumulate it and how to tear it down—will be useful to the reader.

"Didn't your mother ever teach you any manners?" I have never had any problem challenging powerful people, and so probably I have heard this question more often than most. The simple answer is no. My mother died of breast cancer when I was very young. My father, a busy local politician, was left a widower with seven children. I was the youngest, and his only day care option was to cart me around with him from one political meeting to another. He tucked me under his desk with crayons and coloring paper during heated negotiations, kept me at his side during rallies, and used photographs of the two of us on his campaign posters. He would campaign in front of grocery stores with me in a grocery cart. This put me at adult height, so I could catch people's attention, hand out flyers and ask them to vote for Dad. And there was the side benefit that he wouldn't lose me.

To keep me busy when he couldn't keep me with him, my father got me a pony, and I began my life-long love affair with horses. The area where our family lived was still rural enough that a horse and a place to put it were within the means of the working class.

My family has had a long history in labor, and my father was very clear that "union" and "workers" and "America" all belonged in the same sentence. My great-great-grandfather was a founding member of the carpenters union. My great uncle was a leader in the Brooklyn building trades before and during World War II. The International Boilermakers Union helped my father's family make it through the Great Depression. Patty Campbell, the leader of the United Brotherhood of Carpenters in the region at that time, was close to my father, and a key political supporter. During contentious electoral campaigns, I was cared for so well by the "brothers" at the carpenter's union hall that to me they actually were my brothers.

When I was five years old there was a big United Auto Workers strike at the Ford plant in Mahwah, New Jersey. My father was Supervisor in Ramapo, New York. Mahwah was just over the state line from Ramapo, but many of the strikers lived in my father's voting districts, and he actually put a lot of them on his payroll so that they could get health insurance during the long strike. I remember accompanying him to picket lines and hearing him announce that he would help the strikers "hold out for what they deserved." A little later on, there was another strike at a nearby pharmaceutical plant, the Lederle strike (a division of American Cynamid). I remember him coming home all excited because he had just ordered the police to withdraw from the strike and told the company that hell would freeze over before he would let "my cops, paid by the good hardworking men and women of this county, guard a thug company."

The culmination of his political career was a program he called Controlled Growth, which became the forerunner for what is today referred to as Smart Growth. Controlled Growth was a comprehensive land use policy that halted development in open or green space, preserved family farms, and forced developers to pay for building infrastructure (including public schools) that would be needed as their sprawl began to gobble up the environs of New York City. The plan infuriated the developers, who were just as powerful back then as they were in Stamford, Connecticut, where I dug into my first union work, and in greater Las Vegas, where I spent my last four years in the labor movement. Both Stamford and Las Vegas were experiencing rampant development, and were run by Democratic Party politicians who claimed that either government workers could get paid a living wage *or* needed social services could be expanded, but not both. But where I grew up, Democrats challenged big developers to pay for their fair share of growth instead of putting the entire burden on the backs of workers. And when the developers fought back, the politicians stood their ground and won.

To ensure that the effect of a zoning code that favored open space would not diminish the ability of the less affluent to move to the county, the Controlled Growth scheme included plans for building thousands of units of affordable housing. Substantial money was needed for this, and my father took his planning team to Washington and came home with a commitment of federal funds for one of the first public housing projects in Rockland County. This immediately became a flash point in the politics of what was until then an almost entirely white county, where many read "affordable housing" as code for "moving the blacks to the suburbs." What ensued was not pretty. I remember being threatened by classmates whose parents had told them to beat me up. (Finally, one day on the school bus a boy "called me out" over this issue and I kicked his ass with helpful coaching from my big brothers.) It was my father's deep commitment to unions that enabled him to fight a battle that would have driven many politicians from office, and he made sure that the public housing was built entirely by union labor.

I couldn't have articulated any of them at the time, but looking back now I see that these experiences were formative. Ultimately, this was where I got my ideas about what a union is and what it means to be antiracist. It's where I learned that the truly poor deserve the dignity of housing in a nice neighborhood, that actions matter, that corporations should pay their fair share, that bucking the Democratic Party power structure is no big deal, that unions and environmentalists can work together and win, and that progressive social change cannot be made without a leadership ready to take risks.

In junior high and high school I helped organize student protests and walkouts over issues ranging from nuclear power plant construction to the reinstatement of the draft to simple issues of personal dignity—such as the dehumanizing effect on overweight kids of our high school's draconian gym requirements (we overturned the policy).

But by the time I came of age, the labor movement I'd grown up with was nowhere to be seen, and what I found in its place was just awful. The building trades supported nuclear power and opposed every environmental principle I believed in, and the American Institute for Free Labor Development (the international institute of the AFL-CIO) was implicated in supporting Latin American death squads who killed *real* trade unionists.

At the State University of New York at Buffalo, I couldn't figure out why the conservative fraternity kids, pre-law students and jocks had control of all of our student fee money (and did nothing but throw parties). I put together a slate of radicals to challenge these traditional holders of the student government purse, and to the disbelief of just about everyone our slate won every seat in student government by a blowout margin. Suddenly I had a full-time secretary and a small government to run with an annual budget of $10 million. We could send buses to political rallies in DC and Albany, bring speakers to campus, and spread the word on why voting against Ronald Reagan (then running for his second term) was in our interest as students.

I was being mentored and tutored at every step by smart young organizers from the Student Association of the State University of New York (SASU). SASU was legally a nonprofit student-run organization based in Albany, but we thought of it and referred to it as a student *union*. It had been created in the 1970s, along with similar organizations in many other states, as a vehicle for acting independently of, and ideally being an influence on, student governments, which were often conservative. Each campus had to vote whether to affiliate or not, and if the vote was yes, then the campus paid dues to SASU. These dues referendums were opposed by Reagan-reinspired groups like the Young Americans for Freedom who occasionally beat the self-taxation student fee system. SASU's annual budget was well over $1 million dollars by the time I came along, which paid for a full-time organizing staff (the people who had been mentoring me) to run campaigns on tuition rates and larger social issues.

I was soon elected president of SASU and settled into the student seat on the SUNY Board of Trustees. This gave me access to key information needed by the unions that bargained with the sixty-four–campus system. Although I never violated confidentiality laws, I did figure out how to let union leaders know what was going on at the top level of management. SASU also worked with labor unions on issues in the state capital, and this was when I got my first experience of working with real unions on my own, as a young woman no longer under my father's wing.

SASU sent me to a five-day intensive training program at the Midwest Academy of Organizing, which had a big impact on me and my fellow trainees. We decided to create a condensed version of the program that could be completed in a long weekend, and use it to teach large numbers of college students about the fundamentals of power, strategy and tactics. We raised the money from progressive foundations (my first foray into that terrain), and soon I was a trainer in a national student organizer program.

I moved to Colorado, chasing a boyfriend, and in the fall of 1986 we helped organize a protest against CIA recruitment on the Boulder campus, during which 1,200 students were arrested. We then set out together for Guatemala, to learn Spanish for a few months before traveling through the rest of Central America, where we ended up working on a construction brigade in Nicaragua, at the height of the Contra War.

After a year, I returned to the United States and went to Vermont to learn organic farming. This was the real beginning of my environmental work, and soon I was off to California to work out of David Brower's Earth Island Institute on a project aimed at educating the environmental movement about the devastating impact of US policy in Central America. The project became formally known as the Environmental Project on Central America (EPOCA), one of several organizations being nurtured by that risk-taking powerhouse Brower. (The others included the Rainforest Action Network, the International Rivers Network, the Marine Mammal project, and the *Earth Island Journal*.) We were all incubating a more radical approach to the conservation movement, one that did not shy away from attacking multinational corporations and the international lending and financial institutions that undergirded an unsustainable model of the economy world wide.

In 1989, we organized a large conference to showcase the impressive work being done in Nicaragua's national park system under the Sandinista government. The national parks director, Lorenzo Cardenal, was just twenty-eight years old and was using his post to blaze a new path for environmentalism in Central America, arguing that to conserve Central America's vast tropical resources, governments must address the economic crisis that was driving the campesinos into slash-and-burn agriculture. We wanted to be sure that the conference reached beyond the usual confines of the self-identified environmental movement in the United States. I began to chat with the National Toxics Campaign, the Southwest Organizing Project, and the Highlander Research and Education Center (more commonly known as the Highlander Center) in Tennessee. We assembled a diverse delegation of poor people and people of color who were fighting toxic contamination in their own communities, issues their Central American counterparts were almost completely unaware of. By the time we got to the conference in Nicaragua, I knew I wanted to be working with the environmental justice movement in the US.

John Gaventa was acting director of the Highlander Center at the time and had written a book that had a big influence on me, *Power and Powerlessness.*[†] We got to know each other at the conference in Nicaragua, and he suggested that after the conference I move from San Francisco to Highlander to help him start a new program on globalization. A year later, I packed all my possessions into a car and set out for Tennessee. The timing was perfect, as EPOCA had succeeded in building the connections we had hoped for between the northern and southern environmentalists of the western hemisphere. Greenpeace was opening a Latin American branch and Friends of the Earth had hired a Central American issues staff and lobby desk in DC, among other gains. Dave Henson, my codirector at EPOCA, and I created a joint program between the National Toxics Campaign and the Highlander Center on globalization and toxics.

This work took me to Asia, Latin America and Eastern Europe, but also to eastern Appalachia, the toxic corridors around New Orleans, and the environs of the world's largest chemical waste plant, in Alabama. Highlander was a creative hothouse for me. I was mentored by John Gaventa, Susan Williams, and a host of radical educators who called Highlander their political home. What's more, Highlander had been the official training and education arm of the Congress of Industrial Organization (the "CIO" in the AFL-CIO) during the height of the American labor movement, from the 1930s to 1950s, and the archives of the CIO education programs were fifty feet from my desk. Whenever I needed a break, I would wander into the air-sealed archives and

---

† John Gaventa, *Power and Powerlessness: Quiescence & Rebellion in an Appalachian Valley*, University of Illinois Press, 1982.

browse through education manuals for steel workers and miners from the 1930s and 1940s, photos of a young Martin Luther King and Rosa Parks sitting at Highlander plotting the Montgomery bus boycott, and much more. All the work I would later do in labor unions from Connecticut to Nevada had its roots in the time I lived on the hill at Highlander.

Eventually I became Highlander's associate director, but after three years there I was ready for something new. So I loaded up Jalapeño, a horse I had picked up in Tennessee, and drove back to northern California. This was the first of many multi-week solo cross-country drives I would take with my horse as I moved between campaigns. Back then horse people relied on an annual printed guide of rural families who were willing to take in total strangers' horses for the night. I worked on a series of environmental justice projects, mostly on the United States–Mexico border, until I received a call from Margie Fine at the Veatch Program.‡ Veatch was a progressive foundation that had funded every organization I'd worked for, so they knew me well. Margie wanted to recruit me to become a program officer at the foundation. I had just moved to California and didn't want to move back east, and I really didn't want to work for a foundation. But many mentors pointed out to me the strategic importance of being able to direct several million dollars each year to progressive organizations and then to be in an excellent position to assess whether they had actually used it effectively, so I reluctantly accepted the offer and loaded up my horse once again and headed east.

Veatch had a great philosophy as foundation philosophies go: It did not fund advocacy or service or a swath of projects, but instead focused solely on organizations that organized—that used the direct engagement of people as their main strategy. We were specifically interested in giving large, multiyear grants for what's called general operating support, so groups could keep the lights on and pay the rent and their staff. Most foundations do the opposite, making what are called restricted grants for project *work*, as if any project can happen without phones and staff. Veatch's national scope and this special focus on participatory direct action gave me a bird's-eye view

‡ The complete name of the program is the Unitarian Universalist Veatch Program at Shelter Rock.

of the organizing that was taking place across all sectors of the United States.

My departure from Veatch was also my entrance into labor, and that is where the main story of this book begins.

CHAPTER ONE

Whole-Worker Organizing in Connecticut

A political earthquake hit the American labor movement in 1995, when the AFL-CIO held the first democratically contested election in its history. An entrenched old guard lost to a new generation who promised a radical break from the union leadership of the preceding decades. Suddenly, a different kind of movement seemed possible, one that might draw on the militant traditions of the Congress of Industrial Organizations to expand the shrinking ranks of organized labor. A little historical context is required to put this earthquake in perspective.

The American Federation of Labor was formed all the way back in 1886. Many Americans then worked in small, independent shops employing skilled craftspeople. These craftspeople formed a multitude of professional associations, known collectively as craft unions, whose membership was limited to the skilled workers of a single trade. The AFL was formed as a national federation of these craft unions, and it looked out for their interests alone. The strike was a powerful tool in the hands of these workers, since their skills were not widely available in the general population. When they refused to work, it was hard to find anyone to take their place. In the terminology of the labor movement, this is *shop floor power,* and the craft unions of the AFL were so effective in wielding it, through strikes, slowdowns and more, that they had little incentive to become involved in the "politics" of elections, governance, and law. Less-skilled workers, more easily replaced and lacking shop floor power, became the support base for the emerging working-class radicalism of the day, most prominently expressed in the growing Socialist Party. The AFL saw this radicalism as a real threat to the good money their members made in the crafts and was soon explicitly presenting itself to employers as "the conservative alternative to working-class radicalism," an alternative that came to be known as business unionism.

By the 1930s, the US economy had been profoundly transformed by the advent of huge industrial factories, sprawling mega-complexes employing thousands of people on assembly lines. The assembly line took the work formerly done by a skilled craftsperson and broke it down into a series of discrete tasks, each of which required little or no skill to complete. And if the assembly line could be automated, its speed could actually dictate the pace of work. The few tasks that could not be broken down into unskilled steps remained the domain of craftspeople, who constituted a shrinking percentage of the industrial work force and who fought to maintain their hard-won privileges in the craft unions of the AFL.

These giant factories were a social world in themselves, of a kind the nation had never seen. A small island of skilled workers was surrounded by a sea of unskilled workers; blacks and whites went to work in the same building; and recent immigrants bumped up against US-born citizens.

These developments led to a profound debate within the AFL, between those leaders and unions who wanted to stick to the craft union model and represent only the interests of the skilled few, and those who argued for an "industrial union" approach in which all the workers—skilled and unskilled alike—from a single factory, and eventually from an entire industry, would form "one big union." The crash of 1929 and the onset of the Great Depression gave this debate a fierce urgency. The labor movement split, and in 1935 the Congress of Industrial Organizations was formed. The following year the United Auto Workers staged massive strikes throughout the auto industry, which had pioneered the assembly line and now had the highest concentration of semiskilled workers. In the greatest organizing moment in US history, *more than 100,000 workers a month* formed new unions for six straight months. Instead of walking off the job, striking auto workers occupied their factories to ensure that no replacement workers, or "scabs," could be brought in by the boss, and the term *sit-down strike* was born. Militancy and disregard for the law were the norm. Workers (then mostly men) and their wives and families took to the rooftop of their plant with guns, rocks, and whatever other weapons they could find to fight off the well-armed company goons attempting to take the factories back.

When the US entered World War II in 1941, many of these factory workers were sent to fight abroad in an army that replicated the class and racial proportions of the factories. Women entered the labor force in record numbers to keep industrial production humming back home. The unions made a "no-strike pledge" in support of the war effort, in return for which the government offered arbitration as an alternative method for setting wages and other terms of new contracts.

When the war ended in 1945 and the soldiers came home, the CIO took up just where it had left off at the outset of the war: a new wave of militant strikes immediately broke out. But so did the Cold War with the Soviets, and on the home front, the immediate target singled out by the cold warriors of American capitalism was the CIO. Many CIO leaders, organizers and members had also joined the Communist Party. When Joe McCarthy was elected to the US Senate in 1947, the great American witch hunt was on. The Taft-Hartley Act was passed the same year, penalizing unions whose officers refused to sign statements that they were not members of the Communist Party. The CIO buckled. The momentum of the organization was shattered, and eventually most of its communist leaders—who were often the best and the brightest—were purged. In 1955, the empty shell that had been the CIO merged with the more conservative AFL to form the AFL-CIO.

The post-1955 labor movement was a much different animal. In the anticommunist hysteria of the day, unions turned away from any sort of working-class radicalism to a narrow focus on "bread-and-butter" issues like wages. And there was plenty of bread and butter to go around, as the Great Depression and Second World War yielded to an economic boom that saw wages climb to record highs first in the United States and then in other parts of the world. A postwar pact between American labor and capital was eventually codified into a series of institutions and laws that regulated industrial relations.* Workers got high wages, and benefits ranging from pensions to vacation time to the formal right to grieve. In

---

* The Taft-Hartley Act explicitly stated that employers were only mandated to negotiate with a union over the "workplace" issues of wages, working conditions and benefits, setting the stage for unions altogether dropping issues of broad concern to the unorganized working class.

return, capitalists got labor peace at home and support for American foreign policy abroad. By the 1980s, this latter had gone so far that the American Institute for Free Labor Development (AIFLD), the international arm of the AFL-CIO, was implicated in supporting death squads in Central America that killed real labor organizers. I was then a young adult working on environmental justice issues in Central America, and the fact that the unionists I was working with, who were already deeply engaged in a battle with a capitalist class of the most brutal and violent nature, now also had to deal with killer thugs funded by the unions of my country, made a deep impression on me.

Meanwhile, the postwar economic boom that had greased the pact between American capital and labor had come to an abrupt end, in 1973, when a sudden rise in the price of oil, the cost of fighting the war in Vietnam, and increased global competition sent the US economy into a recession. American workers once again needed militant unions, this time to defend the gains they had made during the boom. But the militant unions of earlier times were nowhere to be found. Any real attempt to bring unorganized workers into the ranks of unions had stopped when the communists were purged from the labor movement. At the height of labor's power in the 1950s, roughly one in every three American workers was union member. In 1973, that number began its long decline. In 1980, when Ronald Reagan was elected president, that number had fallen and only 23 percent of workers were in unions. By the time Reagan had left office in 1988, the number had dropped to 16.4 percent.[†] The decline in union membership went hand in hand with the export of industry and industry's union jobs to countries with lower labor costs. From their peak, in 1974, weekly real wages of American workers had fallen 11.5 percent by 1984 and a whopping 17.5 percent by 1994.[‡]

The historic AFL-CIO convention took place the very next year. Representatives from a small handful of progressive foundations were outside the convention hall being briefed on the events inside and their implications for the future of labor. I was among them. As soon as we

---

[†] 'Union Membership and Coverage Database from Current Population Survey', Barny Hirsch and David A. Macherson, *Industrial and Labor Relations Review* 2(56), January 2003.

[‡] *Labor Research Associates of New York*. Based on data from the US Department of Labor, Bureau of Labor Statistics. Wages are expressed in constant 1982 dollars.

walked into the hotel, you could feel the tension. The outcome of the election was very much up in the air, and that outcome would be historic. Peter Olney, who worked with immigrant drywallers in Los Angeles, was there, and Ken Paff of Teamsters for a Democratic Union.§ They talked about social and economic justice and teaching workers to build their own power. What they were describing were the kind of unions I had long wished for. They made sense and they were exciting. Then the slate calling itself New Voices swept to victory inside the convention hall, and suddenly it seemed that the unions envisioned by Olney and Paff might actually come to be. The election made the national president of the Service Employees International Union, John Sweeney, the new president of the AFL-CIO. As the industrial unions declined, SEIU, representing service sector workers such as janitors, health care workers, civil service employees, and others, had become the fastest-growing union in the nation.

I was then working as a program officer for the Veatch Program. Veatch was among a small core of foundations that had been promoting New Labor.⁊ We argued that foundations that funded programs for "poverty eradication" (in the stilted vernacular of progressive philanthropy) should take a look at New Labor, because good unions were the best anti-poverty strategy money could buy. But the more we pushed this line, the more I wanted to get out of the foundation world and actually work in the new labor movement. My job at Veatch had given me a unique view of the progressive landscape, and it was clear that the American left was in big trouble. It simply did not have enough resources, and had even less people than money. There were precious few progressive organizations that could be said to have a mass base in any meaningful sense. Unions, meanwhile, had a lot of people and a lot of money.

In 1997, Veatch helped organize a briefing at the AFL-CIO headquarters in Washington, so foundation people could meet the leaders of the New Labor movement. After John Sweeney and other top leaders were introduced, with much pomp and circumstance, Richard Bensinger was presented as the man who would lead New Labor's drive to bring the great

---

§ Teamsters for a Democratic Union is a rank-and-file movement that challenged the corrupt leadership of the International Brotherhood of Teamsters (IBT), which represents truck drivers and warehouse workers.

⁊ The proper name is the Unitarian Universalist Veatch Program at Shelter Rock.

mass of unorganized American workers into the ranks of unions. For five years prior, Bensinger had been director of the AFL-CIO's Organizing Institute and had recently been given a new position as the AFL-CIO's national organizing director. He was an inspiring guy. No one had to convince Richard Bensinger that American labor needed shaking up. On the contrary, he was ready to do the shaking. Bensinger was among the strategic thinkers who had introduced *density* into the labor lexicon. By *density*, Bensinger did not mean the number of workers you had talked to or even the number you had organized. The density that interested him was the percentage of workers in any given industry who were in unions. Density was the crucial metric. Bensinger was on a mission to wake labor up to the simple fact that if the percentage of organized workers is shrinking, then unions are losing. I know that seems obvious, but it was something many unions had a hard time hearing back then. Their leaders were still boasting about their absolute numbers, which sounded impressive until people like Bensinger came along and pointed out that those numbers might have been impressive in the 1970s, but the economy had grown, the population had grown, and a membership figure that might have represented 35 percent of the workers in a given industry back then could represent less than 10 percent now.

At the meeting, Bensinger talked about how ferocious corporations had become in their efforts to bust unions. The tools that they had begun using in the Reagan era were different. By the late 1980s there was a cottage industry of union busters who specialized in these new tactics; by the late 1990s there were close to 100 law firms that included union avoidance as an area of expertise. As he described workers being fired for the simple act of putting on a union button, my internal sense of right versus wrong and instinct for fight versus flight were raging. How could it be that in this country we had gone so far backward that workers had lost their right to freedom of speech and assembly? When I talked with him after the event, he challenged me to stop organizing meetings of funders and join up with the New Labor team.

Early in 1998, I was hired into the new national organizing department and put to work on the new Geographic Organizing Projects, or Geo Projects for short. This was an experimental program intended to develop new ways to increase union organizing drive win rates and then to accelerate first contract wins for the new unions. These two crucial metrics require a little explanation for those unfamiliar with the ins and outs of labor organizing.

Efforts to organize new unions generally begin in one of two ways. Sometimes an employer does something really outrageous, like cut everyone's wages or health care benefits, or worse, and the workers contact a union and ask for help in forming a union of their own. The term for this is *hot shop organizing*. Alternatively, a union can launch an organizing campaign based on some sort of strategic analysis of a given industry or market, such as which plants are the most profitable or where the bottlenecks in the supply chain are, and then use that analysis to focus the organizing campaign to get the most bang for its buck. In the decades before New Labor's victory in the AFL-CIO elections, American unions had all but stopped doing strategic campaigns and were just hot shopping.

What was worse, even the hot shopping wasn't working. Once union leaders or organizers are confident that a solid majority of workers support forming a new union in the shop, they petition the National Labor Relations Board (NLRB)** to hold an election, so the workers can vote on whether to form a union or not. By the time the New Labor leaders came to power, unions were losing two thirds of these elections.††
What had happened?

What had happened was all of those law firms that do nothing but bust unions, that's what. Before they showed up, an organizer might have been able to file for an election knowing that 30 percent of the workers supported the union and assume that this would grow to a majority as the election date approached. Now, when an organizer filed for an election, the boss brought in a team of professional thugs who had studied the process and really had it down. The tactics used by employers included

---

** The NLRB was established in 1935 as one of the instructional pillars of President Franklin Roosevelt's "New Deal" with labor. It was substantially modified by the Taft-Hartley Act of 1947, and by the 1980s had become a central element in the legal scaffolding that hemmed in the power of labor on all sides.

†† Kate Bronfenbrenner's research at the Cornell School of Industrial and Labor Relations shows that by 1997 only 33 percent of workers achieved a victory after filing to have a union election with the National Labor Relations Board. See Kate Bronfenbrenner, "No Holds Barred," Cornell University ILR News Center, May 20, 2009. http://www.ilr.cornell.edu/news.

firing key workers, changing everyone's schedule for the worse, withholding vacations, one-on-one intimidation interviews that resembled an FBI interrogation more than a meeting, tearing buttons off of workers, manufacturing bad write-ups on workers with an otherwise stellar record, and much, much more (discussed in detail as this book unfolds). This had completely changed the terms of successful organizing, and the unions had yet to find their way in the new landscape.

The numbers got even grimmer when you took into account those few organizing drives that did result in a union victory but then ground to a halt without the workers ever winning a union contract. Due to the complex legal structure that hems workers in on every side in this country, even when workers vote to form a union that's just round one of the battle. Round two is winning the first contract, because the law states that workers don't actually become members of a union until they have won their first contract. If there is no contract, there is no union. So the boss gets two chances to stop the workers from forming a union.

Specifically, the law says that if there is no contract within twelve months of certifying the new union, the workers can vote to "decertify" it. Let's say you are a worker who campaigned really hard in the face of fierce employer intimidation and won your union election. You thought that the war in the workplace was over and you could get back to practicing your trade and living your life. Suddenly you realize that the war has just begun, and now you watch the boss fight like crazy to stop you from getting a contract, threatening and harassing you even more ferociously for another twelve months to stall the negotiation process. And through it all the employer subtly suggests that if the whole union thing just goes away, everything will be easier at work. Hell, you might even get a raise. You just might give that idea serious consideration. Or you might just throw up your hands and back away from the whole confrontation. Either way, the boss wins.

The top priority for the New Labor leadership of the AFL-CIO was to throw this whole ongoing train wreck into reverse. The Geo Projects were designed to be a laboratory for testing ideas for how to do just that. The one I was to lead was called the Stamford Organizing Project. Political power in Connecticut had gradually shifted to the city of Stamford and the surrounding county, Fairfield, where the labor movement had no base to speak of. This hobbled the power of labor in the state legislature. Fairfield County had the highest number of unorganized workers in the state; in some sectors, the highest in all of New England. The Stamford Organizing Project, or simply the Organizing Project, as it came to be known, was supposed to turn this around—to win some union elections and then some first contracts, and to get it done fast.

The Organizing Project was conceived as a multiunion, multisector[‡‡] project in which member unions were to pool resources, share lists, and adhere to collectively made decisions. This might seem unremarkable to someone outside the labor movement—union solidarity and all that—but given the history of interunion competition and turf wars in this country, the sort of collaboration envisioned by the Organizing Project was anything but the norm.

The Organizing Project was launched with four local unions: United Auto Workers (UAW) Region 9a, United Food and Commercial Workers (UFCW) Local 371, Hotel and Restaurant Employees (HERE) Local 217, and SEIU District 1199 New England. Right from the get-go, our attempt to get these unions working together in Stamford opened up a can of worms that seemed to have no bottom. In fact, just weeks after I came on salary, three national unions tried to shut down the whole endeavor at a meeting of the AFL-CIO Executive Council. Their objections to the Organizing Project were varied. The one that had some substance was that the project did not fit into their sectoral approach to organizing.[§§] Another was that Connecticut in general, and Stamford in particular, was not a priority spot, a criticism which might have seemed valid if you were looking at things from a national point of view, but not if you were in a union in Connecticut. As is so often the case with labor, however, the deeper reason for the opposition to the Organizing Project was never spoken aloud and had to be inferred as a subtext to the debate: Three of the four locals unions involved were seen by their national offices as troublemakers. So from the point of view of the national unions, the

---

‡‡ *Sector* is used in the economic sense here. The Stamford Organizing Project was focused on the geographic region of Stamford, targeting four sectors: health care, hotels, retail, and municipal workers.

§§ Having a sectoral approach to organizing means focusing on all the workers in one industry, such as health care. And you might further break down that sector by focusing on long-term care workers. The sectoral approach attempts to build power in an economic group by organizing a higher and higher percentage of its workers.

Stamford Organizing Project was a slap on both cheeks. Not only was this newfangled Organizing Department at the national AFL-CIO meeting with their own local unions, they were plotting with known dissidents.

When I got to New England, I set up my first meeting with the guy everyone said would love me, Warren Heyman of HERE, but he was cold to the point of hostile. Next I met Jerry Brown, the guy who was supposedly going to hate me and didn't know how to play nice with others. Jerry announced we were going to go to lunch, and when we got there he ordered a martini. Now I really knew I was in the labor movement. Environmentalists don't drink martinis at working lunches, and environmental justice activists can't afford martinis anyway. Jerry and I hit it off right away. He had thoroughly studied my resume. He tested me with some smarty-pants questions. I tested him right back. Wonderful. His opening line was something like, "So, it seems you have done some really interesting work. I hope you can teach us something, because we are pretty pathetic in the labor movement. Any good new idea will be just that for me, a good new idea, and it won't be a bad idea until we try it and it doesn't work." I decided to take him at his word.

After I'd met with all the key union leaders and many related labor officials, it was time for a plan. Um, what, exactly, were we going to do? I had a plan, all right, but to move it I knew I would need the help of my main "boss" at the national AFL-CIO, Merrilee Milstein. Milstein was the Northeast's deputy regional director for the Field Mobilization Department of the national AFL-CIO (I learned early on that everyone in labor has an elaborate title; it would take me a little longer to learn that these titles don't mean much of anything). Merrilee and I had hit it off instantly. She was the real deal. She had been a militant unionist for three decades and was a feminist and peace activist as well. Merrilee was also a card-carrying member of the Communist Party, which was not really a recommendation in my book, since I had rarely been impressed with present-day communists. But Merrilee was different. She knew how to translate her communist ideals into a contemporary vision of a militant movement. My hope for what unions might become was what Merrilee had been doing for thirty years. She'd originally come from the New England Local 1199—the same union as Jerry Brown—starting out as a young organizer and rising to become vice president, working with

Larry Fox, 1199's secretary-treasurer, and Jerry, its president. These three militant, creative labor leaders were to be beloved mentors to me over the coming decade.

Merrilee and I convened what we called our Project Board, which included the heads of the participating locals and their lead organizers. After hearing the local leaders walk through their current plans, I proposed that the first thing the Organizing Project should do was conduct something called a geographic power structure analysis, or PSA, of Fairfield County. The concept of the PSA originated in community organizing. You identify the real power players in a given community or area, determine what the basis of their power is, and find out who their natural allies and opponents are. Based on that knowledge, you formulate a plan for enhancing the power of your allies and neutralizing that of your opponents. I had studied many approaches to PSAs over the years, and the one I found most powerful was developed by Anthony Thigpenn, a longtime community organizer in Los Angeles.⁵⁵ Anthony's model measures power both in absolute terms and in relation to specific goals. It is also conceived as a political education tool; the results of each analysis are shared widely with the base. The PSA hybrid I was proposing would be constructed in two phases, involving two different skill sets. Phase one, the quantitative phase, would be an exhaustive study of demographics, voting trends, political donations and the like, done by professional researchers off in a room someplace with a lot of coffee and a fast Internet connection. Phase two, the qualitative phase, would be an equally exhaustive pooling of the collective knowledge of our members, carried out by organizers and worker leaders. My hope was that implemented in this manner, the Thigpenn PSA would become not just a tool for developing strategy for building power, but a power-building process in itself, as workers began to realize they had resources they never even knew about—personal relationships, social networks, and knowledge of their community—which could be mobilized on their behalf.

All of this was basically unheard of in the labor movement. Unions are accustomed to focusing their research on a particular employer:

¶¶ Anthony Thigpenn was the founder-director of AGENDA, the Environmental and Economic Justice Training Project, and CIPHER, a related research think tank.

ownership, financial analysis, OSHA logs,*** violations of any kind in the public record of the company in question. But we were a geographic project, chartered to organize workers across industries throughout a particular area, and a geographic PSA is specifically designed to map how power moves across a given space.

Making a geographic PSA the main item on the agenda of the first meeting of the Project Board was a bold move, and I knew it. No one had any idea what I was talking about, and I was proposing that this PSA should fully occupy the project members for two months. Looking round the table, I could see the mental wheels spinning: "Just who in the hell is this chick the national AFL-CIO dumped on us? She really wants us to take two months out of our organizing to do some harebrained thing she learned in community organizing?" But the whole reason I was there was to bring in some new ideas from the outside world, and the geographic PSA was a big new idea. Here's why.

Good union organizers are familiar with a practice called workplace charting. You make a big wall chart with a grid. One axis plots work shifts at the workplace, the other plots departments or work areas. Then you fill in the names of all the workers by department and shift. But that's just a piece of paper. The chart comes to life through your conversations with all the workers in the facility. It goes with you to meetings, where you hang it up and let workers study it. As you talk to them, you ask them a series of questions that help you assess who their actual organic leaders are in each department and shift. You might ask which person on a shift the others would go to if they wanted to learn how do things better. Or whom they would talk to if they had a problem with their supervisor or a coworker. You proceed systematically, really listening to what people say. Organizers call this process leader ID. A workplace chart is the organizer's bible. It gets marked with colored highlighters, stick-on stars, adhesive file-folder dots, and symbols of all kinds, creating a topography of all the relations among and between the workers, and it gives the organizer an increasingly precise and accurate understanding of how power moves in the workplace. You can look at it and immediately assess the state of a given campaign: how many workers are pro-union, anti-union, undecided; how many have we talked to; which ones spoke directly with

*** An OSHA log is the public record of all violations of the Occupational Safety and Health Association code that have been assessed on a company.

an organizer and which with a coworker; how many have been house-called, and so on. What's unclear about this concept? Apparently a lot, because most unions in this country don't get it. Fortunately, all of the unions in the Organizing Project except the UFCW already used some form of charting, which meant we were ahead of the general curve in the American labor movement. Note that "dissidents" and "good organizing" have gone hand-in-hand in the history of American labor.

But here's the problem: Even the unions who use workplace charting to make a strategic analysis of the structure of power in the workplace do nothing of the sort when they go out into the community. They spend plenty of resources outside the workplace, but mostly on narrow politi-cal campaigns. And they do seek out community allies, such as clergy. But they have no methodology that can be applied systematically for strategically assessing power in the community, that is, no commu-nity counterpart to their workplace charting. The result is that even the unions that do a good job of organizing the workplace do a poor one in the broader community. They make ill-informed choices that don't lead to strategic wins. Often, they lead to disasters.

An example might help illustrate the point. In a workplace organiz-ing campaign, often the first workers an organizer meets are those who might be termed the "loudmouths." They talk back to the boss—but they talk back to everyone else as well. Inexperienced organizers often mistak-enly identify them as natural leaders, when in fact their coworkers rarely pay serious attention to anything they say. More experienced organizers know this, and also know that identifying the real leaders takes more time and a more subtle understanding of workplace dynamics. But when they're organizing support in the community, they'll go straight to the "loudmouth" priest who talks a radical line, without noticing that no one in town outside his tiny congregation pays any attention to what he says, and meanwhile they'll overlook quieter clergy whose large congregations include many of the workers in the organizing campaign.

This is a big problem, because workers need a lot of support inside and outside of the workplace to have any hope of winning. Traditional union strategies are no match for the maze of laws that effectively strait-jacket workers in union drives. If unions are going to save themselves, they will have to become much more effective at building power beyond the workplace. Even more than ten years ago, this was hardly an original observation on my part. What I had to offer at Stamford was a power-ful tool on which to build an alternative approach. As a community and environmental justice organizer I had studied it closely and used it extensively, and now I was in a position to test its applicability to labor organizing with some of the better union locals in the country.

Most of the work of the PSA would be done by my as yet nonexistent staff. The key thing I needed from the unions was access to their workers. HERE had a tiny unit at a hotel. The UFCW had some grocery-store contracts from organizing that had been done before I was born. But the UAW had just organized a big unit of municipal workers, and SEIU District 1199NE had just won an organizing election at the Honey Hill nursing home. I proposed that we bring all these newly organized workers together for a Saturday afternoon session where we'd begin the process of formulating a PSA. The idea of starting this unstructured conversation among workers from different unions doing different kinds of work was even farther out than the idea of the PSA itself, but the board approved. Jerry Brown was actually keeping his promise that "any good new idea" I proposed "won't be a bad idea till we try it and it doesn't work."

The pieces of the PSA began to come together at that very first meeting. The UAW's new shop included the nonsupervisory staff of the Stamford city government. (Yes, it is odd that city staffers would join a union of auto workers, but that's American labor for you.) Many of these people worked right in the main government building, where they'd gained a unique understanding of the workings of city government. We had secretaries who kept the calendars for the city's top officials and knew all about who met with whom in Stamford's corridors of power. We had people from the assessor's office who knew exactly which corporate land values were being assessed low in return for campaign contributions.

The nursing home workers offered sharp insights into which churches mattered in local politics, which pastors mattered, and the relationships between them. I asked if politicians came to their churches to campaign and they answered yes. I then asked about each politician by name, starting with the local city council and going on up to the state attor-ney general and then the state's congressional delegation. Obviously, if every major politician in the state stops by your church to be personally anointed by the pastor, your pastor carries some weight in city politics.

And if only the uncontested candidate for dog catcher comes, that means something else.

The mix of class and race in that first meeting created some amazing dynamics that would continue throughout my time in Connecticut. Government workers, white collar and mostly white-skinned, joined nursing home workers who were generally African-American, Jamaican, or Haitian. Our agenda addressed two main questions: First, who had real power among the religious leaders, politicians, corporate executives, community groups, and others? And second, what was the workers' quality of life? What pressures bore down on them when they punched the clock and left work? Immediately, it became clear that though the unions didn't know much about how power worked in Fairfield County, the workers knew a lot. But to coordinate their knowledge and arrive at useful conclusions, we had to ask them—all of them—the same questions, the right questions, just as organizers do in workplace charting. Organizing is all about the systematic application of method and a deep understanding of social networks.

After that first large meeting, we launched a relentless stream of one-on-one interviews with more workers and then with community leaders themselves. Meanwhile, Ahmer Quadeer, our new researcher, was hard at work assembling more conventional data.

The results were stunning. An acute housing crisis and simmering racial tensions were the dominant themes. Across the board, workers said housing overshadowed all their other concerns. Some of the city workers worried about their inability to purchase a house even with their white-collar wages. For everyone else, buying a home was inconceivable—most of them were struggling to pay the rent. They were also seriously concerned about the declining quality and resegregation of public schools. The city's busing program seemed to be limited to "black kids from downtown bused for over an hour to North Stamford to attend rich white schools."†††

By the time we were done, everyone was satisfied that the PSA had been a worthwhile use of resources, revealing crucial points:

---

††† The city had just ended an acrimonious debate about where to build a new high school, and the mayor had pushed hard to build another one in North Stamford, perpetuating the existing pattern of kids rising early and spending hours on the bus, with no neighborhood school providing an alternative.

1. Stamford had become the economic engine for the entire state, and home to more powerful politicians than any other region. The state attorney general, assembly majority leader, senate majority leader, key committee chairs in both state houses, Senator Joe Lieberman and many more all lived in Fairfield County. Logistically, it would be easier to hold a meeting of the state's most powerful politicians in Stamford than in Hartford, the capital.

2. Fortune 500 companies held absolute political power in Fairfield, as well as a more diffuse but very real social power, from having convinced the population that they should be thankful to corporations for creating jobs and "cleaning up" the city.

3. There was no organized independent power base here to ally ourselves with: no university, no community groups except conservative neighborhood groups, no local or regional offices of the Hartford-based statewide progressive groups.

4. Fairfield County's corporate elite had launched not one but three distinct powerful corporate associations, one of which, SACIA, was arguably the most powerful business voice in the state capitol, despite being headquartered in Stamford. SACIA understood that to move policy and power in Connecticut, you put your headquarters in Fairfield County, not Hartford. (This point in particular startled many people in the room who considered themselves experts on state politics but had never heard of SACIA.)

5. The city planned to demolish all the remaining subsidized affordable housing, as well as whole blocks of private, substandard but still affordable housing, in a coming wave of "urban revitalization."

Several strategies seemed obvious to me. First, we'd have to find creative ways to expose the area's corporate agenda. Conventional union campaigns would not be sufficient, given the local population's lack of contact with the labor movement (note to unions, that's America now). I suggested that affordable housing in particular, and racism more generally, would be the key issues. We'd have to win over the powerful Black churches, and we knew they were hostile to unions. One clear way to change this relationship would be to change our behavior, and this meant taking on the housing crisis. No matter how much workers might win in wage and benefit improvements through collective bargaining, the cost of housing would still condemn them to poverty. Representing the interests of these workers meant rethinking the role labor unions might play in such community issues.

Not surprisingly, these conclusions led to some serious debate on the board. Would taking on the housing issue add to or distract from our goal of worker organizing? Was housing simply a potential area for media work, a way of embarrassing the bosses and political leaders, or was it worth addressing because it profoundly mattered to our members and to the workers we sought to organize? Was running a "social justice strategy" an idealistic pipedream and bottomless sinkhole for union resources, or would a broad culture of resistance rebound to our advantage in every aspect of our work?

Just as importantly, I was proposing that the bulk of this work be done not directly by union organizers but by the workers themselves. But this would mean a major commitment from the best organizers our member unions had to engage their members in unfolding a plan. This was a far cry from what these guys had thought they were signing up for at the ceremony with Sweeney just a couple of months earlier. They'd thought they were getting some nice "community organizer types" whom they could send "out into the community" to get ministers to show up at rallies and write letters to editors. Instead, I was suggesting that we position the workers themselves to be agents of change.

The AFL-CIO leadership in Washington had just declared June 24 to be National Right to Organize Day, commemorating an incident in Los Angeles a few years earlier in which cops had savagely beaten a group of immigrant janitors during the early stages of SEIU's Justice for Janitors campaign. It was the first time in memory something like that had been captured on TV, and it caused a huge outcry from Los Angeles politicians and religious leaders that eventually led to a major victory for the janitors.‡‡‡ The incident became a key moment in the ascent of New Labor, and the leadership wanted to iconize it, through forums held by "community allies" on examples of local bosses treating workers unjustly. I understood what they were trying to do, but I also knew that good community strategy cannot be declared from Washington

---

‡‡‡ Cecil Richards, the current leader of Planned Parenthood, led the Century City Justice for Janitors fight.

but instead must emerge from direct engagement with the particular community.

The national leadership had in mind all the unions around the country whose idea of "community-oriented" *is* a forum, covered by the same lone sympathetic reporter, featuring the same liberal clergy they always tap for such things. But in Stamford we had four unions who had committed significant resources to a real community approach; for us, this Washington-sanctioned event would be a distraction from work we already had under way. But I was trapped, so I held my nose and agreed to quickly put something together, hoping to at least make sure that it didn't do any harm to our bigger plans. We had just identified the most powerful clergy in town, and they were not people with whom our unions had a relationship. We had also agreed that such a relationship had to be built, but by the workers themselves, not the union staff. This plan would be made moot if we jumped the gun and invited them to the forum. So I left them off the list—my private decision. And I relied on HERE to do one of the things they do well: bring in a busload of workers from someplace else to make the event look bigger than it really was.

The focus of the event was the firing of two workers from the Honey Hill nursing home during the organizing drive there. We found a church and rounded up the usual liberal clergy. Working with HERE's ties in New Haven, we got Roger Vann, the dynamic and ambitious head of the NAACP's Connecticut branch, to emcee, and used old connections from the statewide unions to get senate majority leader George Jepsen to show up. It looked pretty good, as long as you hadn't seen our PSA.

The AFL-CIO sent us their secretary treasurer, Richard Trumka, as our "headline" speaker. Rich Trumka is a storied man in the labor movement. As president of the United Mine Workers, he led a nine-month strike against the Pittston Coal Company in 1989 that was one of the seminal events for unions at the time, incorporating civil disobedience and a sophisticated campaign to pressure Pittston on Wall Street. As soon as I heard he was coming I knew I had to make the event work. With borrowed leaders and bused-in workers (HERE did in fact produce a busload of fifty workers in red shirts from their Yale union), we had a packed room.

It was my job to pick up Trumka at the airport and brief him on the ride to the church, where he would deliver the keynote speech: what we needed him to say, who the fired workers were, what the company's name was, and so on. The AFL-CIO people in Washington had warned me that he would hungry when he landed. Exactly what food was acceptable seemed to be an oddly big deal, but hey, he was a big guy from the mine workers' union. At some point I handed the phone to Marike, our receptionist, and asked her to write down all the instructions on what to feed him when we picked him up. Maybe he was on some medically prescribed diet or was diabetic or something—I didn't know. When the time came to go to the airport, Marike handed me the bag of food and seemed all uptight about it, complaining about how many times Trumka's staff had called her about this particular issue.

When he got off the plane I had the impression he thought I was the secretary or driver or something. His immediate interest was clearly the food, so I handed him the bag, introduced myself and tried to begin the briefing. He had yet to make eye contact; he was fumbling through the bag and growing increasingly agitated. And then he blew a gasket: "*Where's the god-damned black pepper for my sandwich?*"

He was really making a scene, yelling at me about incompetent staff who couldn't get his order right and how sick of it he was. I got this sinking feeling I couldn't precisely identify, because it was fairly new to me, but over the next few years I would come to know it well: a feeling at the back of my throat that quietly asked me if I was on the right planet.

Yet the event was a big success by the metrics of the AFL-CIO, and Trumka did in fact give an excellent speech. Suddenly the Stamford Organizing Project was on the map in national headquarters. I think we won the prize for best press coverage of a National Right to Organize Day event, which was exactly what headquarters wanted. As for me, amid flown-in speakers and bused-in workers, the only part that felt genuine was when the two workers who had been fired finally got to speak. But the press coverage certainly put new pressure on the boss at Honey Hill. Soon afterward, the workers won their first contract, and District 1199NE credited the event with helping to tip the balance of power for a victory. Gee, I thought, if lame mobilizing like that produces such results, what's going to happen when we really get going with an organizing plan based on the informed analysis of the PSA?

Jerry Brown set up a lunch date to introduce me to John Cunningham, the previous head of the Carpenters Union in the area. Jerry thought no one understood power in Fairfield County better than Cunningham, and that if he took me under his wing he could be enormously helpful. I broke the ice by mentioning my childhood experiences with a box of crayons on the floor of the Carpenters Union hall and my father's friendship with Patty Campbell. Cunningham exclaimed, "You knew Patty Campbell?" It turned out that Campbell had gone on to become the national president of the Carpenters Union, and Cunningham had been one of his key allies. Well, we were off and running. Just as with Jerry, I had an instant liking for this guy. He was big, maybe closer to seven than six feet in height, and had an infectious laugh. We drank Irish beer and talked all about everything he knew. Before the end of lunch he announced that he was going to start introducing me to the Fairfield County power structure.

First on his list were the local carpenters union leaders and George Jepsen, the majority leader of the Connecticut state senate, who was from Stamford. Cunningham set up a long, relaxed lunch for Jepsen, the carpenters, and me. Jepsen was to Cunningham what my father had been to Patty Campbell—a lawyer the carpenters had decided to support and propel to as high an elected office as they could. These Friday lunches were a regular Cunningham thing, and I was told to plan my Fridays so I did not have to return to work in the afternoon. When I didn't get it, they explained that I'd "need to be able to drink a lot of red wine."

Thus began a series of Friday lunches with powerful people and lots of red wine. Life could have been worse. At that first lunch, we'd told the carpenters about our ongoing analysis of the city's "redevelopment" plans, and they wanted to hear everything we knew. I said I'd be happy to share our PSA with them, and I began dreaming that they might even join the Organizing Project, which would have been huge, because theirs was the only big base of workers in Fairfield County, and they were already committed to rebuilding their density.

Unfortunately, the national Carpenters Union pulled out of the AFL-CIO shortly thereafter, so I was prohibited from formally inviting them into the Project. Nevertheless, we worked very closely with the carpenters for the duration of my time in Stamford.

A few weeks later, Ahmer and I went to Bridgeport to present a modified version of the PSA, emphasizing all the construction stuff, to a room of about twenty-five white male carpenters and one Latina sitting in the back. I remember wondering who the heck she was, because wow, did she ever stand out in that room. When I returned to my office, Marike, now our office manager, said that a persistent woman named Myrna Iton had called for me a couple of times, and a résumé under that name had arrived on the fax machine.§§§ Marike added, "She told me to tell you she just heard you speak and she wants to work for you." I looked at Myrna's résumé and noticed she had been doing real community organizing in California. I called her up: She was the Latina I'd seen floating in the sea of white male carpenters. We met the next day and I hired her on the spot, though I worried that the carpenters might not be happy with me.

Myrna immediately understood everything I was attempting to do in the campaign. Everything. She could finish my sentences, and we had just met. Like me, she had never worked for a union until a short while before, when she'd signed on with the carpenters, but she had prior organizing experience. And like me, she had grown up in a political family, in her case a Salvadoran family during the civil war years of the 1970s and 1980s. Here was someone who could actually handle the entire project of what I had begun to call comprehensive charting. She could also handle leadership development training. And she spoke Spanish and French fluently—the French would be a tremendous asset with the Haitian workers and their clergy.

After several weeks of comprehensive charting, we began to analyze what we had in terms of community ties. Religious institutions were the most obvious. But the PSA showed clearly that the progressively inclined white ministers on whom the unions often called had few of our members in their congregations, and furthermore did not have much political punch in Fairfield County, and certainly not in Stamford. There were black clergy who carried plenty of political weight and had lots of our workers in their congregations, but the unions had no connection to them. Except, of course, their rank-and-file. We began organizing the District 1199NE and UAW rank-and-file by church, holding weekend sessions in leadership training for churchgoing workers. One or two workers per church agreed to request a meeting with their minister, not

§§§ Myrna Iton is now Myrna Melgar, living in San Francisco and continuing to do some of the best affordable-housing advocacy work in the country.

as union members but as congregants. Their message was to be "Please help us get a contract, not because you believe in unions, but because you believe in me as a member of your congregation, and you know my family suffers."

The local unions in the Organizing Project were getting tense about when any of this work would pay off. Our mandate, after all, was to accelerate getting organizing wins and first contracts, not to slow the process down. Then came the first meeting between some of our members and their pastor. This was the Rev. Robert Perry of Union Baptist Church, according to our PSA the most powerful Black minister in all of Connecticut. He was head of the state Baptist Conference and a leader among the clergy. The workers were quite nervous going in, but they did a fantastic job, just as they had practiced. Rev. Perry was a frail old man battling ill health. He was reserved, quiet, and cautious. He was clearly aware of his authority, and circumspect about when and how he made use of it outside his church. After carefully hearing his parishioners out, he agreed to write a letter to the mayor demanding justice for his church members as they sought a better life. Suddenly, we had the most important black leader in the city taking on a powerful and popular mayor over a union contract fight. What made this beautiful moment even sweeter was that the letter also referred to the campaign the UAW was running for a contract for the newly organized municipal workers, though the workers who had met with Rev. Perry were mostly from District 1199NE. I was to see this over and over: the turf wars that consume labor leaders don't matter to the rank and file. In fact, the workers often don't even notice them until they suddenly erupt and create a catastrophe. Sadly, there will be a lot more about that situation later in this book.

As time went on we learned just how nervous workers were about meeting with their religious leaders to ask them for support. They might stand up to their boss at work by putting on a union button, which union organizers invariably think is the scariest thing a worker can do, yet they struggle to muster the courage to ask their minister for a meeting. Note to labor: Workers relate more to their faith than to their job, and fear God more than they fear the boss.

Giving themselves strength in numbers was the key. If they went as a group to meet their minister, their request for help was likely to be successful. The training sessions we were running for these meetings were crucial, and role-playing was the crucial component.

Several weeks later when I went to follow up with Rev. Perry—which would also be the first time I met him—he confided to me that he hadn't had many good experiences with unions. In fact, he'd had a very bad one with the building trades over the construction of his church. Eventually I heard this story in one form or another from every single Black minister in Fairfield County. There was no question that not one of them would have responded to an overture from even the best union organizer as they responded to their parishioners. Soon workers were giving regular reports to their ministers on union developments, and some even changed their usual seats at church so they could worship together.

When Rev. Perry's letter arrived, Mayor Dannel Malloy took notice.⁵⁵⁵ The mayor was white, Irish, Catholic, and ambitious. He had come of age politically in a post-union Fairfield County. He was a Clinton Democrat, pro-business, and depended for campaign contributions not on the unions but on the Fortune 500 corporations headquartered in Fairfield County. He was completely oblivious to the possibility that his treatment of unions might matter down the road if his aspirations included a run for governor.

There were a number of extremely ambitious politicians around the county, most of whom hardly waited to be sworn in to their latest office before beginning to campaign for a higher one. This made for a very competitive political environment that offered numerous tactical opportunities to a union campaign that played its hand smartly. Hell, Joe Lieberman would soon be running for vice president of the nation. Where was Joe from? You guessed it: lower Fairfield County.

Politicians in the region began paying attention when they saw the churches and unions operating together. The decisive moment in the campaign came when District 1199NE started to organize several nursing homes owned by Vencor, a national nursing home chain based in Kentucky—and a Fortune 500 corporation notorious for union busting. Vencor then fired a worker leader. If a firing like that results in workers

---

⁵⁵⁵ The former mayor of Stamford is now governor of Connecticut. Many people in the state now appreciate that we taught this politician that workers and their organizations matter in the new economy as much as they did in the old.

starting to take off their buttons or renouncing the membership cards they just signed, that negative momentum can be hard to stop. It was time to put our emerging coalition to the test.

The worker Vencor fired was Mary Cadlet, and they had chosen badly. Mary was a deeply religious woman who attended an area church. She was older, articulate, Black, and she'd been a certified nursing assistant for about twenty years. She stood in perfect contrast to their ruthless, anti-union southern company. Until then we had mostly been holding small private meetings with workers and their religious leaders, and we were beginning to hone our tactics. Vencor had no idea what they were up against.

We called for a rally in front of the nursing home at shift change the day after Mary was fired. A whole entourage of ministers showed up, along with state senate majority leader Jepsen and a number of other politicians. Rev. Winton Hill of the African Methodist Episcopal Church arrived in his clerical vestments and declared that there would be "no more Mary Cadlets in our town, no more at all. The religious leaders are now watching and all God's children have the right to self-improvement through their union." The press coverage featured big headlines announcing a new alliance in town and ran photos of ministers and politicians hugging Mary Cadlet. We went back to the nursing home the next day and passed out the newspapers at shift change. Two weeks later the workers voted by a decisive margin to form a union.

It was a very particular dynamic that made all this work. The workers got the ministers, and the ministers gave the politicians the "cover" of responding to the summons of religious leaders. The politicians would use this cover when their big corporate donors asked them why these pro-business Democrats were suddenly speaking out for unions.

The leaders and organizers of the four member unions of our Organizing Project were taking note of these developments just like everyone else. Everyone understood that an organizing campaign that had been on the verge of collapse had scored a decisive win. And after the Vencor workers voted to form a union, the clergy joined them at the bargaining table, demanding that the fired workers get hired back. We began to hold all our bargaining sessions in churches instead of hotels, a change suggested by the ministers themselves. Not only would it be easy for them to "drop in" and talk with the workers, but the ministers also understood that the workers would feel stronger if they were in their houses of faith. We won two first contracts in Vencor nursing homes where District 1199NE had failed before. A little more than one year in, the Organizing Project had five organizing wins and five first contracts. And from there things just snowballed.

The ministers decided to host a multicongregation meeting on the housing crisis. We supplied the research, data, and analysis, and they supplied an overflowing crowd of nearly a thousand parishioners. There was fire in the pulpit as minister after minister stood up and proclaimed that Stamford needed a housing policy, and then added, "And we need a wage policy. How come our people get bad housing and bad wages?" Media began reporting on the role of the unions in a new housing "crusade."

Three months later, the Public Housing Authority announced an "improvement through privatization" plan at the Oak Park housing complex, where a lot of new union members lived. We knew from our research that this was in fact a "demolition plan" to get subsidized housing out of Stamford. It is one thing for a union to not prioritize housing issues even though many of its members are struggling to pay the rent. It is quite another for a union to ignore the fact that many of its members are about to have their housing torn down—even though this is routine. If the unions were going to represent the housing interests of their members, now was the time to do it. We agreed that union staff organizers would team up with members and door-knock the entire housing complex the following weekend, and we would turn out as many as we could to attend the "informational session" the Public Housing Authority was required to hold to discuss the privatization plan.

There was tension growing in the office again because the UAW in particular was not yet on board for a housing fight. The AFL-CIO was also concerned that I was wasting a lot of staff time on this non-workplace stuff. I knew in my bones we were at another watershed moment and we could seize it by saving Oak Park. The housing work was producing a ton of new organizing leads. We were making connections with unorganized service workers in droves, and they loved us because they thought we might help them save their homes. This was very real. Our organizers saw it every day when they were working the next union campaign: Instead of slamming the door in their faces, unorganized workers welcomed them in.

This was why I had signed on with labor—because I believed that just this sort of work was possible. Now it was happening, and there was absolutely no way I was going to let it go. But to keep the momentum I needed a strong ally from among our member unions, someone who could defend the housing work with a voice that the others would accept as authentically labor. In other words, I needed Jerry Brown. Jerry was not among those questioning the work, but he wasn't loudly defending it, either. He really didn't much care about it one way or the other. But Jerry was a leader who paid attention to his rank-and-file, and I thought that if he could actually experience what his members were experiencing, he would be right there with us.

It so happened that Jerry was coming to town for some contract negotiations, and I had the members ask him if he could stay a while and tour the Oak Park complex. We had overlaid our membership database with the lists from the housing complex and found that a full third of the Oak Park units were occupied by brand-new members of Jerry's union, 1199NE. Two of these new members, one Haitian and the other Jamaican, took Jerry on a walking tour of the complex. Jerry met their kids and saw what we saw: these projects were lovely—low-rise, two-story buildings surrounded by green grass and nice old trees, right near the Long Island Sound. Just what you would want in public housing. When Mayor Malloy looked at the same vista, did he see what the developers that backed him saw? Why did these working-class, dark-skinned immigrants get to live where the ocean breeze ran cool all through the summer? Let's tear it all down and make some real money! By the time Jerry had finished his tour, I knew I would not have to worry any more about defending the housing work to the unions.

Our researcher discovered that before the city could demolish these publicly owned buildings, the law required that some tenants be elected to serve in the "Public Housing Authority planning process" and that the Housing Authority planned to get "volunteers" for this function at the upcoming "informational meeting." We decided to shut down the meeting by leading a walkout, leaving the Housing Authority without their needed "volunteers" and stalling the planned demolition. This would be the moment for the new labor movement of Fairfield County to confront the power structure of the city of Stamford. And it would be a surprise attack. We went into high gear, with media trainings for a leadership team of union members who lived in the complex, the whole bit. Some residents invited their ministers to come. And the members, not the staff, did the final night of door-knocking, often with hordes of kids in tow.

To the utter shock of the Housing Authority bureaucrats, hundreds of residents and several TV crews packed into the elementary school for the meeting. Without asking anyone's permission, the ministers opened the proceedings with prayers asking God to prevent the Housing Authority from tearing down anyone's home. The crowd went wild, the TV cameras rolled, and the members simply took over the meeting. In their new-found role as rank and file tenant-union-church leaders, they announced that the housing demolition was never going to happen. The Housing Authority bureaucrats literally fled the meeting. The morning paper's headline was "Unions to Back Residents' Housing Fight," and the article quoted extensively people who identified themselves as union members who lived in public housing.

By now our researcher had learned that the city had slated all public housing complexes for demolition. Our idea was to organize every last one. The problem was where to find the organizers to do it. The Union Summer program seemed like a possible answer. This was another initiative of the New Labor leadership. Unions were becoming cool again, and there were college students who actually wanted to spend their summers working for low pay and experiencing the new labor movement. Which was wonderful, except no experienced labor organizer would send a college student out to talk to workers in a real union organizing drive. There is just too much at stake. One bad house call with a worker leader and your whole campaign can tank. As a result, many Union Summer programs were handing the students busywork that was boring them to death. We decided to pull in a big Union Summer crew and put them to work organizing in the housing complexes. The "summeristas" would talk to real people and do a real job, only with a lower risk factor.

The Stamford Organizing Project quickly earned a reputation on the national college scene. First, because apparently we gave them the worst housing of any Union Summer program, ever. You just couldn't find affordable housing in Stamford—which was why we were doing housing organizing. We wound up buying mattresses, pillows, blankets, and reading lamps and putting the students on the floor of the vacant office just below ours in downtown Stamford. There was no shower, so we bought them all a gym membership at the downtown YMCA. There was no kitchen, so we gave them a daily food budget to eat all their meals out. Well, they were there to work, so they weren't going to be spending much time eating, bathing, or sleeping anyway. And that was the bigger, better part of the program's reputation: Stamford was the place where every student talked to real live workers, did house calls, learned how to move people in one-on-one conversations, and more.

Shortly after we shut down the Oak Park "informational meeting," the mayor announced that he was done bargaining with the municipal workers and that the only way they would get a contract was through arbitration. The mayor had pulled the same stunt on the cops and fire-fighters in recent years, and used the arbitration to force concessions from all of them. This was the big reason why nearly 600 municipal workers had called the UAW and asked for help forming a union the year before. The UAW won the union election by promising to turn back the tide of concessions. But negotiations for that notorious first contract had been dragging on since I had arrived in Stamford. The UAW had a formidable opponent in the mayor, who was considered politically untouchable, the "next big thing" in Connecticut politics. His nickname was Golden Boy. There was just no way a union could get traction against this guy while fighting for the narrowly defined interests of fairly well-off municipal workers. But that wasn't what the Organizing Project was going to do.

The UAW wanted to call for a March Against the Mayor. It was May. We decided to plan the march for the day before the Union Summer students left town, and challenged them by putting them fully in charge of the turnout for the march. Now the "summeristas" had a meaningful project of their own.

Throughout the summer the mayor was harassed by college students fired up with the passion of youth and workers who were facing the imminent loss of their homes. To say he did not enjoy this new kind of attention would be putting it mildly. This was not the image the Golden Boy needed to project if he was to launch into the next level of state politics. The Mayor's Night In was just one example. Every two months the mayor hosted an open forum to meet with constituents about whatever they wanted to discuss. He was totally unprepared when a crowd of a 150 showed up one night to confront him about the plan to demolish public housing. The story in the paper the following morning began, "A crowd of about 150 Oak Park residents and their supporters electrified the usually low-key bimonthly Mayor's Night In last night…"

By the day of the March Against the Mayor, Golden Boy was starting to come unglued. He was going to church leaders to ask them, beg them, not to show up at the march. He offered the churches new resources and a "seat at the redevelopment table." The major newspaper, always close to the mayor, wrote an editorial calling the march "too confrontational," alleging that it was "unfair to take the fight to his house, his neighbors, his kids." Everyone on our side of the fence meanwhile was having a ball, enjoying their newfound power. The march came off, with fewer ministers in attendance than we had hoped for, but enough to show the mayor he couldn't out-organize the movement. The next day's headline read, "Workers, Tenants Protest Outside Malloy's Home"; the article reported, "The peaceful march, punctuated by chants and civil rights songs, was the latest in a series of protests of Malloy administration policies that demonstrators say are creating a socially and economically divided city."

Not too long after, the mayor announced that he was stopping the arbitration proceedings and going back to the negotiation table with the UAW.

The Organizing Project was accomplishing all of this in spite of the fact that only two of our four member unions were actually doing any organizing. Then, along came the janitors Local 531 from Hartford, very much a SEIU outfit (in contrast to District 1199 New England, which had been fighting affiliation with SEIU pretty much ever since joining it). When the New Labor upheaval elevated John Sweeney to head of the entire AFL-CIO, Andy Stern had taken Sweeney's place at the helm of SEIU. One of Stern's first priorities had been to take on Gus Bevona, a self-serving union boss who ruled the big New York City janitors' local, SEIU 32BJ, with an iron fist. Stern used SEIU bylaws that allow the national union to place corrupt locals into "trusteeship" to bounce Bevona from his penthouse palace in New York, though not without giving Bevona a "severance package" worth a cool $1.5 million. (Bevona was hardly desperate for money, since his annual salary had been $450,000 for running a union whose members made an average of $32,000.) The downfall of Bevona paved the way for the janitors local in Hartford to join the project more than two years in, and we went on to organize 2,000 janitors in record time.

The Stamford Organizing Project was just one of four experimental Geographic Organizing Projects that the New Labor leadership of the AFL-CIO had launched simultaneously around the country. The idea was to compare different approaches to the problem of accelerating the process of organizing workers into unions and winning them a first contract, which was seen as the national labor movement's most urgent problem.

Research comparing the rate of decline in the unionized percentage of the national work force with the time it took to organize new members and win them a first contract had clearly shown that the American labor movement was sliding into oblivion. The New Labor leadership invested millions dollars in experimental programs like the Geo projects, all of it from union dues paid by millions of workers from all over the country who needed their unions to survive.

So, how did we do? By the time the janitors in Fairfield County had their union, there was no question that our experiment was complete, and the data showed our tactics in Connecticut had worked. The Stamford Organizing Project had helped 4,500 workers successfully form unions and win first contracts that set new standards in their industries and the market.**** Beyond that, the Stamford Project had saved four public housing projects from demolition and then won $15 million for improvements to that housing. We'd also won the nation's strongest "one-for-one" replacement ordinance, protecting thousands more units of affordable public housing, plus an "inclusionary zoning policy" from which the workers in Stamford will benefit for years to come. Finally, the

---

**** In 2000, the number 5,000 was a big deal. More important was how many individual NLRB elections, first contracts, and political races we had won in a very short time frame. A few years later, the organizing unions would seek to achieve organizing wins in the tens of thousands. But along with those metrics came some consequences, which I will discuss in their place.

Project had actually shifted political power in the city, with two new city council members and one school board member elected in union-led campaigns. Meanwhile, the other Geo projects hadn't even got to square one: The three of them together had failed to organize *a single worker*, although each of them had received significantly more money than the Stamford project.

In a rational world, after sweating out the early disintegration of the three Geo Projects in which they had invested so much, the people in the National Organizing Department at the AFL-CIO would have popped the cork on a bottle of champagne when the fourth succeeded so well, and congratulated themselves on being such wise and prescient leaders. Then, having invested so much money in their most urgent problem and actually finding a promising approach to a solution, they would have immediately put even more resources into a new experiment to see whether what had happened in Stamford could be scaled up and made to work in other parts of the country. The Stamford staff, now seasoned organizers who had lived and breathed the successful synergy between labor and community organizing, would have been dispersed across these new projects designed in the Stamford mold. None of this happened.

Just as the Organizing Project was coming to a successful close in Connecticut, John Sweeney's attempt to reform the national AFL-CIO in Washington, DC, was shipwrecking. The unions that had put top people into the AFL-CIO when Sweeney was elected began to repatriate their staff. Among them was Kirk Adams, who resigned as head of the national AFL-CIO's organizing department to return to his home union, the SEIU. The Stamford organizing team got hired into positions further up the union food chain, but not into situations where they were encouraged to apply the lessons of Stamford. In fact, their Stamford experience was rarely even mentioned.

As the Organizing Project racked up victory after victory, we assumed that eventually other unions would want to see which items in our toolkit might be useful in their economic sector and region of the country. In fact, I wrote a complete training manual of some 200 pages on how to conduct a power structure analysis in a union setting, how to do "comprehensive charting" and how to assist the members in selecting which non-workplace issues their union should dive into. Sadly, I have found no way to circulate it through union channels. And though the Stamford Organizing Project has been the subject of a number of books and articles, there has been no forum within labor in which the broader strategic and political lessons of the Stamford experiment could be discussed. Here, then, are a few of those lessons.

It is critical to have a strategic mindset that considers the challenges the workers face in their lives as either "workplace" or "non-workplace" issues, instead of the "community/labor" binary so prevalent in union thinking. The latter model implies that workers are not members of a community and that community members do not spend most of their time at work, and that therefore "labor" issues are the proper domain of unions while "community" issues are the domain of someone else. But members do not divide their lives into "job concerns," which warrant energy and attention, and "everything else," which is somehow trivial. We found that it was actually important to replace "community/labor" with "workplace/non-workplace" in the everyday speech of our organizers and to talk about organizing "whole workers."

Leadership development was critical, but note that we didn't understand that concept the as labor commonly does. For us, leadership development meant empowering the workers to be central participants in their campaigns. This was not just for show, to make them feel good about having "ownership" of the campaign. It was because they really were the only ones who could build the necessary ties between the union and their own communities. When union staff try to do this job in place of the workers, they blow it.

The Stamford Project was the lowest-funded of the Geo Projects, but it received serious resources nonetheless, and that level of support was absolutely essential. Key among the resources required was a staff of experienced organizers, not entry-level ones. Too often unions hire a "community organizer" who has never really organized anything, or subcontract this work to front organizations, often with foundation money.

Beginning with a thorough geographic PSA was key to everything that followed in Fairfield County. The broad lesson here is that unions should analyze the structure of power in the wider world in which their members live as carefully as they analyze the power structure in the workplaces and in the corporations that own them. The workers themselves are a key source of knowledge in this regard, but they are often unaware of the strategic nature of the knowledge they have. Showing them how to put it altogether takes a lot of time, invested by skilled organizers. But the cost of trying to shortcut this step is not being able to strategically assess the importance of the various issues the members face.

A community union *must* reflect its community. That sounds simple, but, well, take a look around the labor movement. In Stamford, we talked about race all the time. Our staff organizing team was racially diverse, multi-multilingual and overwhelmingly female. We had huge, unwieldy meetings with translations in Creole, Spanish, and English. Workers would say there was no place else in Connecticut where people bothered to translate for them. And we paid for child care at all of our meetings—good child care. That might sound trivial, but neither unions nor community organizations typically provide this. We found that if you make child care available, mothers will turn out in droves.

So much of the debate around union organizing strategy never leaves the realm of jargon and ideas that never touch the ground, that it is important to spell out what organizing whole workers means. These workers were changing their entire lives, not just their work lives, and they were doing it from the foundation of their union. They were bargaining with their bosses, not begging. They were taking over government meetings and running them themselves. They thought and spoke of themselves as belonging to a workers' movement, not just a single union. They understood that this movement they were a part of had both the right and the obligation to engage in direct, militant action on issues that were of vital concern to the communities in which they lived. And they were winning everywhere. They were fundamentally building worker power, and it was an experience of community, class, race, faith, and personal liberation.

CHAPTER TWO

The Yo-yo: Into and Out of the National SEIU

After Stamford came the midnight phone call of November 7, 2000, the mad dash to Florida, and the excruciating spectacle of the national union leadership conniving with the Democratic Party to make sure the Democratic voters of Florida stayed at home with their mouths shut as their votes were stolen and the White House was handed to George W. Bush, Dick Cheney, Karl Rove, John Ashcroft, and Donald Rumsfeld.

I couldn't tell you today what I did when I flew home from Florida. It's all a blur. But I was certain I was done working for the AFL-CIO. I guess I'd known senators and lawyers wouldn't understand this stuff, but I had expected more from my leaders in "new labor." Meanwhile I had hardly ingratiated myself with the people who actually ran the national labor federation. When I returned to the Stamford office, I privately told my top leaders I was finished.

Jerry Brown and Merrilee Milstein were my mentors then, and Jerry wanted me to leave the AFL-CIO and work for him at District 1199NE, but I needed a break before deciding whether I could call labor my home. Jerry asked if I would stay on long enough to help them with an upcoming nursing home contract campaign. This was going to be a major effort and could lead to a very big strike, covering seventy-eight nursing homes in two states, so I could hardly say no.

There really isn't anything like a strike. Thousands of people put their life situations on the line, and there is no way to learn how to do it except by doing it. Working on Jerry Brown's senior leadership team through enormously complicated negotiations and preparations for a major strike was like getting a crash course in bargaining to the brink and past it. It wasn't an easy course to enroll in, because after Ronald Reagan made it legal to permanently replace striking workers, most unions just stopped striking, shelving the most powerful weapon in labor's arsenal. By February 2001 I was living in Merrilee's house in West Hartford and working out of the Hartford headquarters of 1199NE.

As negotiations broke down and the strike edged closer, it became increasingly clear that the national SEIU and its president, Andy Stern, hardly supported us. Every morning at the 7 am briefing, we'd discuss how the workers in each chapter were holding up, and then Jerry would update us on his discussions with the industry, the governor, the legislature, and finally our own national headquarters. This last part was always painful. By the time the strike began, Jerry and Stern were openly battling over strategy. Stern wanted to cut "growth deals" with nursing home operators nationally by working with them on common interests. To get accords with big corporations that would help to expand the union numerically, Stern wanted to show bosses he could tame his militant local leaders. The action itself was the largest nursing home strike in US history. John G. Rowland, the Republican governor, called out the National Guard. The press reported that Governor Rowland was spending *five million taxpayer dollars a day* to fight against the people who cared for Connecticut's elderly.

We didn't know it, but Stern had begun talks with Rowland about what a settlement would look like. And then, suddenly, the national SEIU simply cut off all financial support to the 1199NE: no more money, no more communications support, no more nothing. Instead, to the dismay and disgust of many of us, Andy Stern himself rode into town—to cut a deal with the union busting governor.

I had been working in labor for three years. I had developed a new model of worker-centered comprehensive campaigns in the Stamford Organizing Project and weathered the electoral storm in Florida. I had been ready for a break after that, and Jerry Brown had convinced me to stay on through this strike. Now I wasn't just ready for a break, I *needed* one.

I had learned more in those three years than I wanted to know. I had seen the ugly underbelly of the new labor movement as well as its outward promise. I had also had more fun, laughter, and passion and cried more of the good kind of tears than I had ever had in my life. This is why people always do go back to labor. Labor is the only place you can get the resources you need to fight like that, to know that much possibility.

My rhythm is a bit different from most people's. I can go for long periods, years actually, without a day off, on less sleep than is probably good for me. And then I make up for all the missed weekends and late nights by taking a real break, preferably someplace that is culturally and geographically far away from my work environment. It's a rhythm that fits in well with the pacing of campaigns, which demand extraordinary commitment for limited periods.

Now I needed to get outdoors. I can't clear my head indoors. For me, being outdoors involves skiing or horses or bikes or kayaks or running and probably very large mountains. They may seem odd sports for a labor organizer, but they've been passions of mine since my youth, when skiing was not yet the very expensive, corporate-run, glitzy scene it is today.

It was July and I wanted to ski, so I boarded a plane for New Zealand. Snow and cold and sunshine and adrenaline and physical challenge and sore muscles—these would be my therapy. I didn't have much money, but I figured I could somehow survive for at least three months—a skiing season.

I'd been away six weeks when the day that in New Zealand was September 12, 2001 shook the world. Even after I learned that my family in New York City was safe, I wanted to fly right home to them, but they insisted it made no sense, that I should stay where I was. By late September the snow had melted and I was out of money. I found my way to the southern tip of New Zealand and began working on a sheep farm directly under the hole in the ozone layer. Geographically, that was about as far from the American labor movement as I could get without leaving Planet Earth. This was real New Zealand, far from the tourist path. I was given my own pastures, an enduro-style motorcycle, and a team of sheep-dogs, and I was out of bed at 4:30 every morning for birthing, branding, vaccinating, you name it. It wasn't skiing, but it was outdoors and it was hard work. I got to live with a local farmer and since it was the height of birthing season I was actually banking good money. I spent a month as a sheep farmer, working 24/7, and earned enough funds to later travel all of New Zealand.

I kept abreast of the news back home: the Patriot Act, the war in Afghanistan, the impending war in Iraq. One day my cell phone rang—in itself unusual, as I'd mostly used it to get unlost in this foreign country. I answered and heard the voice of Jerry Brown.

"Is this McAlevey? Time to get home. This is way too long a vacation. There's a big campaign we need you to run in California for Sal Rosselli. Can you be at a meeting in Los Angeles next week?"

I swear to God, there was no "Hello," no "How are you," nothing. I love that guy. He cracks me up. I asked him for some details. The campaign was statewide, for a first contract from Catholic Healthcare West, the eighth-largest hospital system in the nation, following an unprecedented agreement to organize 14,000 hospital workers. I told him I would think about it. In truth, I didn't think all that long. I'd been months in New Zealand. Now I booked my flight back to the US, with a stopover in Los Angeles to meet Sal Rosselli and Mary Kay Henry.

Sal headed what was then SEIU Local 250, northern California's health-care union. With around 45,000 members, this was one of the largest locals in California and one of the largest health-care locals in the nation, which made Sal a powerful labor leader. Mary Kay had come up as an organizer for the national SEIU, working first primarily in California, and now for the entire western region. Mary Kay and Sal had just helmed a successful organizing campaign at Catholic Healthcare West (CHW). The organizing agreement, which obliged the huge corporation not to oppose the organizing drive, was the biggest the national SEIU had ever signed with a hospital company. With employer neutrality assured, the workers voted to form a union.

The next step was for all 20,000 of them to get their first contract, which would take a major campaign involving the national union, Sal's Local 250, based in Oakland, and Local 399 in Los Angeles. Sal thought he should have the biggest say in deciding who would run the contract campaign, since his local had been a major player in winning the accord and had received at least half of the resulting new members. Urged by his close ally Jerry Brown, he had advanced my name. I was a known entity to the key people at headquarters in Washington, so the stars seemed aligned for me to jump into the new job. Fresh off the plane and still smelling like sheep, I sat down to discuss things with Sal and Mary Kay, and by the time we got up to go I thought I was hired.

Except nothing happened. Instead, I got odd mixed messages from Mary Kay, who was clearly not comfortable with me; I didn't know why. I couldn't get her to return my calls. Though Sal assured me it was all going to work out. But soon a whole month had gone by and instead of a job all I had was people saying nice things in seemingly random voicemails. I needed to work. I was genuinely nervous about the state of the country and of the world, and I had no income. As the weeks went by, the situation grew increasingly strange, reminding me of the feeling I'd had before I left for New Zealand, that those on the top floors of the house of labor played games with people—including each other.

By late January 2002, I had accepted a position as the new senior program officer at a large liberal foundation based in New York. After just two months on the job, I knew I had made a mistake. I was antsy. I wanted to run organizing campaigns, not fund them. Then came another call from Jerry Brown.

"McAlevey, a great and unusual thing has happened. Andy Stern just named Larry Fox head of SEIU's national health-care division. This is good. Very good. We need you right away. I know I always told you not to work for the national union, but forget that, Larry is the real deal. Call him up and get to work for him in whatever capacity he needs you—he knows all about you already. I have to go. Call him." And with that, Jerry hung up.

Within a week I had resigned from the foundation job and was one of four deputy directors Larry Fox had named to the national health-care division of the SEIU. My title was National Deputy Director for Strategic Campaigns. Working for Fox was perfect for me. I enjoyed his thinking instantly. He saw the big picture. He was deeply radical. He was equally adept in the CEO milieu and hanging out with workers.

Larry sent me to Pittsburgh, where my job was to take what I had learned in Stamford and put it to work in Pennsylvania. Our local in Pittsburg was getting set to launch an organizing campaign at the University of Pittsburgh Medical Center (UPMC), a lucrative hospital chain, already big and growing fast, with more than a dozen hospitals, plus cancer and surgical centers, senior communities, outpatient clinics, and much more. The local had a great team of senior organizers who all worked in the 1199 tradition from which they came. And they were experienced at organizing nurses, an unusual accomplishment in the SEIU health care division, which had been much more successful with hospital ancillary workers. UPMC had become the galloping giant of the hospital market, replacing steel as the biggest employer in western Pennsylvania. Everyone understood that to raise standards for all hospital workers and patients in Pennsylvania, the UPMC workers would need a good deal of support to form their union.

As soon as I got to Pittsburgh, we set to work to hire someone who could conduct the conventional research side of a geographic power structure analysis. This time there was no resistance to the idea. In fact, the local folks were eager for one, in large part because of the particular situation in the Pittsburg area. Steel was gone. Coal was gone. There was a new economic power structure, and the union had to have a clearer picture of who really ran it. My first few months were spent training staff and leading the PSA. Our researcher dove into the detail work that required computers and statistics, doing deep digging on key people, and compiling recent win-loss ratios on political campaigns by each political team, nonprofit outfit and corporation in the region. At the same time, we talked face-to-face with literally thousands of workers about what they knew and who they knew in the region. Early on, I had the researcher scan for upcoming local elections where we might be able to quickly interject ourselves in a meaningful way.

We found that both the Pittsburgh City Council and the Allegheny County Council were potentially very important to the UPMC organizing campaign: Both had jurisdiction over land use and other points of leverage we could use in what we now believed would be a multi-year campaign. I argued for the same next step we had taken in Stamford: running members of the union for safely Democratic seats, ones where the election was essentially decided in the Democratic primary. This strategy has a big pay-off for a union trying to build regional power, because primaries cost far less money than general elections and you can kick out pro-business Democrats that you would otherwise have to fight further down the line. And there were a lot of those; this was what the military calls a "target-rich environment." We mapped our members by election district and precinct, and the local organizers began to interview those who lived in the two districts where we thought we had the best shot.

Within a few weeks, we had our candidates, a white nurse for a suburban seat on the Allegheny County Council, and a Black certified nurse's aid for an urban district of the same body. And away we went: community approach, strategic use of the PSA, rank-and-file workers challenging the hostile elements of the Democratic Party power structure—a comprehensive strategy grounded in our conventional research and the workers' own knowledge, and it was *rolling*. So, I thought, you *can* take lessons learned in one campaign, like Stamford's, refine them and apply them to another, like Pittsburgh's. Then it happened.

Apparently, we had violated some unwritten code regarding how political decisions get made in the SEIU. The local union was accustomed to calling its own shots in local electoral politics. They understood that coordinating with the national union and the state AFL-CIO made sense on statewide and national races, but these were two small races in Pittsburgh. Nevertheless, word came down from Larry Fox that Anna Burger, SEIU's executive vice president for the eastern region, was furious that the national health-care division (i.e., me) was setting strategy for political races in "her" territory. Fox countered that his staff *did* make decisions for comprehensive market campaigns like the one we were running in Pittsburg. Burger insisted that her national staff assigned to the east coast made all the political decisions there. In fact, there was a structural ambiguity within the national union, and we in Pittsburgh had quite accidentally walked into it. I figured it was no big deal. They would work it out at the top; we would begin to coordinate with whomever we needed to and carry on. I had no idea how petty the power struggles at the top of the national union were.

The tug of war between Fox and Burger ramped up, and next thing I knew Burger was declaring that this had happened only because I personally didn't know the first thing about electoral politics and was incapable of thinking strategically. Really? In my relatively short time with the union I'd run three successful campaigns for local offices. Score, 3–0. Before that, I had run several other electoral campaigns and won. We had not arbitrarily chosen our two candidates; they had emerged from a meticulous power structure analysis based on reams of research and the collective knowledge of the local workers. We had spent months crunching numbers, assessing possibilities, analyzing win rates and calculating the money it would take and the strength of our membership. But Burger apparently needed some ammo for her turf war with Fox, and she found it: I hadn't conducted a poll.

Polls are a crucial tool in conventional electoral politics, and no one decides to run for office without some data suggesting that victory is possible. Beyond that, polls can be used in creative ways in all kinds of political struggles. And it was true that we had not taken a poll, not spent $50,000 calling 600 people on the phone. Instead, we'd done an entire geographic PSA that had included one-on-one discussions with thousands of people, people we'd sat down with and engaged on a wide variety of matters. It was what Larry Fox had asked me to do: go to Pennsylvania and replicate on a larger scale what I had done in Connecticut. It was a whole other concept of "polling," it was different and it was better. It pooled the collective knowledge of the workers themselves in a way that provided a far more detailed understanding of power in the region than conventional polling could and empowered the workers, as they came to understand the value of what they knew: a resource they never even knew they had. And from there we had systematically worked our way up to develop a comprehensive strategy for western Pennsylvania designed to take on the powerful UPMC. We were doing *more* than running a couple of candidates for local office—we were doing whole-worker organizing.

This would not be the last time I'd be called on the carpet by the national SEIU for actually talking and listening to workers instead of having a professional pollster do it and report back to me. It was the first time, and the labor elite's serious dependence on polls was news to me. In a weird way it made sense: Since unions had stopped actually listening to workers, how could they know what people thought if they didn't hire a polling company to tell them?

Anna Burger was absolutely adamant about it, and ordered that a poll be taken on our two candidates in the districts they would run in. This made absolutely no sense, I said. "We already know they won't poll well; we are running a stealth campaign. No one even knows their names yet." I patiently (OK, maybe not so patiently) explained our strategy of getting the most electoral bang for our buck by running surprise candidates in districts that were so solidly Democratic that we could win office simply by winning the primary, where the money involved would be less and the impact of our volunteer hours would be more. The poll went ahead nonetheless and produced the shocking revelation that people hadn't heard of our candidates. Within twenty-four hours Anna Burger had told the Pennsylvania local to shut down the campaigns and withdraw the two members from the races.

But the local didn't back down. They had done too much work, they had raised expectations, they had two members who were officially in the race. You can probably imagine how delighted Anna Burger was about this. She next ordered the national union to pull most of its resources out of the effort. One of those resources was me. The word that was actually used was "banished" as in: I was now "banished," not just from the electoral campaigns, not even just from the SEIU local in Pittsburgh, I was "banished" from the entire eastern region of the SEIU. Months later, the nurse won her seat on the county commission and the certified nurse's aid narrowly lost her campaign.

I was left once again wondering if I should leave the labor movement altogether, because what happened in Pittsburgh was the dumbest thing I'd ever been involved in. When you do political work, there are always all kinds of things that make you frustrated or angry, but in terms of plain stupidity the waste of our efforts there was in a class by itself. For a moment I doubted I had a future with the SEIU at all. Larry Fox, however, wasn't having any of it. And I was learning so much from him, and I really enjoyed working for him. But he would have to find me an assignment far from Anna Burger's realm of influence. I didn't have to wait long.

Larry was on the phone.

"Jane, get on a plane tomorrow for Kansas City. We need you to go stop the sale of a large not-for-profit hospital system in the Midwest. Oh, and, well, we think it might be too late already. Most folks assume it is too late. But if we have a chance at all we have to go for it. It will be very important."

Kansas City? Was he kidding? Block the sale of a hospital company?

"I don't want to go to Kansas City, and anyway I would rather go on a campaign that involves workers."

"I understand that, Jane. And I am your boss, and I just said it's important. I am not asking you to go, I am telling you to go."

I boarded a plane directly from Pittsburgh. I hadn't even had time to go home to New York following my "banishment." I had no luggage with me except the little bag I brought to Pittsburgh from New York each week. And that is how I wound up in Kansas City for three months with three days' change of clothes.

At stake in Kansas City was the conversion of a large regional not-for-profit hospital chain into the local pawn of a for-profit multinational corporation. The local chain was Health Midwest, with fifteen hospitals on both the Kansas and Missouri sides of the Kansas City metropolitan area. It had good facilities and real estate holdings and a few crown jewels like Menorah, the beloved hospital of the Jewish community on the Kansas side, and Baptist, the primary hospital for the large Black community on the Missouri side. The only briefing information I got was that Tenet Healthcare, then the number one target of our national hospital organizing campaign, had the insider angle.

Tenet Healthcare is an industry giant, employing more than 60,000 people in more than ten states. It has also been notoriously corrupt. In 2002 one of Tenet's California hospitals was raided by federal investigators. The government alleged that Tenet was guilty of Medicare fraud, that its hospitals had lined their coffers with taxpayers' money by encouraging elderly patients to undergo unnecessary and invasive coronary procedures. In 2005, this investigation resulted in a lawsuit against the company claiming that Tenet had robbed the Medicare system of more than a *billion* dollars. By 2006, Tenet had paid over two billion dollars in fines, penalties, and settlements in a multitude of cases. That's a difficult operation to sustain, and by 2008 Tenet had lost 73 percent of its value, making it the nineteenth-biggest loser in the Standard & Poor 500 Index for the decade.* Its execs were still sitting pretty, however. While the shareholders lost three quarters of their investment, CEO Trevor Fetter was raking in $3.64 million a year.†

But this was 2002, and Tenet was still riding high. When I landed, our research department knew next to nothing about Health Midwest. Another SEIU deputy director, however, John August, was better informed, because while working for a different union he had organized the only two union hospitals in the Health Midwest system. So John knew some nurses there and knew the basics of the hospitals. And Louise Milone, in our capital strategies department, knew the attorney general of Missouri. That's what we had—an organizer who could tell me about the two hospitals he had organized for a rival union and a capital

---

* Elizabeth Harrow, "Worst 10-year performers: Medicare fraud accusations catch up with Tenet Healthcare," *Blogging Stocks*, July 27, 2008.
† Forbes.com CEO Compensation Special Report, April 22, 2009.

strategies person with a relationship to the attorney general in one of the two states involved. And SEIU was virtually unknown in Kansas City; it had no presence there aside from a small amalgamated local with little shops across a smattering of different kinds of worksites—the kind of local that barely does any good for its members. No one even knew SEIU was really in Kansas City with a local like that.

As soon as I woke the next day I began to read the newspapers, scanning for everything I could find about the Health Midwest system. And I started rummaging through my brain for someone I could ask about the power structure of the area. I called a few foundation executives I knew and asked who they were funding in Kansas City, and was reconnected with a great save-the–family farm group in Missouri I had once given a grant to back when I worked in the foundation world. Bingo. The non-union connections began to work. One person pointed me to the next, and the community ball began to roll. Now I had names to use from the area when I called a couple of local clergy who were longtime left-leaning faith leaders. I phoned the Black ministers I had worked so closely with in Stamford, and sure enough, they had a couple of connections, too.

After three days in Kansas City, the good news was that I had met some of the most influential ministers in town and had a lead to the top rabbi on the Kansas side. The bad news was that—everyone told me—the sale was all but complete. The Health Midwest board had already essentially agreed to it in closed sessions. A done deal, pending the final approvals required for such an enormous financial transaction. And I was out of clean clothes.

I called Larry Fox.

"Larry, it's Jane. Tenet Healthcare has Health Midwest. So, I am going to book a flight back to NYC. Sorry, we are too late here."

"Look Jane, I didn't hire you for that kind of answer and I didn't send you to Kansas City to tell me what we can't do. You're supposed to be the one who wins, right? Call me when you have a better answer, and a strategy, and then tell me what you need. Don't call back before then."

And he hung up. Wow. I hadn't heard Larry talk that way before. I guessed the stakes were high, but the funny thing was I didn't know exactly what they were. That level of corporate strategy was not my department back then. Now I guessed that somehow stopping this sale was key to the national campaign to organize Tenet itself. I also knew

I wasn't flying home unless I didn't want to work for Larry anymore. I called him back and said I needed a researcher, who could stay in DC but would be working with me full-time. I needed a communications person too. But I also needed a few more days to sort out my strategy.

One thing was clear: This was a community fight, not a union fight. The SEIU not only had no power in Kansas City, it didn't have much political juice in Missouri or Kansas either. And the issue affected the entire Kansas City community. I was doing breakfast, lunch and dinner with local journalists, religious figures, political office holders in the districts with the hospitals, and more. Everyone left those meetings with a full stomach and a clear picture of exactly why selling their nonprofit community-owned hospitals to a sleazy for-profit corporation like Tenet was a bad idea. People didn't know much about for-profit hospitals back then—how megacompanies were gobbling up smaller hospital chains, then shutting down the less profitable ones, which were often the only hospitals serving poor people in a given area. I had printed out the list of Health Midwest's board of directors at Kinko's—I was still operating out of my hotel room—and working every connection to them I could find. My first and almost my only encounter with a union during my entire stay in Kansas City was with the American Federation of Teachers; oddly enough, the few nurses in Kansas City who were unionized were members of the AFT. And the teachers' union was hardly helpful. On the contrary, I had to scramble just to get them off my back. They were convinced that I was in town to pressure whatever company was buying Health Midwest into signing an organizing rights accord with the SEIU, which the AFT imagined would be a first step in an effort by the SEIU to steal their members. And why not think that? It was a common practice between unions, as I'd someday have good—or bad—reason to know.

But that sad experience came later. Now I thought all I had to do was contact the head of the AFT in the area, Gary Stevens, introduce myself, and simply promise him that I wasn't there to organize the Missouri and Kansas hospitals out from under him. How naïve. I had our chief of staff in DC phone the head of the AFT national health-care division and promise that the SEIU was not moving in on their turf in Missouri and Kansas, but the AFT remained unconvinced. I asked Stevens for a meeting so I could brief him on my real mission. He told me he'd set it up with him and one other guy, but when I walked in, he had about thirty-five nurses in the room sitting in a big circle surrounding one empty seat, which was for me. It was almost comical, but the result was more like tragedy, a failure to connect that was an accurate reflection of the depth of distrust between unions in this country.

I would have to forget the unions and rely on the community alone. One week in, I had assembled a team of influential religious leaders who were ready to act. Not surprisingly, not one of them had any connections to unions. The first shot across Tenet's bow came from Rabbi Mark Levin, whose congregation had provided the bricks and mortar for Menorah Hospital and represented a significant patient base there. What's more, he had connections to sitting Health Midwest board members and the civic power structure. At the end of our meeting I asked him to write an op ed for the newspaper, and he wrote a scathing piece, published in the *Kansas City Star,* about why the hospitals shouldn't be sold. Home run.

A few days later, working with religious leaders and some local politicians, we held the first informational picketing across from the biggest hospital. Thanks to the rabbi's opinion piece, the press covered the picket. Ministers were preaching about why the hospitals should not be sold. This little campaign was coming together. And then I had a real stroke of luck.

To this day I don't know exactly how it came about, but my cell phone rang and on the other end was someone who would not identify himself but claimed to be a Health Midwest board member. He said he knew who I was and he wanted to know my real intentions. I told him I wanted to stop the sale of Health Midwest to Tenet Healthcare, that Tenet was really bad news. In fact, Health Midwest should not be sold at all—letting go of Kansas City's excellent nonprofit hospital system would be a terrible mistake.

He agreed to start talking to me. He clearly was who he claimed to be, since he had insider information about the sale that I desperately needed. He still wouldn't reveal his name or his number, which was blocked on my phone, but he said he would get in touch with me as he thought necessary. I told him I would call him Deep Throat, after the anonymous inside tipster of the Watergate scandal. He laughed. He told me our campaign was having an effect on the board members, that people were beginning to question the sale. That was all I needed to hear.

Now we needed more ordinary people. The clergy were great for writing opinion pieces and placing calls to attorney generals and other regulators, but we needed public action. Washington had sent me a very talented communications person, Joyce Moscato. We took out ads in the weekly African American paper describing how Tenet had closed hospitals in black communities. The national SEIU sent in extra staff to listen to all the messages on our Campaign to Save Our Community Hospitals 1-800 machine. The staff would call people back and provide them with phone numbers for the Health Midwest board members and local politicians.

Then we set up what's called a patch-through phone system, so our young staffers could ask people if they wanted to be put directly through to their city council members and state legislative leaders to demand that Health Midwest not be sold to Tenet. This was before the Internet was quite up to a job on this scale, so our SEIU national call centers really had this phone patch through stuff figured out.

One of the local ministers insisted that I speak at the rally. That is not generally the way I work, but I wanted him to feel ownership of the event. I got quoted in the press saying, "It's time for Kansas City to stand up and say that we don't want for-profit health care." Not the most inspired political rhetoric, but it got the point across. And then suddenly I was in trouble again. I got a call from Larry Fox.

"Jane, you are not authorized to say that SEIU is opposed to for-profit healthcare. You are only authorized to be against Tenet Healthcare."

"Larry, I am running a genuine campaign to block the sale of a community nonprofit hospital chain to a for-profit system. To pull this off I have to actually educate people about the real issues involved. Am I supposed to get people into the streets to block the sale to Tenet because that is in the narrow interest of the SEIU, but leave nothing in place for when their hospitals get sold to a different for-profit corporation that will be just as bad for their communities but which the national union doesn't care about?"

Larry replied that he was fine with me running the campaign just the way I was running it, but Andy Stern was angry about the quote. I just needed to be more careful and not get quoted condemning all for-profit health care. This was another reason why I liked working for Larry Fox.

It was fall now, and local political campaigns were in full swing. I asked the national union for maximum political contributions for certain local candidates so that I could get into all the fundraising events and talk to every political power player. I had already found an ally in Gary Kemp, the head of the Kansas City Building Trades. Gary was old-school in a good way. He didn't like the idea of the local hospitals being sold and he made sure I knew when important political fundraisers were happening and also brought me in to speak at the Building Trades Council meetings. We were getting resolutions passed at town council and church meetings, all demanding that the sale of the hospitals to Tenet be stopped.

Deep Throat called to report that the Health Midwest board was going to convene a special meeting to discuss the sale. He said it was make-it-or-break-it time.

I asked my religious allies to call the *Kansas City Star* and request a meeting with the editorial board. The *Star* was an important community institution (as local papers once were). When I walked into the *Star* building with our religious team leaders, the national CEO of Tenet Healthcare was just walking out. Holy schmoly, this was big.

By the time the Health Midwest board finally met, the proposed sale was the biggest story in town. TV cameras were lined up outside HM headquarters. All night, the local news programs were running breaking-news interruptions every time someone walked out those doors. That's the point where the energy just drains from an organizer. There's nothing more you can do. I just lay down in the hotel room that had been home for three months, mindlessly watching the tube and waiting. And waiting. Finally the story broke: After an all-night meeting, the Health Midwest board had rejected the sale to Tenet. A minute later, my cell phone rang, and for the first time ever Andy Stern was on the other end.

"Jane, that was one hell of a job. That was incredible. Jesus, that was good work."

Within weeks, Larry Fox had signed an organizing rights accord between Tenet Healthcare and our national union, giving us organizing rights for 30,000 hospital workers. It was the biggest accord SEIU had ever won. This was industrial-scale organizing! And Tenet seemed desperate to get us off their back. To be clear, many talented people across the country had been working the Tenet campaign for years; stopping the Health Midwest sale was simply the final blow.

Before leaving Kansas City, I broke bread once more with the religious leaders who had been so crucial. Deep Throat called to congratulate me and wanted to identify himself, which he did, though with the caveat that I was never to share his identity with others. He also wanted me to meet "my enemy," as he called him. When I walked into their restaurant brunch meeting at the bagel café, this corporate honcho from Tenet shook my hand and said, "When you want to do that for us, you can make a million dollars a shot by blocking mergers and acquisitions." I smiled. We compared notes. He was deeply interested in knowing a few of the plays in my playbook. I withheld them. I thanked Deep Throat and flew home to New York, to a real home and clean clothes.

After a few days off, Larry Fox was on the phone again.
"Jane, your next assignment is going to be bigger. You need to go to DC to meet with Stern about it. Be polite, Jane, and don't say no whatever you do. You won't be working under me for this assignment. Stern wants to borrow you."

Stern began our first meeting by expressing his appreciation for the Kansas City win, and then he asked me to head up what would be the national union's first real congressional policy battle. There was a simple reason why SEIU had until now stayed out of big congressional issue fights: they just hadn't had the chips to play at that table. SEIU is strong in a handful of state legislatures—California, New York, Washington, Illinois, Oregon, Pennsylvania and Connecticut—where it has a lot of members and a sophisticated local. Passing national legislation requires a broader national presence. The union can move fifteen or twenty US senators, but no more, and the same proportion in the House of Representatives. Even if unions air-drop money into political work in states where labor is weak, there's no actual base of members to do anything with it. The inescapable fact is that it is hard for unions to drive national policy with less than 7 percent of private-sector workers unionized nationwide.

But now, in the winter of 2003, SEIU was confronted with a real crisis that would play out in Congress. President George W. Bush had just vetoed an important Medicaid funding bill. Medicaid is a crucial safety net program for the poor and its budget provides a significant chunk of the salaries of SEIU members working in hospitals and nursing homes. Of course, those very same Medicaid payments also account for a big chunk of the total revenue for the corporations that run those hospitals. Stern wanted to see if the union could put together a coalition that included hospital owners, who shared some of our concerns about the federal funding for Medicaid—a coalition with enough breadth and depth to get a win in Congress on a major national issue. As with the Tenet buyout of Health Midwest, everyone thought this campaign was a big stretch, but the stakes were so high we had to try.

Stern asked me specifically if I could tap into some of the connections with community and environmental organizations that had been essential to the win in Kansas City. I immediately remembered Larry Fox's call during that campaign, telling me Stern was furious that I'd been quoted in the press opposing for-profit health care. I told him that as long as SEIU was ready to find real common ground with others on Medicaid, I didn't see why not, but I did mention my fear of inviting community players to the table when we needed them to help fill in our missing twenty states, if we weren't going to back them afterward. Too often, unions use their allies for what they need and then dump them. I told him I didn't want to be involved in that.

When I was getting up to leave his office, Stern said, "So, you will be coordinating the federal fight. The starting budget is six million dollars. If that's not enough, let me know. We probably can get more if the employers sign on to the campaign."

Um, right. This is why I was still in the SEIU. I like campaigns that have to be completed in less than two months, start with $6 million budgets, and might win something that will have a real impact on the lives of millions of poor people.

I would be working under Kirk Adams, Stern's chief of staff and a key architect of the national SEIU's emerging big-picture corporate strategy, which included finding enough common ground with hospital owners to work with them on issues like Medicaid and Medicare funding, thus demonstrating the union's value to their bottom line, then using it as leverage to win organizing rights agreements.

I began where I always begin: a power structure analysis—this time, a very quick one on the House and Senate to learn exactly whom we needed to move to win. Then, just as in local organizing campaigns, we proceeded to leadership ID, though this time, instead of identifying which workers were the leaders on the shop floor, we were identifying which senators and representatives were the real leaders on the Medicaid fight: who carried weight on the powerful budget and appropriations committees, the states they came from, their vulnerabilities, the political teams they played for, and so on. Next, we created a chart, overlaying a map of SEIU membership over a map of the congressional leadership, discovering the gaping holes and identifying allies—such as the Center for Community Change, ACORN, and faith-based organizations—with a presence in those holes, who might join a cooperative campaign to put the money Bush had cut back into Medicaid and maybe even—who knows?—add some more. Many of these antipoverty groups I had known for years.

Talking with them, I learned that restoring the Bush health-care cuts was not the only thing on their congressional agenda. There was also a major push to change Medicaid eligibility rules so that more poor people would be able to access the money we were trying to win back. Not surprisingly, these groups wondered whether unions or especially hospital owners would care about eligibility rules. I wondered the same thing. No one during my briefing at the SEIU had even mentioned this. I realized that the SEIU leadership needed to be briefed on why the eligibility rules mattered so much to these potential allies. I set up a meeting in Washington with the leaders of many of the antipoverty and direct-action groups that had reach into the key states we needed to win. I asked Stern to be in the meeting and kick it off, and to make a real commitment to them on the eligibility issue.

By this time we had brought some key hospital corporations on board. They didn't have much more geographical reach than the union did, but they had weight with Republicans. And they had influence in a few crucial Southern states where the SEIU had nothing. I made a series of maps showing the states and congressional districts where we needed to win. One map identified areas the union could carry, another the regions the corporations could carry. Then I overlapped that map with a similar one for the community groups. These maps demonstrated that if we could get everyone working together we could win—but that was a big if. Obviously, the union hoped that my personal credibility with the anti-poverty groups would make them forget labor's reputation for burning its allies. The eligibility issue was not a priority for SEIU, neither was it a problem. The real question involved the corporations: Would they at least agree not to oppose those changes to the eligibility rules that were most crucial to the antipoverty groups?

In the end we ran two parallel meetings. The first included our national and regional community allies. I was the convener and chair of this one, with Andy Stern representing the SEIU. The second meeting included representatives of the corporations, chaired by Kirk Adams and Larry Fox. At each meeting, I gave a slide show laying out the strategic overview of how we could win and exactly which player was going to cover which members of the House and Senate. I pulled no punches about where all the players' interests converged and where they diverged. The main point was to show that we could win, but that winning would require a real coalition of forces that were often adversaries.

Everyone got on board. The corporations agreed to kick in their lobbyists and money. The latter was critical, as we had come to the conclusion that we needed considerably more than $6 million just to carpet a few key congressional districts with TV ads. The community groups promised to mobilize their troops, and very quickly there were direct actions taking place in target states across the nation. It was a coordinated assault: SEIU ran the air war, and the community groups ran the "ground war."

It worked. The billions Bush had cut from Medicaid was restored, and then $20 billion in additional new funding was added. We had kept our word on the eligibility issue and also won some improvements in the eligibility rules, though not all the antipoverty groups had hoped for.

Once again, Stern called me in to congratulate me. Just as with Kansas City, this win had strategic implications for SEIU. We had shown the corporations that the union could be a key ally in moving federal funding issues that were crucial to them. Fox and Kirk Adams asked me to make a presentation to the national union's executive board on how we won. They wanted me to review the entire campaign from the first steps: the power structure analysis, how we used the PSA to chart the maps, and how we had managed to get the strange bedfellows we'd mapped to work together. I was excited. This is what I had come to labor to do—to see what would happen if you put the kind of resources labor commands into the service of a politics that takes coalition building seriously. I was there to open some windows in the stuffy house of labor.

Then came another of those weird calls. I was in my DC office. Larry Fox phoned from Connecticut and asked me to go to his office down the hall, close the door, and call him back.

"Jane, I have some bad news. I am sorry I have to be the one to tell you this, but Anna Burger is not going to allow you to make the presentation to the board. In fact, she has decided to keep you away from the meeting entirely. She doesn't want you to be part of the discussion in any way." I heard him take a deep breath.

"In your place, Anna is going to have her political department people talk about the campaign and take the credit for it. I know, Jane, this is very, very bad. I have already tried to push back, along with some other fans of yours in high places, but Anna really has it in for you. I am truly sorry." Silence.

"So, Larry, what do you think? I have just played a key role in pulling off two important long-shot campaigns for the national union, and that doesn't seem to matter against petty personal politics stemming from a couple of local electoral campaigns in Pittsburgh that were simply the result of the national union having ambiguous lines of authority. I have already been banned from the Eastern region. Now I am being taken away from big national campaigns and punished by the Queen of Petty. Will this ever change?" Silence.

"No, I don't think so. A few of us have assessed it: Anna really has decided you are someone she doesn't like to have around."

And it wasn't just me. Some women in SEIU had approached me with their own Burger stories.

I realized that what separated me from these women was that I understood there was life outside the labor movement. This was one of the things that had made me valuable to labor, but it was also my escape valve. I often spoke with mentors from outside the union, and now these people offered me starkly different advice from what I was getting from women in the national SEIU. In fact, most of these mentors were surprised I had lasted in labor for as long as I had—five years, at that point.

Fox came back from the board meeting and told me that Burger had introduced the big presentation on the congressional win before handing it over to her staff. They framed it as the work of their political department and never so much as mentioned my name or the indispensable role played by our community-based allies.

This time Larry said he would do nothing to convince me to stay with the national union, and accepted my resignation graciously. He asked if I would accept some consulting work with a couple of locals that wanted me immediately. Not quite sure what else I was going to do, I agreed. Larry told me that Sal Rosselli had just suffered his first big defeat in a long time, out in California, and was searching for ways to turn it around. I called Sal for a briefing. He told me to just get on a plane.

Rosselli had sent a team of good organizers into Fresno, an agricultural city in the heart of California's Central Valley, where they had succeeded in helping 10,000 home care workers form a new union. That was the good news. But they had just got slammed in the first contract fight and actually *lost* it. The contract had to be approved by the Fresno County Board of Supervisors, and in my initial assessment, Rosselli had grossly misjudged how different the political landscape of Fresno was from his base in the San Francisco Bay Area, the most progressive region in the nation. And no first contract meant no union.

I agreed to take on the effort to resurrect the first contract campaign. Rosselli had put Dana Simon in charge of the effort for the local. Dana was the real deal. He knew how to organize, and he actually liked talking with and listening to workers. I told Larry Fox I needed a full-time researcher to move to Fresno for two months to conduct a PSA under my direction. I reminded him that since I had resigned from the national SEIU, it was in his interest for me to leave that crucial skill somewhere in his research team. He quickly agreed and sent Sara Rothstein, a super-sharp young researcher whom I had recruited into SEIU from prior work we had done together.

Anthony Thigpenn, my longtime colleague and good friend who had created and then taught me the power structure analysis technique I was using, lived in Los Angeles. Anthony was devoted to community organizing in his home city, but he had a long-term interest in changing California state politics. And changing California politics for the better meant changing the political equation in the Central Valley, and Fresno was the valley's seat of power. I asked Anthony if he would be willing to help me with the campaign, and he agreed. This was shaping up to be quite a team, with the likes of Anthony Thigpenn, Dana Simon, and Sara Rothstein. Look out, Fresno!

Over the next two months we conducted a very thorough PSA, and the results strongly suggested that the conventional wisdom that big agriculture controlled the Central Valley was wrong. The agricultural titans who had ruled this area like feudal lords had been displaced as the Valley's dominant power by big developers. And the road to the developers was not through the Fresno County Board of Supervisors, where Rosselli had focused his efforts, but through the Fresno City Council, which had decision-making power on land use.

I knew these conclusions would be a hard sell with Rosselli's Local 250, in Oakland. Here I was, waltzing in from New York with this PSA thing, telling them that some of their fundamental assumptions about how power worked in their own state were wrong, and that the county supervisors, who ultimately voted on their contract, were not their real target.

We finished our analysis and Sara Rothstien presented it to Rosselli, Simon, and a small group of other people concerned, including Arturo Rodriguez, the head of the United Farm Workers (UFW). The PSA contained maps of political contributions, win-loss records of the key political teams in the region, and more. We showed how a handful of key real estate developers could actually move the county supervisors to approve the home care contract, and that the political interests of these developers lay with the Fresno City Council. Therefore, if Rosselli's team could shift its focus to the council races that were crucial for the developers, they could wedge the real power players to get the supervisor votes they needed.

Fortunately, Arturo Rodriguez and his political director at the UFW, long considered the experts on political power in the Central Valley, thought the PSA was spot-on, and that we had just documented exactly what they had suspected: that the power equation in the Valley had fundamentally changed. We then made a series of recommendations that Local 250 needed to implement right away: key allies to make in the community, policy positions to take on some important Central Valley issues, and local city council endorsements to obtain. In short, we recommended a comprehensive strategy that changed the entire approach the union was taking.

Soon afterward, the Fresno County Board of Supervisors reversed themselves and approved the Local 250 home care contract, covering 10,000 workers.

Shortly after the Fresno win, Larry Fox called again, to say he had reconsidered his approval of my resignation, and that actually he and Eliseo Medina, SEIU's executive vice president for the Western region (and occasional challenger of the notion that Anna Burger would inherit the reins of the national SEIU when Stern moved on) had a new challenge they very much wanted me to accept: moving to Las Vegas to revamp our highly inept, maybe even corrupt, Nevada local. I said no way. Then Larry and Eliseo went into double team: Larry reported that Las Vegas was key to his analysis about which health-care markets would matter in the 2004–2008 time frame for big-scale hospital organizing; Eliseo assured me that he could protect me from Burger. The Southwest was his region and he could provide sufficient cover to keep me out of harm's way.

Eliseo was a compelling figure. His career as a labor activist began in 1965 when, as a nineteen-year-old grape picker, he participated in a crucial United Farm Workers' strike. For the next thirteen years he'd risen through the ranks to become the UFW's national vice president. Then he moved to SEIU and helped revive the San Diego local, building its membership from 1,700 to over 10,000 in five years. He was a key strategist in the Los Angeles building service workers' strike, which in April 2000 resulted in the largest wage increase in the fifteen-year history of SEIU's Justice for Janitors campaign.

As I looked around the world outside labor, nothing seemed all that exciting. The entire progressive movement was gasping as if in a massive asthma attack. The Bush-Cheney-Rumsfeld-Rove machine was on full attack.

Then, like the brilliant organizers they were, since they couldn't overcome my common sense, Larry and Eliseo appealed to one of my passions: horses. Larry told me over and over that land in Vegas was so cheap that I could get a little place where my horse could live with me. Jalapeño, the horse I had acquired while at the Highlander Center in Tennessee, was still mine, though I had not seen him all that much during the New York City–DC–Pittsburgh–Kansas City–Fresno whirlwind tour. Finally, he convinced me to just go to Vegas for a visit. The week I got there, in a true twist of fate, happened to be the week of the National Rodeo Finals. Hmmm, this was interesting. Who knew Vegas had so many cowboys? Over the next several days I went alone to the rodeo every night and then to the myriad cowboy dances in the casinos. In the morning, I would go hiking at beautiful Red Rock Canyon just outside the city. Hmmm. Red Rock Canyon was stunning, and there appeared to be horses up in there.

I relented and said I would accept the position and move to Vegas.

CHAPTER THREE

Bumpy Landing in Las Vegas

It is hard to convey how odd it was for me to move to Las Vegas. I didn't own a TV and never had. I'd never put so much as a nickel in a slot machine (and that's still true). Sheep farming in New Zealand is my idea of entertainment. Moving to a place built on glitz and glamour, a fake city whose skyline is a collection of replicas of real cities I actually like, had been nowhere on my life's radar screen. But there were lots of good reasons why a union that wanted to organize the hospital industry would make Las Vegas a priority, and Larry Fox had them figured out. And though the details are complicated and a little arcane, they are worth explaining because they offer some insight into what goes into an intelligent strategy to organize workers on a large scale.

To start with, some of the key national and regional hospital chains SEIU had targeted for unionization ran hospitals in Las Vegas. What's more, these hospitals really mattered to the national companies, because they made truckloads of money for their parent corporations. You have to understand the system of hospital billing and insurance companies to appreciate this. When you injure yourself at home and you have health insurance, you go to a health care facility that's "inside" your insurance company's network, and the insurance company can work how everything is billed to its own advantage. But when you drive to Las Vegas from Los Angeles (and 300,000 people do that every weekend), or fly in for a weekend from somewhere in the Midwest, your local hospital doesn't come with you. Vegas hospitals are delighted to see you walk in the door, because you are an "out-of-network" charge that they can structure to their own advantage and then collect from your health insurance company. Las Vegas has 44 million tourists coming and going each year, and whenever one has a heart attack after drinking too much and losing their house at the roulette table that's another juicy patient for a Las Vegas hospital. If you are interested in organizing a campaign to unionize a whole national chain, send some organizers to one of their hospitals in Vegas and you will definitely get their attention.

If you are a national union and you want to organize an entire industrial sector, if you are smart you don't start with the weak, underperforming shops, even though those are the ones where workers are most likely to be underpaid and pissed off. No, you start with the high-performing, income-generating outfits. You assume you are going to win the organizing drive (this leaves out the vast majority of union organizing), and when you do, you want to end up sitting across the table from an employer who actually has some money to pay for a good contract. Now, this presumes you care about winning a high quality contract (even more unions fall out of the mix). But you care about this, because you want the workers at all the hospitals in the market to see what is possible to win with a union. Finally this presumes that your national union is actually going to stay focused on the local campaign and keep putting resources into it long enough to win a good first contract—and now we have left out virtually *all* of the unions. Amazingly, when Larry Fox was the head of national health-care organizing, the SEIU actually behaved in this intelligent manner.

To go on from here, I need to explain a little about hospitals. Most health-care markets are served by a combination of five common types of hospitals: faith-based, academic medical centers, publicly owned, nonprofit, and for-profit. Actually, some states don't allow for-profit hospitals or health care, and that's a good thing. My home state of New York, like most of the Northeast, does not permit publicly traded hospitals to operate at all. Many politicians and journalists I have met, and certainly most workers, don't even know that there are states that entirely ban the kinds of hospitals that dominate Las Vegas. This is one reason there are so many good hospitals in New York and Boston: It is actually illegal in those cities to set up a hospital or health care company whose core purpose is making money rather than healing patients. Have you ever heard anyone with cancer say, "I am jumping on a plane to Vegas to get some quality care?" I didn't think so.

The for-profit hospitals deliver the worst care in the country, hands down, and sue me for this sentence so I can depose all your records in court and have some real fun. This is not to say that the other types necessarily deliver high-quality care. Plenty of them don't. But the worst patient care is consistently found in for-profit operations. Like all corporations whose purpose is to make money, the for-profits want the least regulation possible. That means no environmental groups or laws, no community organizations to account to or laws that mandate health care for the poor, and above all else, *no unions.*

For-profit hospitals didn't even exist in this country until a regulatory structure that favored them was set up during the Reagan administration. And once for-profit hospital corporations had crawled out from under a rock, they headed straight for Las Vegas, and undid a lot of Nevada's health care laws. The Las Vegas hospital market is now unique, in that it is actually dominated by national for-profit hospital chains.

Not coincidentally, Nevada is what is called a right-to-work state. The labor laws in Nevada are totally different from those in what are commonly called union security states. In a union security state, once the workers in a shop vote to form a union by a simple majority of the votes cast, every worker in that shop has to join and pay dues. In a right-to-work state, though a majority of workers vote to form a union, each individual worker can decide at any time to join or to leave it, which has all sorts of implications for how one goes about organizing and sustaining a strong union, which I will get into later. When you look at a map of the right-to-work states, you are also looking at a map of the "red" states in presidential politics, the states with the worst schools and the most poverty, teen pregnancies, and other community ills.

Not only is Nevada a right-to-work state, it is also profoundly corrupt. Its most powerful political players are casino owners who until recently were all "mobbed up" with the mafia. Paying off politicians with "bag money" is still a common ploy, and people who make the wrong enemies still occasionally wind up in shallow desert graves. After the casino owners, the next-biggest political players are in the mining industry, guys who are all about stomping out any kind of environmental regulation. It's a situation that doesn't favor local health and safety.

Las Vegas, with its right-to-work laws, its casino owners and mining corporations, its corruption and its 44 million tourists a year engaging in insalubrious activities, is the Shangri-la of low-quality, bottom-feeding, for-profit hospital chains.

Just what sort of political power do these corporations have? When I arrived in Vegas, the biggest for-profit hospital in town was Sunrise, owned by the Hospital Corporation of America. The family that controlled HCA also controlled the US Senate. That would be the family of Bill Frist, then the Senate majority leader from Tennessee, HCA's home state and national headquarters. Of course, there is a tradition in this country that if your family business is making money hand over fist you might want one of your own in the US Senate just to keep the wheels greased, but not many actually get to be majority leader. Now when your family business is a big for-profit hospital chain, you want to make sure that the Senate doesn't go off and do something stupid like regulate health care (or, God forbid, nationalize it). And though Frist and HCA are an obvious example because their connection to political power was so public, the other for-profit hospital chains with cash cows in Las Vegas have been no less powerful in their own way. Certainly they have the power of money. The CEOs of these companies consistently make the biggest salaries in health care. Alan Miller of Universal Health Services (UHS), with an annual compensation in excess of $20 million, is not only the highest paid CEO in the health industry but also one of the highest-paid in the entire country. Meanwhile his company delivers care so bad, its patients might do better in Bangladesh.

Oddly enough, precisely because these corporations are publicly traded, they are more vulnerable to what are known as corporate campaigns or pressure campaigns. Unions have pension funds with millions—no, *billions*—of dollars that they can move around the stock market and use as a weapon against the for-profits. It's quite a bit more complicated than that sentence implies, because the main thing pension funds need to do is earn a return for retirees. And because the pension fund boards are part management and part labor, etc. Stockholding unions can participate in investor calls and learn early on when any potential legal action, violation or other problem might be communicated to shareholders. These for-profit hospital corporations are easy to embarrass because, quite frankly, they stink. This makes them more vulnerable to campaigns that get nonunion shareholders to add their pressure to the union's. Where bureaucracies that are supposed to police hospital quality are understaffed and can't do their job effectively, unions can help them by using organizing campaigns to expose inferior care and by demanding investigations that can be put to use in the shareholder campaigns. And finally, because these big for-profits are national in scope, if unions want to organize workers on a large scale there's some logic to going after the big national companies against whom you can invest a lot of energy on the front end and hopefully come out the other with an organizing accord that covers hospitals in multiple states.

If you're trying to organize a corporation like CHW that is a regional player trying to go national, that's even better, because the company needs things from politicians and regulators. At best this might be a politician you had put in office. Short of that, any player with whom you have some positive influence. And short of that, someone for whom you could create serious problems.

What Larry Fox had figured out was that the hospitals in Las Vegas not only mattered to their corporate owners in terms of cash flow and profit, but they were at the intersection of every major hospital organizing campaign the national SEIU was looking into. There were two national for-profit hospital chains with their claws deep in the Las Vegas market. The Frist family's HCA had four hospitals there. Universal Health Services (UHS) had four and was planning to open a fifth. A third big player was Catholic Healthcare West (CHW), which had two hospitals and had purchased the land for a third. Finally, there was the Clark County public hospital, which served the poor and, incidentally, outperformed the others in terms of quality of care indicators. That sums up Vegas: The poor people's hospital run by the county was a beacon of quality measured against the bottom feeders of the private sector.

So what about my team, the union? Plainly put, the SEIU local in Las Vegas was an embarrassment. The union couldn't organize lunch for two, let alone a campaign for new workers. Politically, SEIU was barely on the radar screen of Vegas politics. The casino workers' union was the dominant union in town. In the confusing way that the names of many unions don't reflect their full membership, the casino workers' union was called the Culinary Workers Local 226. It was affiliated with the Hotel

Employees and Restaurant Employees Union, and in fact was HERE's biggest local in the nation. There was also a teachers' union affiliated with the National Education Association, and the Carpenters Union had a strong presence as well. In the gossip circles of Vegas power brokers, politicians would say the casino workers and carpenters unions had money and people, but the teachers just had money. No one bothered to gossip about SEIU.

Even the *name* of the SEIU local was sad: Local 1107, chosen because it is casino slang for a perfect hand of cards. One year in, I began to ask the members if they might want to change the name: "Building a union is not about gambling; it's about power. Do you want a name that's about gambling?" Two years in, we voted to call ourselves SEIU Nevada.

Though I had been working in the national health-care division for two years, the only thing I knew about the Vegas local was that it was underperforming. The only organizing of nonunion workers they did was when the national union air-dropped a campaign for a "hot shop"—a shop whose workers had actually called the union and *asked* someone to come organize them.

There is a myth that Vegas is a "union town." Labor people outside all know that HERE's local did a stellar job of winning good contracts for the maids and servers in the casinos, converting crummy low-paying service jobs into middle-class careers. The casino worker contracts are as good as it gets for service workers in this country. That is no small feat and you can read about them in numerous articles and books.* John Wilhelm, leader of the national parent union, UNITE-HERE,† made his name in Las Vegas rebuilding what was an awful union and turning it into a powerful union serving its members. D. Taylor, the union's current leader, is an incredibly savvy and able leader. When you consider what the average maid or food server makes everywhere else in this country, and you understand that this union in Las Vegas fought sometimes bloody struggles to win good contracts benefitting mostly female members—contracts that provided full employer-paid health care, decent wages,

---

* See Mike Davis, "Armageddon at the Emerald City: Local 226 vs. MGM Grand," *The Nation*, July 11, 1994, and Harold Meyerson, "Las Vegas as a Workers' Paradise," *The American Prospect*, January 15, 2008.

† The Hotel and Restaurant Employees Union (HERE) merged with the Union of Needle Trades, Industrial and Textile Workers (UNITE) in 2004.

some retirement benefits, vacations, and some rights on the job—you can see why this union is a big deal.

In truth, Las Vegas is not a union city; it has a union street: Las Vegas Boulevard, universally known as the Strip. The power of the casino workers is highly concentrated along this two-mile stretch of amazingly tacky gambling Fantasylands. Union density on the Strip is high, both for the service workers who staff the casinos and the construction workers who build and regularly rebuild the Strip with even more garish monstrosities. But go just a few blocks off the Strip, and even the casino workers aren't union. The Vegas suburbs aren't union. Reno isn't union. It made me a little crazy when I would say I was organizing in a right-to-work state and people answered, "Yeah, but Vegas, that's a union town."

As if the local corruption, the state's right-to-work laws, and the political power of the casinos and mining interests weren't challenging enough, there is yet another peculiar aspect of Las Vegas that makes it inhospitable terrain for growing unions: the transient nature of its population. Not only do 44 million tourists come and go each year, the actual residents also come and go, and with astounding frequency. In the past twenty years Las Vegas has grown by an average of 5,000 people per month. But even that doesn't capture all the moving going on, as the 5,000 new residents are actually the difference of 10,000 arrivals minus 5,000 departures of old residents every month. It's a gold rush dynamic: Rust Belt refugees and Midwesterners stream in searching for decent-paying jobs in either casino service or construction. Latin American immigrants stream in seeking work building houses for those 5,000 new residents a month. Very few of them end up staying long enough to care about much of anything that actually happens in the city. They move so often that maintaining voter lists is a joke. Not surprisingly, the city has a high percentage of adults without children, and anyone who actually gets a good job and settles down and has kids soon discovers that Vegas has none of the social support structures for families that are considered the norm in other American cities.

So, who the hell would want to go try to organize new workers into the SEIU in Las Vegas? No one.

You can't say I don't like a good challenge.

Before I left DC, I was told by the national leadership that if I found dirt so deep that cleaning it up would require unseating everyone on the local executive board, I should not hesitate to recommend that the national union place the local in trusteeship. No one in the national union really knew exactly how bad it was in Vegas because no one had paid enough attention.

When I got to town the first person I met was Vicky Hedderman. Hedderman had held the post of rank-and-file president of the local for almost a decade, which was not a great recommendation, given the sorry history of the union during that time. It was crucial that I understand who Vicky really was, and even more importantly how she had managed to hold on to her jobs for two decades. Yep, it was crucial to understand that. Unfortunately, I didn't.

I didn't understand it partly because the structure of the Nevada local was different from what I was used to. In the Northeast, the SEIU locals still had the original structure given to them by the communist organizers of District 1199 before 1199 had merged with the national SEIU. By the time I got to Vegas, the 1199 structure had become the norm for SEIU across the country. In this model, staff are considered members of the union just as the workers are, which militates against the sort of divisions forming between staff and workers that I would find in Nevada. And since staff and workers are all members, they can run for the union's elected offices, like president, vice president for this and that, secretary treasurer. The Nevada local followed a tradition common among the public sector unions built in the late 1960s and early 1970s, when government workers won the right to collective bargaining.‡ In this model, the staff are not actually members of the union and cannot run for elected office. Instead, members elect officers from their own ranks, who then hire a single, powerful staff person, the executive director, who then hires everyone else.

Every organizational structure has advantages and disadvantages. On the face of it, the structure of the Las Vegas local might seem more democratic. The problem is that in this age of huge and complex corporations using sophisticated professional union busters, it takes a

‡ The right of public-sector workers to collectively bargain was a victory of the civil rights movement, since most Blacks who had decent jobs were in the public sector, which until then had been denied the right to organize.

professionally trained staff to run a union. The 1199 model acknowledges this up front: the trained staff run for elected office, and the members vote on them, so union elections hold the staff directly accountable for their actions. In the Las Vegas model, once the elected officers from the rank-and-file have hired their staff executive director, he or she hires the rest of the staff and begins running the day-to-day operations, and too often you end up with weak functionaries holding largely ceremonial elected posts standing between the staff who run the union from the members they ought to be accountable to. Hedderman's position, rank-and-file president, was a perfect example of this. Though her title implied that she was the head of the union, the union's constitution actually didn't give her much power. The real head was the staff executive director.

From the moment Hedderman first began her rise through the elected offices of the Las Vegas local, she'd managed to take advantage of a series of perks for the various titles she held that always amounted to her not actually having to work at her job full-time as a unit secretary at the Clark County public hospital. Unions in the public sector often try to get what are called lost-time clauses into their contracts, mandating that the employer pay employees for time spent on union work. Most unionists regard this as a good thing, but I am entirely unconvinced. In the Clark County civil service contracts, the union had negotiated for a "bank" of lost-time hours, and the distribution of these hours was approved by none other than the rank-and-file president. So, if you were elected to the union post of, say, chief steward at a county facility, assuming the local's president was loyal to you and vice versa, he or she simply signed a payroll sheet each month stating that you were not at work at your actual job because you were doing union work.

One specific clause, which appeared only in the main county contracts, stipulated that if the rank-and-file president came from the Clark County payroll, then the county would have to keep paying that person at full salary even though he or she worked full-time for the union. Hedderman proudly and often explained to me that the union never even tried to negotiate this language into any other contract, so it all but guaranteed the county workers control of the local's presidency. This was because only the a county worker could campaign for union office by saying, "Elect me, I can be your *full-time* advocate." Hedderman understood that hell (or Vegas) would freeze over before any private company would sign a contract that committed it to paying the salary of a union president.

This was more obviously sinister when one looked at the other public sector contracts—the public health district's or the quasi-publicly run convention center's—where the union might easily have won the same language but chose not to. And since contract negotiations were done with little participation by anyone, the members in the other government units thought there was some legitimate reason why only county workers could be president.

Vicky essentially fixed it up so she became rank-and-file president in perpetuity, with a salary paid by the boss. Beautiful. And the union constitution didn't really assign the president much in the way of work. Actually, there was one thing she worked at tenaciously: hanging on to her position. Her strategy was filing grievances on behalf of her members in the county hospital.

A grievance is a legal complaint filed by a union alleging that the employer is violating some point of the collectively bargained union contract. Filing grievances on behalf of individual workers might sound like a great thing, but the reality is quite different today. In the mid 1930s through 1940s, in workplaces with extremely dangerous conditions, such as mines and steel plants, with much stronger grievance procedures in place that could lead to immediate resolution of dangerous conditions, grievances must have made sense. But in the twenty-first century service economy, with its weak unions in a weak labor movement, the grievance process is about as effective as shoveling sand with a pitchfork. Once a grievance is filed, the issue leaves the collective hands of the workers and gets plugged into a stifling chain of legalisms and bureaucracy. It often takes *years* to actually get the thing resolved, and the final decisions are made by lawyers and bureaucrats far removed from the workplace. A union that spends all its time on grievances has very little real power. But if you have the workplace effectively organized, the kinds of problems that would eventually become grievances are resolved on the shop floor, where the managers actually have to listen to their employees or face a more immediate form of dispute resolution: direct worker action. And frankly, sometimes union officers file grievances on behalf of real slackers who actually are screwing up on the job, and then the union has to waste precious resources defending them. An organized shop can smell that bullshit as soon as it starts.

Grievances are very effective, however, in creating a base among the membership for the leaders who file them. In the absence of any real collective worker power, a union leader can agree to handle a grievance with a wink and a nod that says, "Remember me at the next election." Since a union like this has very little vitality, turnout for its internal elections tends to be quite low, and a small network of members grateful that their grievances were filed will often be enough to return the same lame leadership back to power again and again. Good organizers can spot these unions a mile away. They call them grievance mills, and what Vicky Hedderman had going for two decades in the Las Vegas local of the SEIU was the quintessential grievance mill. I knew none of this that first day when I walked into Hedderman's office to meet her. I hadn't even read the local's constitution and bylaws yet. All I knew was that she was longtime rank-and-file president of a really ineffective union, the kind of union that has contracts expiring and gets few workers involved in their own negotiations, and I was there to change all that, and so most likely she and I were not going to be best of friends. When I shook her hand, I wanted to blurt out, "What the hell have you been doing for twenty years?" What I said was, "Hi, very nice to meet you."

Generally speaking, this problem of not playing with a full deck—stepping on toes I didn't even know were there, confronting adversaries whose source of power I did not fully understand, stuff like that—was a *constant* condition of my life in the labor movement. At first I thought it was the result of my relative inexperience in the arcane minutiae of unions, and certainly this was true in part. Only later would it occur to me that it might also be the result of conscious decisions higher up, made by those who wanted me on their team because I knew how to win a tough campaign, but who also wanted me vulnerable, so that when my belief in building real worker power conflicted with their vested interests, they could get rid of me.

Not that I was the only strong player they could have sent to the table in Nevada. But if you consider the convolutions of that rat's nest of a local, factor in a corrupt right-to-work state and a phony city built on gambling and prostitution where the temperature climbs above 110 degrees for days on end, it will probably dawn on you—as it soon enough did on me—why the SEIU, searching for a sucker to take on such a circus, had to dig all the way down to a lefty troublemaker like me.

I did hold one card that trumped anything in the hand of even someone as entrenched as Vicky: if conditions were bad enough, I could call headquarters and recommend that they trustee her local. And Vicky knew that things were bad. She also understood that if the local were trusteed, she'd have to go back to being a full-time unit secretary in the public hospital. On the other hand, if she supported my candidacy for the executive directorship at the local's executive board meeting, as the national union was recommending, she could go on drawing her salary while avoiding her job in the hospital. Yeah, it made me want to puke, but you have to pick your battles, and I had some major ones breathing down my neck.

When I arrived in Nevada, I was being paid as a consultant to the national union. I still had to formally be hired by the executive board, which was 100 percent loyal to Hedderman. An early example of just how willing Hedderman was to play ball with the Stern forces was the actual negotiation regarding my hire. When I sat down with Vicky to talk about the process with the board, she said she had typed up a contract for five years and would have the board approve it "right away." Just like that. I actually pushed back, in defense of worker democracy, saying I thought I should have a one-year contract instead, so that the workers could fire me with no questions asked the next year. That idea didn't come from SEIU headquarters or from Hedderman. It came from Jerry Brown and me, brainstorming on the phone about the best way to introduce some fair-minded procedure into this poorly run local union.

The way Hedderman and the prior executive director had run the union had created serious tension between members in the public and private sectors. The Clark County civil service workers originally formed their own small union, and then decided to affiliate with the SEIU in the late 1980s. This sort of thing was quite common. When government workers won the right to collectively bargain, many simply voted to form independent associations at whatever government institution they worked. The City of Las Vegas workers also formed their own union years ago, chose not to affiliate with any national union, and are still independent today.

Another of Nevada's quirks is that the Clark County government is the real power in the state. Nevada has a libertarian ethic and no income tax—and a large chunk of property and sales taxes go to local governments, as does a large portion of the far more lucrative hotel room and airport taxes. So the lion's share of all the dollars those 44 million tourists a year bring into the state stays right in Clark County, giving it more money and therefore more power than the state itself. If you exclude prisons and schools, Clark County even has more public employees. So for the national SEIU, affiliating the Clark County civil service was a smart move.

When I landed in Vegas, the Clark County civil service workers and their counterparts at the county hospital enjoyed total control of the executive board of Local 1107—they always had. And they had decent contracts. Life was good for the county workers. And they had started the union, so hooray for them. But I had been sent there to organize new members—in fact, to totally transform the local into the sort of organizing powerhouse we had built in Stamford. There weren't many public sector workers left to organize in Vegas, so all the growth would necessarily have to come from the private sector, specifically the workers in the local hospitals that were so strategic to the giant health care corporations the SEIU had its sights on nationally. And any organizing drive that added big numbers of private sector workers to the rolls of the local would be seen as a direct threat by the county workers who controlled the union. Wonderful.

These kinds of tensions have emerged at local and even national unions all across the country, the direct result of New Labor's "turn to organizing." Loads of new members inevitably disrupt entrenched balances of power. It is the same dynamic that makes it so hard to interest politicians who are in office to support campaign finance reform: the simple fact that they are in office makes them like the system the way it is—why would they want to rock the boat by changing anything?

But although the county workers in the Vegas area were generally pleased with their pay and benefits, the truth was that they shouldn't have been. The contract with Clark County had expired in 2002, and nearly two years of negotiations followed, resulting in a new contract that was full of disappointments. Even after all that bargaining there were outstanding disagreements, and at some point the Clark County manager and the union had simply agreed to most of the contract while leaving the final details of the exceedingly complex pay system unresolved. So although the contract was supposedly settled when I arrived in late February of 2004, there was actually one small issue still outstanding: *pay*. Unfortunately, I didn't know this. Neither did anyone at the national SEIU in DC. And most importantly, neither did most of the public sector workers themselves. But Vicky Hedderman and the four executive board members from the Clark County civil service knew, and they also knew how bad it was that this problem was "not yet resolved."

What a mess. And that was the Clark County civil service contract, supposedly the real feather in the local's cap. What I found in the private sector contracts was even worse, as I next discovered that the local also had two private sector contracts that were about to expire. One of these contracts was already in its "window" period—bear with me while I explain that. The details of these laws can seem incredibly arcane, in part because what they actually mean and do is deliberately hidden under layers of legal gibberish. So if your eyes start to glaze over, remember that this is just what the people who wrote the laws hoped for. They wanted to bore you right out of your rights. I'll try to make them more interesting.

Let's say a union has a contract with a corporation and it's set to expire. Under private sector law (and there are all sorts of strange little deviations for crazy reasons everywhere), the union must "trigger" renegotiation of the contract no more than 120 days and no less than 90 days, before the date the contract expires. These 30 days are called the "window period," and during that time workers can petition to throw the union out entirely. Officially, the employer is prohibited from circulating such a petition; it must come from the workers themselves. In real life, each time a contract expires, all management has to do is find one worker who wants to grow up to be just like them to run what is technically called a decertification petition ("decert" in organizer slang), and an election ensues on whether to throw out the union. As if that weren't enough, workers can also petition to disaffiliate from the parent union and join a different union instead. This triggers an election battle between the two unions, with both unions sending teams of frantic organizers into the same shop, attempting to convince the workers of the superiority of one union or the other. In union talk this is called a raid, and is considered one of the slimiest operations a scumbag union can do. And of course, unions do it all the time.

The insane laws that make decerts and raids possible were not thought up by nice people, FYI. They were carefully constructed to weaken unions and hurt workers. They are one important reason (among many) why unions began to decline in the early 1970s. And they are the law of the land, whether you live in a right-to-work or a union security state. If you are running a union local, you learn pretty quickly that you better have a really good system in place to deal with all this craziness. Miss one of these dates and it can sink your entire operation. This actually happens.[§]

Now let's return to the question of just how bad things were at Local 1107 when I arrived. This is how bad: There were two contracts at two private hospitals about to expire, one of them already in its window period, and negotiations had yet to begin. No survey had been distributed to the workers at the two hospitals asking what issues they wanted to address in the next contract. In fact, the workers hadn't even been told their contract was expiring. Neither had the national union been informed. And neither had I, the new executive director. Thankfully, the outgoing executive director had at least managed to send in the little piece of paper notifying the employer (and federal government) that it was time to renegotiate.[¶] But that was all.

Welcome to Vegas. There were two hospitals with expiring contracts and nothing had been done. The union had no discernible power in any field. The workers were weak as hell in terms of anything that had

---

§ Some argue that that the legal framework for decertifying unions has a plus side as well, in that it provides workers with bad unions the chance to jump to more effective ones. I am skeptical of this argument. Who, in the end, gets to decide whether an existing union is bad enough to warrant being raided by another union? In practice, this evaluation is made by the leadership of the raiding union, which has every incentive to view the existing union as unworthy. And what a waste: with less than 11 percent of the national workforce unionized, there are endless opportunities to organize workers who have no union at all.

¶ The notice is sent both to the employer and to the Federal Mediation and Conciliation Service (FMCS). The FMCS is a quasi-governmental agency created by the federal government whose purpose is to facilitate the collective bargaining process. The FMCS is legally neutral and generally stays completely outside the negotiation process unless there is a problem. In practice, it is less offensive than the National Labor Relations Board (NLRB), the federal regulator of unions and an agency that is totally aligned with employers, oops, I mean the White House and Congress.

to do with organizing or mobilizing. And I'd been sent there to clean the place up in general, and specifically to organize new hospital workers into the union. Everyone in Washington assumed that meant organizing workers at nonunion hospitals, but I could now see that it also meant organizing all the workers in the two hospitals who had union contracts but had chosen—for apparently valid reasons—not to be members.

The two hospitals were named Desert Springs and Valley, and they were not just any two for-profit bottom-feeders. They were owned by the same company, Universal Health Services, one of the largest hospital chains in the world. The CEO, Alan Miller, was one union-hating deeply ideological scumbag capitalist. He and his corporation were notorious for using every slimy trick in the book to keep unions out of their cost-cutting, nurse-exploiting hospitals, nearly all of which were (not surprisingly) located in right-to-work states. Desert Springs and Valley were among the very few union-organized UHS hospitals in the nation, and the only reason they had a union was that UHS had bought the hospitals after the organizing campaigns had already been won.

This Las Vegas assignment was beginning to look like a nightmare, and so I did what I had been promised I could do as a condition of accepting it: I called Jerry Brown, my old leader and mentor from District 1199 New England. Back when I was getting talked into Vegas, I'd insisted on a few things, one of which was that the national union would pay Jerry to coach me. How naïve. First, Jerry would never have taken a penny from the Stern gang in DC. They had thoroughly, viciously screwed him when he led District 1199 into the SEIU. Second, by proposing this I had remarked myself in the eyes of Stern's people as a "Jerry's girl"—and Stern's people detested Jerry. In the end, Jerry agreed to be my mentor for no charge.

Everyone involved in shoehorning me into the Nevada local—Jerry Brown, Eliseo Medina, and Larry Fox—had agreed that I should present myself as a seasoned hand at negotiating contracts, when of course I was not. I had hardly even *read* a union contract. But I agreed to play the part and in exchange I got Jerry as my designated coach. I remember thinking, "How hard can this be?" I had met plenty of people in unions who were negotiators, and frankly they were not always the sharpest knives in the drawer. Hell, if they could get a contract, so could I. But none of us had any idea that I would be confronted with not one but two big negotiations, both already way behind the curve, as soon as I got off the plane.

"Hello."

"Jerry, it's Jane. Umm, shit, Jerry, there's two nurse contracts about to expire here and absolutely nothing done."

"Shit. That's bad, McAlevey. Ah, well, you need to get the two contracts, read them from cover to cover, work with the members, identify just two or three key areas where you can make some improvements, and leave everything else for the next time. There just isn't time to for you to wage a big fight if they are expiring and nothing has been done."

Whew. Thank God I had Jerry to calm me down and help me with a plan. Sounds great. Just figure out what are the worst parts of the contracts and make them better. Oh, and get a flyer out calling for a meeting of the members in each hospital, and by the day of the meeting you'll have read the contracts, be ready to ask the workers about their priorities, and also tactfully explain, "Sorry, but since nothing has been done at all and your contract is expiring, we only can fix a few things. But we can come back and make it all better in a few years." Well, at least I had a lot of experience getting flyers out.

I called in the rep for the two hospitals and said, "Get a flyer out for a meeting." In a typical union, the "rep," or representative, also sometimes called a BA or business agent, is the key staff person once a contract is in place. Reps usually handle the filing of grievances and arbitrations and help workers get ready for negotiations. Some actually negotiate contracts—it all depends on the union. The rep for Desert Springs and Valley had been with the casino workers' union before being hired by 1107. When I met D Taylor, the leader of the casino workers, he told me that this same rep had been fired by his union. And this rep was not the only casino union reject on my staff. In fact, D Taylor made me promise that I would not hire anyone he had fired without calling him first.

I soon decided that it would surprise me to see this guy tie his shoelaces correctly. I asked him to make a flyer, but he was so flummoxed by this task that I made the damn thing myself and instructed him to pass copies out to the workers, to blanket the hospitals. He was a little startled and wanted to make sure I didn't just want him to call the couple of workers he knew at each place and invite only them. I said no, *everyone*.

That night I took the contracts home. When I started reading I couldn't believe my eyes. They stunk. I hoped there was something about the language I didn't understand. I decided to get up early in the morning and read them again; maybe then they would make sense. I actually had nightmares that night. Morning came too soon, and in the full light of day the contracts went from bad to worse. What was the point of these agreements? Who the hell had written them? Who had voted for them? Why? My head was spinning.

"Hello."

"Jerry, I think we have a problem here. Honest. Everything seems bad in these contracts, everything."

Jerry being Jerry, he probably assumed that McAlevey the social justice organizer had had some fantastic notion that union contracts should say something good. So he told me to send copies of the contracts to him via overnight mail. Whew, again.

Two days later my phone rang. Five years later my ears are still ringing.

"Jane, we have a problem here. These things stink. They're horrible. They are the worst contracts I have ever seen and I have been doing this for thirty years. You can't sign your name to these. You will have to renegotiate most of the language in both of them."

I thought I was going to pee in my pants right then. Here I was, in Las Vegas, Nevada, sent to help workers in the most important industrial sector the national SEIU needed to grow the union, and in two private-sector hospitals that were part of a huge national for-profit hospital chain their contracts were expiring. Plus the expiring contracts sucked. I had no organizers and no allies, and I hadn't met a single worker. Oh yeah, and I had never negotiated, and there were all sorts of technicalities of the collective bargaining process I had no clue about. I had only one thing in my corner, and that was absolute confidence that neither Jerry Brown nor Larry Fox would tell me I could do something I really could not do, and they were both adamant that I could wing this.

There was actually a reason that even after organizing workers for five years I had never read a contract, and to understand it you have to remember that what was supposedly new about New Labor was its emphasis on organizing new members instead of just renegotiating contracts and filing grievances for existing ones. Many union locals had dug themselves so deeply into the latter rut that digging them out of it was a Herculean labor. One of the tactics of the new national leadership at SEIU was building an absolute firewall between organizers (who worked to bring in new members) and "servicers"—the reps and negotiators (who negotiated contracts and helped administer them for existing members). The campaign I had led in Connecticut was about organizing, and I had been all but prohibited from spending any time reading contracts. As a strategy for changing an entrenched institutional mindset this made sense, but as a strategy for building a strong union it was all wrong. In fact, this was why the Desert Springs and Valley contracts smelled to heaven. Back in the 1990s, the national SEIU had parachuted some skilled organizers into Las Vegas to help the workers form the union, then left the job of winning first contracts to the inept Las Vegas local.

What Jerry Brown and Larry Fox knew better than most was that winning a good contract was not about legal technicalities but about strategy and power, and power came from organizing. They had each seen me engaged in intense fights that required an understanding of power and strategy, and this is why they kept telling me I could do this too. After getting through those first negotiations, I understood this, and in the Las Vegas local we tore down that firewall between bargaining and organizing and threw it under a truck.

I hung up the phone with Jerry and called Larry, at the time the head of the SEIU National Hospital Division.

"Larry, did Jerry tell you what he found in the two nurse contracts?"

"Yeah, that's too bad, Jane, sorry to hear that. On the other hand, look at it this way: if you have a really big fight and win really big, then reforming the local will be easier. The workers across the union will know you are really talented and terrific. Ah, this is actually going to be fine, yeah, sure, go get 'em and everything will be fine."

Gotta love that man. Every setback became an opportunity for organizing. That was why he'd been such a good guy to have running the hospital division in Washington, and also why it was such a loss when Stern forced him out.

My very first task was to sort out the membership numbers in the hospitals. This is the essence of what's different about unions in a right-to-work-for-less state. How many of these nurses were even in the union? Supposedly our local had a computer system to give us just that kind of information, but—surprise—it didn't work. OK, no problem, I can just get those numbers from the person called the organizing director. About two minutes with her and I knew yet another reason why the local union was in so much trouble. When I asked her why the hospital workers hadn't been informed that their contracts were expiring, she said that was someone else's job. When I asked her about the reporting systems between her and her staff, she said she didn't have any. I asked her if that was why she hadn't known that her rep hadn't told the workers about their expiring contracts. Nothing.

I suddenly remembered someone in Washington who'd been assigned to a few short-term campaigns in Vegas telling me that one test of whether I could reform the local would be whether I had the nerve to fire the organizing director. Well, nerve is one thing I have plenty of. I called her into my office, handed her a polite resignation letter, and said, "You can sign this or I am firing you. Your choice." When she told me she had friends on the board, I told her I had not an ounce of time for bullshit and she could resign and get her accrued vacation time or I would fire her and she would get nothing. Done. I was a little nervous about informing the staff that she had resigned after I'd been in town just one month, but when I told them, you could see them visibly relax. Their shoulders dropped. People began to smile. It was like I was suddenly Snow White and there were birds swirling over their heads.

If the computer system doesn't work and the organizing director doesn't even know it, the only way to determine the number of union members in a hospital is by actually counting membership cards. But when I tried to do this, I quickly discovered that the rep had been lying about how many cards he collected each week. In a right-to-work state where workers can join or quit the union every day, it was explained to me, the reps typically have a weekly quota of cards they are supposed to get members to sign. This guy vanished without a trace one day— before I could fire him. I remember telling D Taylor, the casino union leader, at our next breakfast meeting that I had begun firing bad staff, and he told me that when they'd fired that rep it was for "lying about his numbers." Turned out he did signatures and handwriting like multiple personalities and had been using them to fill in and sign rafts of membership cards, turning these in while actually doing nothing. And the staff troubles didn't stop there. Of the eight staff I found when I walked into the Vegas office, eventually all but three had resigned or been fired.

I soon became adamant about organizers referring to how many *members* they had recruited each week, not how many cards they had collected. Some organizers found this annoying and trivial, but to me there was nothing trivial about changing our language from "I got three cards this week" to "I recruited three new members this week." It was a question of what sort of culture our union would foster. Eventually, members would do the recruitment, but I am getting ahead of myself.

Before the rep vanished, we held the first meetings at the two hospitals, based on the flyer I had made myself. The turnout was awful. Only seven workers showed up at one hospital, and even fewer at the other. These were saints, the sort of people who show up out of sheer principle, simply because they believe having a union is the right thing to do. I sat there thinking that there was no way I could do this without at least one good organizer for each hospital, and I needed them yesterday.

Amazingly, there was an organizer named Morgan Levi working right out of our offices who was just terrific. She had been sent to Vegas as part of a campaign run by the national union (not the local, of course) to organize a couple of hospitals in town. The workers had caved in the face of pressure from the boss and the campaign had gone belly-up. The union had filed charges against the boss, and Morgan was staying around to keep the workers involved as the legal fight worked its way toward resolution. It was important work, but it wasn't nonstop, so Morgan had a lot of time on her hands.

"Hi, Larry. The organizing team has this great young organizer out here named Morgan. I need you to reassign her to this local, now, so she can help me with the catastrophe called the UHS contract campaigns." Long pause.

"You know, Jane, that's not going to be easy."

This time I was not just being naïve. I did know, and Larry knew I knew, that the national union absolutely prohibited organizers from getting involved in contract campaigns—that crazy firewall between contract bargaining and organizing. Over time I would conclude that this is a key reason unions can't organize anymore, maybe as big an obstacle as the screwed-up labor laws. Eventually I realized it is at the core of the problem with Andy Stern's vision for labor. Seems to me SEIU wants growth at any cost. Period. So all the talent is assigned to bringing new workers into the union. The new members are then passed to a different team with one tenth the talent who are supposed to help them actually get a contract and *build their union*, which of course doesn't work, and SEIU ends up a hollow giant.

But Larry Fox knew that if we were going to organize the rest of the hospitals in the Las Vegas market, we had to win a good contract for the workers at Desert Springs and Valley who were already members. Otherwise, why would unorganized workers at the other hospitals want to join us? No contract was almost better than the Desert Springs and Valley contracts as they presently stood. For a month I had been all on my own: running the day-to-day of the entire union, meeting with all staff, assessing them, firing them, taking over the management of the money, starting to assess whether we could play a role in upcoming County Commissioner elections, meeting with the executive board one on one to introduce myself, writing and preparing new language for the two contracts, meeting with local political leaders to say hi—you name it. On top of all this, I was acting as the only on-the-ground organizer for these two hospitals, going in at lunchtime and meeting with the workers to begin the leader ID process and by getting the existing few leaders to collect bargaining surveys that asked workers what improvements they wanted to make in their nearly expired contract. I can do a lot of stuff at once, but I was drowning and the clock was ticking, fast. So Larry took the plunge and spent some of the political capital he had with the national union getting me Morgan Levi. Incredibly, Larry's detractors at national SEIU headquarters would later use this issue to get him out of key decision making in the union.

The minute I had Morgan, everything changed. One good organizer is worth a hundred so-so reps. No kidding. And Morgan was a natural. She had graduated from Dartmouth at a time when labor briefly became cool on college campuses, and went straight into organizing. Since leaving college she had done nothing but talk to workers. She had learned an extraordinary amount, she fundamentally got organizing and had real charisma. It didn't hurt that she was beautiful and funny and liked to laugh.

Morgan got to work sorting out what the hell was really going on in the two hospitals. In a few days she had more bad news: We had even fewer members than either the screwed-up computer or the dishonest rep had reported. And the first of the two contracts would expire in less than a month, the second in less than two.

Jerry Brown and Larry Fox insisted that I literally drop every other thing I was doing and focus like a laser on these contracts. But to do this I needed the support of the executive board which as I have mentioned was controlled by public sector workers who were not at all pleased that the new executive director wanted to spend her time on private sector hospitals. I was very honest with them and appealed to their sense of justice. "Look," I explained, "You've been surviving without me for years. The workers at these two hospitals are about to get screwed. Let me focus on getting them a contract, and then I will return to running the union and dealing with everyone else." They agreed.

In actual fact, there was no way I could *really* drop all the other work. For one thing, the local was so utterly dysfunctional, it generated a constant stream of crises that simply had to be dealt with. For example, the national SEIU had run an organizing campaign the year before at the ambulance company that served Las Vegas. In keeping with national union policy, after winning the election to form a union, the national handed the job of landing the first contract back to its inept local, which then sat on its ass and did almost nothing. Under the screwed up US labor law, as mentioned earlier, even if a union wins an organizing campaign and gets a majority yes vote from the workers of a given shop, the workers don't actually become members of the union until their first union contract is settled. And if one calendar year passes and there is no first contract, the boss—um, I mean the workers—has the right to run a decertification campaign for what is legally called a permanent window, which in normal English is called *forever*—until the workers win a first union contract or the union gets thrown out. You can't imagine the kinds of intimidation bosses will pull out of the hat in a "permanent window." The first of May would mark one year since the workers at the ambulance company have voted in a union, and they were on the verge of throwing in the towel. Why fight to keep a union that can't win a contract? And if they did, it would send a big message to every worker in Nevada that there was no point in dealing with the SEIU; all the resources the national union had put into the organizing campaign would go straight down the toilet; and, worst of all, the workers would be left without a union.

Before I could even think about the ambulance workers, as the new executive director I got hit with what's called a "prohibited practice charge," because for a full year the local hadn't done anything to resolve the outstanding pay issue in its contract with the county civil service workers. This document was served to me personally—a welcome-wagon gift from Tom Reilly, the powerful county manager who clearly had trained his sights on the inept union that represented his labor force. I had only been in Vegas a few weeks and suddenly I was personally legally accountable for stuff the old leadership hadn't bothered to deal with. Tom Reilly was a big cheese in Vegas, very popular with the gaming elite, the public, and also with his county commission, the body that voted on our contracts with county civil service workers. Our contract with the county expired in two years, and Reilly smelled blood. The local SEIU was low-hanging fruit. No one on the county commission liked our union. There was nothing about it to like.

Furthermore, as the incoming leader of the local, I was well aware of the jealousy that the public sector workers felt toward their private sector counterparts. I also knew that their complaint, that "private sector workers get all the attention from the national union," was actually true. While this favoritism made logical sense, considering that future growth in the Nevada union would be almost entirely from the private sector, the local nevertheless claimed to represent both public and private workers, and if it didn't effectively do that for them, the public sector workers would be better off elsewhere.

As much as I needed to focus on the contracts at Desert Springs and Valley hospitals, I also had to do *something* with all this mess in the union's public sector. And it couldn't just be defensive, putting out fires, there had to be some sort of proactive component. First, because a good offense is the only way to go if you intend to eventually win anything, and second because playing offense suits my nature. If we aren't doing that, then I'm not interested.

To launch our offensive we desperately needed allies on the county commission, and by chance there was an election coming right up. I set up a quick meeting with D Taylor and asked him if there was any opportunity for our local to get involved in any of the upcoming local political races. He replied that there was a seat up for grabs on the county commission itself. He had to remain neutral because he had ties to all five Democrats competing in the primary, but since I was new in town and didn't owe anyone anything, I had room to move. And the seat was in a Democratic stronghold, so whoever won the primary would win the seat.

Here we are again with why I love primaries: You can spend less money and still win big. And along the way, work to reclaim the Democratic Party from its abyss.

I took D Taylor's tip as a "go" and ran as fast with it as I could. As I mentioned, in Nevada elections for the Clark County Commission are almost more important than the governor's race, and are certainly more important than elections for the state assembly or senate. Just to give you an idea: If you want to run for the Nevada assembly you need about $20,000 in the bank to be taken seriously. To run for a seat on the Clark County Commission, you need about $2 million. So I asked SEIU in Washington for a bunch of money, and I assigned one of three smart staff the local had to gather some worker leaders and sort out the candidates. If we could put someone on the County Commission it would be a huge help when the time came to negotiate the new contract with the county, and it would also show our public sector workers that the union actually was paying attention to them. Winning big in politics is everything if you work for government, because elected officials ultimately sign off on your contract. And there was even more icing on this cake: A win would be a fast way to signal to the outside world that a whole new SEIU was coming to the state of Nevada.

Fortunately, I don't seem to need as much sleep as most people. So I extended my workday, which now began at four in the morning and ended at ten or eleven at night. I committed a couple of hours a day to the public sector and in the remaining seventeen focused like a laser on the for-profit hospital contracts.

The events that followed merit retelling in detail, because they laid the groundwork for the victories the local would win in the following years. Furthermore, it is the details of this story that convey the sense of *social movement* that was palpable in everything we did. To me this is absolutely crucial. The prevailing view in labor is that most of what we actually did in this campaign is impossible. But that's because most unions are engaged in this technical thing called labor organizing. We were building a movement. The difference is critical, but you have to know the full story in order to really get it. Finally, this story goes right to the heart of the tension in the New Labor movement. New Labor is all about bringing new workers into unions and reversing the long-term decline of unions in the United States. But to New Labor unions like SEIU, "organizing" means signing an agreement with a corporation bringing 20,000 new workers under your jurisdiction. To me, "organizing" means bringing workers into a deep personal engagement with their union, their fellow workers, their boss, their community, and all of the social and political issues that shape their lives. Most labor leaders today think that ideal is not possible in the self-centered, plugged-in, globalized country this nation has become. The story I am now going to tell proves them wrong.

CHAPTER FOUR

Round One: Reorganizing Desert Springs and Valley Hospitals, and Why Labor Should Care More about Primaries than about General Elections

Among the tiny handful of workers who showed up at those first meetings at Desert Springs and Valley hospitals back in early March were Bev Phares and Cass McPheron, both from Desert Springs Hospital. Bev was an Intensive Care Unit registered nurse and Cass was what they call an LPN, or a licensed practical nurse. Under the byzantine rules of the NLRB, LPNs and technicians are both legally part of what's called the tech unit. At Desert Springs, the old SEIU local had been so inept as to agree on separate contracts for nurses and techs that did not expire at the same time and so had to be bargained separately. Registered nurses have much more clout at a hospital than any other staff, including the techs, and the predictable result was that the Desert Springs techs were locked into a terrible contract that wouldn't expire for another two years. The techs at Valley Hospital weren't in the union at all. Once upon a time they had been, but when Universal Health Services (UHS) purchased the two hospitals they immediately ran a campaign to decertify the union at Valley, and presto, the corporate owners had emerged with unionized nurses and nonunionized techs at Valley Hospital.

Bev and Cass held seats on the local's executive board as the chief stewards for their units, but when I met them they told me, "We don't go to meetings."

"Ummmm, why?"

"Those meetings are awful. We don't do anything. No one talks to us. It's just a handful of government workers who spend the whole time yelling at each other about their own issues. So we stopped going."

For years Bev and Cass had been holding the union at Desert Springs together. They were the sort of nurses who are the real saints of the health care unions, salt-of-the-earth true believers. They were in their sixties. They had been through the worst of nursing, back when women were supposed to go into the caring professions as an act of charity, nurses wore dehumanizing uniforms, and male doctors treated them however they pleased. They'd worked incredibly hard every day for a horrible employer under conditions no employee should have to endure, and somehow still managed to love their patients. They had an awful union but they stuck it out.

Well, I didn't know anything about bargaining a contract, but I did know how to organize workers. I set up the meeting in a diner near the hospital instead of the office, which was too far away for nurses coming off twelve-hour shifts. We sat down and began our introductions. We talked about how long they had been nurses, how long they had been in Vegas, how long in this hospital, how long in the unit they were in and on the shift they were working, something about them—their families, whatever they wanted to say about their lives outside of work—and the one most important thing they would want if they could have anything they wished for from the new contract we were going to win.

I could feel my shoulders relaxing. Thank God, I was hanging out with workers again. One thing I did not like about working for the national union was that I was always around staff and leaders, not workers. These women were tired—not tired of nursing, but tired of their bad boss, their bad hospital, and their bad union. And they let it all come out. The more they talked, the better it got. Asked what was the one thing in the contract they most wanted to change, most of them said, "Everything." I said, "OK, it isn't that you won't get more chances to propose more ideas, but I just want to know your top priority." All right, then, they wanted a fully employer-paid health-care plan for themselves and their family (what we call dependent coverage). These health-care providers had been made to pay more and more of their wages for their own care, upward of $400 per month. And they wanted raises, and respect, and new "floating rules."

Floating rules allow hospitals to shuffle nurses through the different units that make up a hospital. Managers justify "floating" to the public by saying things like, "If we have a crisis on the medical-surgical floor and we have an ICU nurse on another floor without a patient, are you telling me we can't bring that nurse down to care for the patient in medical-surgical?" This is total bullshit. Nurses act, immediately and within their skill level, in any real life-threatening emergency. What all the pressure for "floating" is really about is money: Hospitals put patients at risk by mandating that nurses trained for one unit move to other units at a moment's notice to make up for the intentional short-staffing that inflates the income of scumbag for-profit hospitals. People die from this practice, and nurses lose their licenses.

We still didn't even know exactly how many of the eligible workers at Desert Springs Hospital were in the union, but I knew it wasn't more than 40 percent. I explained that there was no way we were going to win much of anything until we got to at least 70 percent, and that if we could hit 90 percent, unified and organized and combative, we could win on a lot of the issues they had raised in their opening remarks—that is, we actually could change "everything" in the contract.

Where did I get this number of 90 percent? I figured you never get *everyone* to agree on anything. At least 10 percent of any cross section of people will disagree, and a union is a cross section of America. It isn't a church or an environmental group or the Democratic Party, where people decide to participate because they agree with a core set of beliefs or goals. A union is an organization of the workers hired by a boss to get something done. Ferdinand Marcos in the Philippines, Baby Doc Duvalier in Haiti, the Communist regime in Poland—they all got at least 10 percent of a vote just before getting run out of their countries with pitchforks. So 90 percent seemed like a reasonable bet.

This was one of those moments when not knowing "how things are done in unions" proved to be one of my strongest assets. As I would later learn, firefighters and cops get 90 percent union membership because they run their unions like a military operation. I would not be surprised at all if the casino workers' union is at or close to 90 percent. Other than that, most unions in right-to-work states never get anything close to 90 percent membership.

Fortunately, the nurses I was talking to didn't know any more about "how things are done in unions" than I did, so I didn't get laughed out of the room. Instead, they expressed genuine concern, saying that just about everyone working in the hospital hated the union. I suggested that one way to start changing that would be to engage their coworkers in a face-to-face discussion, asking each worker what his or her priorities would be for the new contract. We had already been meeting for a few hours, but we spent another hour creating a survey about just that. We made a plan to get copies to them at work the next day.

"Jane, we only conduct this discussion with the people we know are members, right?"

"No, most nurses are not even in the union."

"But why should someone who hasn't paid dues all this time get to have an opinion?"

"The best way to get everyone to join up is to talk with them. We want everyone to realize that the way to make things better is to come together."

I told them that since nothing had been done until now and the contract was about to expire, we needed to send the boss a formal request proposing a date for negotiations so that we wouldn't get hit with a bad faith bargaining charge (legally, an unfair labor practice). I suggested that we also send Universal Health Services something called an information request for both Desert Springs and Valley hospitals, on everything that unions are legally entitled to know in the collective bargaining process: hours worked, wages paid, overtime, cost of the existing health-care plan, data on floating, and so on. It would take a well-run hospital a couple of weeks to compile this information; hospitals like these would probably require a month or more. So not only would we get information we really needed, we would also buy ourselves some time. I later discovered that the Vegas union had never before sent a full information request before bargaining.

That night Bev called to say that one of the nurses she had brought down to lunch was not a union member anymore because she had grown so disgusted with the old union, but she had agreed to rejoin after our meeting.

"We need some more shift-based meetings fast, so that I can bring more people to meet you, Jane. Then they will realize we have someone good here."

"Bev, you are the reason people are going to join or not join in your unit. Our really urgent priority is identifying nurses like you in every unit and shift."

"You mean the union people?"

"No, I mean in each unit and shift we need to identify who it is that the majority of the nurses go to when they need help or don't understand something."

"And what if they are not in the union?"

"Well, once we figure out who they are, it will be our job, yours and mine and the others' in the union, to get them to join."

Correctly identifying who the real leader of the workers is on every shift, every day, and in every unit is one of the most important ingredients in any workplace campaign. When campaigns lose, inadequate leadership ID is often a major factor. This is hardly an original insight, believe me. Every school of thought about union organizing puts leadership ID front and center, and training sessions, manuals, and seminars are devoted to it. And yet I would say that in my ten years in the labor movement, a large majority of the organizers I met couldn't get this step right. There are a lot of reasons for this, beginning with plain old laziness. Good leadership ID takes a lot of time, and I am not talking about mindless, punch-the-clock time. I am talking about fully intellectually engaged time. And honestly, there are a lot of lazy staff in unions. But let's assume you have motivated organizers who actually go out and engage with the workers. The first workers they will encounter are what we might call the loudmouths. Then there are the workers known as the tough ones who talk back to the boss. There are the confident and highly skilled ones who just get everything they need for themselves as individuals—not pensions or health care, of course, but a better individual deal with the employer. There are the popular good-looking ones, and the nice ones everyone likes to chat with in the break room. Then there are the left-leaning or progressive workers who immediately like the union organizer, exclaim, "Thank goodness you are here now," and offer to help do anything. And there are the quiet ones, and the not-so-friendly ones. And we could go on. Most organizers stop at the worker who is excited to see them and really wants to build the union. Or maybe they ID the one that the other workers say always stands up to the boss.

What they miss is the one who actually leads her colleagues day in and day out.

The real leader is generally not the one an inexperienced organizer would pick out of the crowd, yet she does have a handful of recognizable characteristics. She is really good at what she does; in this case, she's the best nurse on her shift and in her unit. She is committed to helping other nurses who want to provide good care for their patients. If she thinks a request for help is genuine, she will make time for it even if she doesn't have a minute to spare. She is the nurse all the doctors want. Rarely have I met a real leader who wasn't also the top nurse on the unit, or at least among the best. And every shift has one. The challenge is that this person may well not be pro-union, and for all kinds of reasons. An organizer (paid or unpaid) must then engage her in a substantive way on the issue or issues she most wants to change in her hospital, and help her come to the conclusion that forming a union is the best if not only way to make those key improvements. The second crucial step that organizers tend to miss is identifying the issue that is the most important to each worker they talk to, and early in the conversation. Why? Workers aren't clones; they care about different things, and if the organizer can't repeatedly zero in on the issue crucial to each worker and make him or her understand that only mass collective action is going to resolve it, at some point the organizer will probably lose that worker.

The smartest bosses know the same thing the smartest organizer knows: who the real leaders are and what their issues are. And in a hard organizing campaign, the boss who knows this is working that nurse every day, just as the union organizer is.

Word was spreading about the "new negotiator" and the upcoming bargaining. I began holding weekly shift-change meetings, so I would be at or near the hospitals at least once a week, bright and early at 7:30 am and then again in the evening. And now I had a real organizer with me, Morgan Levi. With Morgan in action, I was able to turn some attention to the other fires that needed either putting out or stoking. Morgan kept me in her back pocket for those times she would get stuck with a particular worker. Not because I was a better organizer, but because it would make workers feel like they were being heard: "Oh, you need to take that concern right to your negotiator, she needs to hear about this."

In a perfect world, before you sit down at the bargaining table with the boss to start working out the details of a contract, you hold a real election for your bargaining team. Before you do that, you identify who all your key leaders are and persuade them to run in the election. But we didn't have a snowball's chance in hell of doing anything like that if we were going to open negotiations in time to avoid an unfair labor practice charge. I mean, we didn't even know how many members we had. It was early April, and I had been in Las Vegas for all of five weeks.

Jerry Brown had coached me to "always bring some workers along to bargaining," and I figured the only way to accomplish that at this point was to invite every single member who wasn't on shift to attend the negotiations—and bring whomever I could round up from Valley Hospital, whose contract would expire just one month after the contract at Desert Springs. I also wanted the staff at each hospital to begin to see themselves as working for the same big corporate boss and to realize that we were all going to win or lose together. Nothing like this had been done before in Vegas, and it confused some of the longtime members.

Bev Phares asked me, "Jane, are you sure that *anyone* can come to negotiations?"

"Yes, labor law is very clear on this. The bosses pick their side and we pick ours."

Bev persisted, "Jane, this is not how we have ever done this." She said it was just her and a couple of nurses and the previous executive director, and he did all the talking.

This was getting fun. Yes, bring every single person you are signing up! Yes to real union democracy! There's no time for elections. They can't bust us for it. Jerry says to bring some workers. What do I care about "how things are done in unions"?

When the date for opening contract bargaining was set for early April, I thought, "What the hell are we going to do? We haven't even collected enough surveys to know what our priorities are." I called Jerry, who said, "Just open the table, review the status of the information request, put it on the boss and make him look like the one who is not ready, since he won't have given you all the information you asked for. Just get the process going and it will create momentum and excitement. Workers will always get excited by negotiations if they are allowed to come."

OK, we could stall with the information request. But there was no way I could get any substantive proposals together. And once you put a proposal on the table in labor negotiations, you can't take it back—that is, you can weaken it, but you can't strengthen it. So you have to make a strategic calculation as to how much you can credibly ask for, so that once it gets chewed up and stomped on you still get what you really need. We weren't even close to that kind of nuanced assessment. But if we had nothing, we could get slapped with a bad faith bargaining charge. (I was learning all this law on the phone from Jerry.) And as an organizer I knew that the first session had to feel meaningful to the workers. No one wants their time wasted, ever. People were going to have to take a full day off to attend what would be a short bargaining session, losing twelve hours of pay for a few hours of talk. *Something* had to happen in those few hours to make it worth their while. And we had to have some fun. Seriously. Any experienced organizer knows that no matter what you are doing, if you want people to come back for round two, they have to have fun and experience something meaningful in round one.

The hamster on the little wheel in my organizer head was running for dear life. What if we did an opening presentation in which every single nurse we could cram into the room got to speak directly to her concerns? Since I had no idea what their actual priorities were, could I just give them the floor? It might be a tremendous experience for the nurses, and it would just burn through the minutes. Perfect. Only this was way outside the box, and Jerry didn't see any point in it at all. He actually thought I was being silly. Still, I had a hunch that I wasn't. These women had a lot to say about the hospitals. At Desert Springs, they could have run the place better than the management did.

I proposed the idea to the nurses at our next meeting. We could do a slide show presenting recent research that showed improved job conditions for nurses was linked to improved patient care, and end by showing how much money Universal Health Services was making nationally, and that they could certainly afford the contract we would eventually propose. The nurses loved the idea until I suggested that they make the presentation. You should have seen the look on the faces of the long-timers, the ones who every couple of years had sat in the room with the old executive director and never said a word, and then a few days later were handed a contract that had clearly been settled in a room they were not in.

Good organizers know that a key ingredient in any winning formula is moving workers past their fear and into self-confidence. So I said, "Look, you are the nurses here. I'm an organizer. Who is going to be smarter about telling management how to run a better hospital: you nurses who have been here forever, or me?"

"But but but but but…"

"Look, this is silly. I don't even know what the details are of intubation and why certain nurses shouldn't be floated to a unit where intubation might happen. You have to do this. I'll make a PowerPoint presentation, you can look at it and fix it, and we can all practice it together. Each of you will only have to take one slide, OK?"

I stayed up all night getting the presentation ready for its first showing, at a 7:30 am meeting of the night shift nurses coming off work.

The nurses loved it. There was very little they wanted to change. Universal Health Services was demanding that the negotiations take place in a hospital conference room. US labor law requires a "neutral" location, but this was not going to be a conventional negotiation. I figured if UHS was dumb enough to invite us into the hospital, we should take them up on it, because by this time I had decided to throw the playbook out the window and invite *all* of the workers—not just union members but any nurse at Desert Springs or Valley who wanted to come. If the meeting was in the hospital it would be much more accessible to them. People could even stop in on their lunch break. Hell, they could stop in for 15 minutes on their cigarette break (this was Vegas, remember). Some of the nurses thought I was making a huge mistake, but I assured them we wouldn't win a damn thing if we didn't grow the union fast, and that meant being totally transparent.

We all met early for a final rehearsal of the presentation. We practiced the PowerPoint, and then we practiced it again. I explained that in the new way of doing things I would never, ever put something across the negotiations table that they had not first approved. We had not told UHS about the presentation; we were bringing our own screen and projector. I wanted the boss to be totally surprised. On the big day, we had the tables all lined up, with me in the middle of one and ten nurses flanking me on each side. Delegations of nurses from Valley Hospital and techs from Desert Springs were at either ends of our tables to express their solidarity with the Desert Springs nurses. Behind us was a second row of about ten nurses. We had carefully spread out the seating so the room seemed completely full. We had our proposed agenda up on the screen. Since I knew it was important to the registered nurses, I was dressed to the nines, in a stylish black suit and pearls. This was the new union and we were *in control.*

When the doors opened and the management team filed in and took their seats, the look on their faces was priceless. The real honcho on their side was Rick Albert from Foley and Lardner, a big law firm in California that specialized in what their website calls union-avoidance. That's normal with big national corporations. They would never trust their line managers from a single facility to negotiate a contract. This was the first time any of them had met me. I had kept myself intentionally obscure until now. As soon as they were at their seats, I introduced myself to Rick Albert from across the table and asked if our proposed agenda met his approval.

He was obviously taken off guard. He said sure, but he wanted a list of everyone who was sitting with me to verify that they were actually workers and not union staff. Right into the trap. "Even better," I replied, "Let's start with a full round of introductions. That way we can all meet everyone here. How about you guys go first and then we will go?"

We had even planned which worker would start at what end of the table, so that we looked totally together. When the first nurse stood and identified herself and described her work experience, we were on a roll. No one goofed, though there were quite a few trembling voices. I tallied it all up and pointed out that since we had about 350 years of nursing experience in the room, we ought to be able to make wonderful patient care improvements.

Then we launched into our slide show. For each slide there was one nurse presenting and another sharing anecdotes that would bring to life the serious problems created by short staffing, mandatory overtime, floating, low pay and more. Each nurse had picked her own slide, so they were all were speaking to their main concerns. Each had a paper copy of the slide show with her own notes jotted down. And we had practiced. An hour later, the nurses were rock stars. They'd hit the presentation out of the park.

In negotiations, both sides have the right to call a caucus, or break, at any time, no questions asked. I suggested that perhaps management wanted a caucus to discuss the presentation and return and give us some feedback. What I was really thinking was that if I felt like exploding then so did the nurses. They had just done something completely new to them: standing up and telling their managers what they wanted, and being heard. I thought we needed a *human emotion* break. Albert took the bait, and the UHS team got up and filed out of the room looking a bit bewildered. When the door closed behind them, the room burst into laughter, applause and tears. The nurses were exchanging high fives, smacking the table, hugging me, and calling other nurses on their cell phones. The nurses from Valley Hospital kept saying they couldn't wait to tell everyone at Valley what had happened and start their own negotiations. Morgan saw what I saw: Our contract campaign was in gear, and we were building a union. This was going to be fun.

Somehow I got the room to come to order and asked everyone to be seated, because we still had a lot of work to do to win. Everyone got very serious. I reminded them that we were still less than half the hospital and the boss knew it. To actually win these wonderful things in the presentation we would first need to win 90 percent union membership. And that 90 percent would have to be educated, unified, and mobilized. Here again, I was fortunate that these nurses were as inexperienced when it came to unions as I was, so they didn't know what an absurd number I was asking for. I explained that time was of the essence. And *they* had to do it; Morgan and I could only help.

"Jane, shouldn't we be wearing our union buttons or something?"

"No, not until a majority of nurses are ready to wear them. Otherwise we will show weakness instead of strength. When the time is right, everyone should put on a button all at once. Remember, this is a right-to-work-for-less state, and management would love to get a visual measure of just how weak the union is right now."

I introduced Morgan as the new organizer for the campaign, and she unveiled an oversized wall chart and got right to work explaining what a powerful tool "charting" could be. The chart was laid out as a grid with the units of the hospital listed horizontally across the top row and the shifts listed vertically down the left column. The name of each worker was in its correct column and row, with union members highlighted in yellow. We were taking our organizing prowess and putting it to work in a contract fight. Eventually we would chart the entire union and require every organizer to maintain an up-to-date wall chart of every facility in it.

Morgan asked the nurses to review every name on the chart and make a list of all the nonmembers they knew. She explained that this was not a perfunctory exercise; they had to engage these people in real conversations about their jobs and how bargaining might make them better. Everyone in the room realized that for our core group, an "organizing campaign" meant moving from a nice idea to a reality.

We decided we should make a flyer announcing that negotiations had begun and *everyone* was welcome. Morgan took photos of the nurses and got some quotes for the flyer, and promised she would be back before the day shift was over if there were volunteers to leaflet at shift change.

We didn't realize it at the time, but new systems were emerging then and there that we would hone into a finely tuned instrument over the next few years, improving it every time we used it. All of us had learned that speaking at the bargaining table is a powerful experience for workers, *if* they are prepared, organized, and rehearsed. I explained that in most contract negotiations, 90 percent of a settlement was arrived at during the final 10 percent of the negotiations (thanks, Jerry), and that probably the workers should do most of the speaking in the first, longest phase, and I should do most of it during the end run. This made sense to everyone. Privately, I also knew that this would give me 90 percent of the time to learn how to negotiate before I actually had to put my currently non-existent bargaining experience to the test.

Two days after our presentation, union membership at Desert Springs hospital had grown by something like 10 percent, but Valley was lagging. It was a bigger hospital, and there had been no negotiations there to get the ball rolling. Morgan was overwhelmed trying to organize both hospitals. I was overwhelmed trying to—well, I was just overwhelmed. I called Larry Fox with the great news about the opening session and told him I needed more organizers. Larry knew it and so did Jerry. They contacted Diane Sosne at District 1199 Northwest in Seattle, one of the best locals in the national SEIU, who sent us a solid organizer named Teresa Tobin. At about the same time we hired Jamie Ware. Jamie was a Vegas native and really dressed and acted the part, with tight pants, stiletto heels, and tops that prominently displayed her considerable cleavage. She was like a character out of the CSI television show. On several occasions I actually told her to change her blouse to something that wouldn't be quite so distracting to everyone involved. Jamie was inexperienced but promising, and we desperately needed help. We assigned her to work under Teresa at Valley hospital, while Morgan and I dug in at Desert Springs. I had told the nurses at Desert Springs that we needed twice the attendance at the next bargaining session. They thought this was impossible, but I just kept asking them if they really wanted to win "everything."

The new Las Vegas SEIU was now in contract campaigns at two hospitals, running a political campaign in a heated Clark County Commission race, fighting off the decert at the ambulance company, and urgently trying to find and recruit new staff. I could handle all that. It was the rewriting of the two contracts that was wringing my last nerve. Organizing, mobilizing, spitting in the face of power—that stuff comes naturally to me. Writing is like going to the dentist. Writing contract language is like going to a dentist who has run out of novocaine.

In "normal" union work, the only time you have to write every article of a contract is when you are writing the first contract for a newly organized shop, and then you actually get to start from scratch. I was confronted with 200 pages of existing garbage clauses. I sat in the hospital cafeteria every day working with nurses to fashion proposals on absolutely everything: wage scales, staffing, regular hours, discipline, vacations, layoff procedures, on-call pay, the numbingly elaborate floating rules. There were more than sixty distinct topics in all. On the plus side, I got to hang out with nurses.

Larry Fox, thank goodness, sent us Sara Rothstein, the wonderful researcher I had worked with in Fresno. Sara worked out the cost of each of our proposals and also showed how the boss could pay for it.

We were under huge pressure, because the second bargaining session at Desert Springs was scheduled just two weeks after the first one, and we were legally required to have real proposals ready to pass across the table. At the same time we were counting on doubling the membership over the coming weeks by inviting everyone to participate in developing new proposals. The trick was to determine what we could commit to at this early stage that none of the potential new members would want to change. Jerry told me not to even go near the wage scale, which can actually be divisive for obvious reasons. The nurses explained that we couldn't formulate new floating rules for the same reason. So we honed in on things we were pretty certain everyone would want, like across-the-board cost-of-living wage increases and 100 percent fully employer-paid family health care.

I am not someone who generally worries a lot, but it was obvious that in pretending I was an experienced hand at this I was going way out on a skinny limb and it was a long way down if I fell. Bargaining is a game in which everyone plays for keeps. One mistake and workers can lose things that really matter. I called Jerry and begged him to fly to Nevada to watch my first real bargaining session. When he agreed I felt instantly better, though it did cross my mind that screwing up in front of my mentor could be worse that screwing up on my own. At any rate, my knees were knocking the morning of that second session. I was nervous about turnout. It was crucial that we show everyone—the boss, Jerry, and most of all ourselves—that we were growing. We had already given the boss a truly outside-the-box experience at the first session, and now we had to top it if we were to keep the momentum going.

I arrived at the hospital to find the room packed with eighty nurses. Jerry sat in the far back with his hat literally pulled over his eyes, studying every move Morgan and I made. The bosses' side of the table again looked baffled, and they made no objection when I suggested that all eighty nurses introduce themselves. After this lengthy prologue, the nurses began presenting their own proposals and passing them across the table. As before, we had carefully rehearsed who would present which proposal at what exact moment. Letting the workers themselves speak on substance issues was another thing that just seemed obvious to us but is rare in union bargaining.

Just as I was about to call for a lunch caucus, the door opened and a group of nurses in scrubs and skull caps—clearly just out of a procedure—walked in with lunch trays of cafeteria food and sat down on our side to watch. Morgan immediately handed me a note:

"Holy shit, it's the entire cath lab day shift. Do something!"

The "Holy shit!" was because Morgan had been working her chart for days, and it was covered with color coding showing exactly who in the hospital was a member, who had given us a bargaining survey, who had attended the first bargaining session, who was a real leader, and who was resolutely anti-union, and she and I knew that the cath lab nurses all hated the union. And the bosses knew it because there were cath lab nurses who confided in them. The cath lab is a strategic unit when you're organizing a hospital, particularly a hospital like Desert Springs, which advertised itself as "the heart hospital." There is a pecking order among hospital nurses that is all about skill and demand, and cath lab nurses are right at the top. Beyond that, unlike nurses in "closed" units (such as labor and delivery), cath lab nurses have routine contact throughout the hospital, and in a heart hospital they are the very root of the nurse grapevine. Win them and they can bring along an emergency room and help with ICU, the GI lab, the step down unit and others. At Desert Springs, we had serious problems in the ER and cath lab. There was a notorious anti-union diehard in the cath lab named Sean who Morgan was convinced would make or break our campaign. He wasn't with the group that had just walked in, but that was just because he was off work that day.

The "Do something!" in Morgan's note meant that I had to think of a dramatic way to show the cath lab nurses their new union in action before their lunch break ended and they returned to the lab.

I decided that I could stay hungry for a while. I called for a short caucus and selected a proposal I knew we could move quickly and presented it for discussion. In minutes we had arrived at an agreement and the workers were practicing their lines. We called the boss back in and the workers made the presentation. Then I called our lunch break and did a quick debrief with the workers in the caucus. The whole thing was finished before the cath lab nurses' fifteen-minute break was over.

After that we began distributing "Take a Union Break, Come to Bargaining at Lunch" flyers. As long as the employer didn't get it that negotiating on the hospital premises was a gift to the organizers, we would get all the mileage out of it we could. Rick Albert, the union-busting lawyer from California, was probably so accustomed to sitting across the table from conventional labor negotiators, it simply never occurred to him that any union would let workers walk in whenever they felt like it to see what their organization was doing. And we were inviting *everyone*, union member or not. We had three simple rules: Keep a poker face; Workers can talk a lot, but only when planned; and Workers should pass me notes any time I said something they disagreed with or thought was wrong, and even more importantly any time the boss said something they knew to be wrong. More generally, they should pass a note if they wanted to say something. These notes just flew across the room. When a note made a really important point, instead of introducing it at the table myself, I would ask for a five-minute caucus and prepare the worker to present it.

At lunch Morgan pulled out her wall chart and explained it all again, because so many new workers were present. Everyone could plainly see where we were weak. She then taught the nurses to use a tool that made signing up coworkers a more precise operation: a shift schedule. The only way to put together an accurate comprehensive hospital-wide shift schedule is to have workers bring you the individual units' schedules—it's one of those constant nagging tasks of labor organizing. Morgan had done this, had made the master schedule, and now she showed every-one how to put together the chart and the schedule to pinpoint workers throughout the hospital, and suggested they take membership cards and spend the rest of our lunch caucus signing up new members. No time like the present! After gulping a few bites of lunch, everyone took an assign-ment, and in a little while they were all back with the signed cards from new union members. A festive, mildly competitive atmosphere began to develop around this recruitment.

When Jerry and I got into the car at the end of the day, he started laughing.

"Ahh, Jane, when I said always bring some workers along to bargain-ing, I didn't mean the *whole damn hospital.*" Long pause. "I have never seen workers speak the way these nurses just did. Never. I want to think about this, but I think it's great."

I almost crashed the car, I was so relieved.

The next day, two cath lab nurses joined the union.

Negotiations were due to open at Valley in late April. This time the UHS corporate team wouldn't let us bargain at the hospital. I assumed this was because they were getting smarter, but it turned out they just didn't have an appropriate space. They gave me a list of casinos and suggested we book a place to negotiate. I recommended to the nurses that we should never agree to bargain in a casino. It just felt wrong: Workers don't gamble for a contract, they negotiate, and you win or lose based on your collective power, not on luck. Everyone agreed. What I didn't say was that I knew there were drinkers and gamblers in our ranks—this was Vegas—who would find being in a casino pretty distract-ing. To the bosses I simply said we were nurses and couldn't force our members into smoke-filled casinos. Our staff combed through churches near the hospital, we hadn't had time yet to understand who attended what faith, where. There weren't many—again, this was Vegas—but they found a Congregationalist church that had space for our main bargaining room and a lockable room for the management caucus, as UHS had demanded.

We walked into the room on the first day of negotiations to find a giant mural of Jesus, arms outstretched, looking down on the space where our tables would be. Management would spend the whole bargaining period staring at Jesus blessing the workers. Everyone loved it, and the workers who were religious could hardly believe it. This time we were actually ready with our proposals, as we were using the same ones for both UHS hospitals, fine-tuning them for Valley or Desert Springs only where necessary. And our numbers were stronger as well. We'd been at 32 percent membership when we started organizing in earnest just one month before; now we were at 50 percent.

Seventy-five nurses packed the house at that first Valley bargaining session. The room had a perfect bursting-at-the-seams feel. We made an opening presentation on priorities, just as we had done at the Desert Springs negotiations, and then went right on to propose the entire new contract, article by article, that very first day. The workers did everything. By now we had honed this tactic, with an additional twist: The workers would always present, but if the boss interrupted or asked questions, I would handle it. Knowing that they didn't have to answer to a union-busting lawyer made all the difference in raising the nurses' comfort level about speaking.

When the bargaining session was done, I turned to Morgan with a straight face and said, "OK, Morgan, 90 percent membership. Go do it." She replied that was flat-out impossible. So I pulled a Larry Fox on her. I looked her straight in the eyes and said, "Morgan, that's not the answer I want or expect from you. Go make it happen, and come back and see me when you're done." A year later, Morgan would have the new staff in stitches retelling this exchange, and how at the time she was convinced I had lost my mind. But really we were having a hell of a good time on the campaign. It *was* crazy, but the craziest part was that it kept working.

The next week Morgan walked into my office. "Look Jane, I can't crack Sean, the cath lab leader at Desert Springs, and without him I can't crack the ER, and without them there's no way to get the kind of membership numbers you are asking for. Sorry."

"OK. Let's get Sean into a meeting with me."

Ouch. Morgan was both offended that I thought I could do what she couldn't, and relieved that I would try, because then I would understand why 90 percent membership was a ridiculous goal. Morgan couldn't believe anyone could organize a worker better than she could, which was one reason she was such a fantastic organizer. In fact, I didn't think I was a better organizer than Morgan Levi, but I was the big cheese in our little local, so I figured a special meeting with me would stroke this guy's ego. Which is not a put-down of Sean, either. It's just human nature: Sometimes our pride requires a little boost before we can change our mind, especially on opinions we have been quite public about with our colleagues. Later that day Morgan phoned and said, "You're on, Jane. He wants to meet the big negotiator."

Talk about pressure. Morgan and I reviewed the game plan for the meeting. She knew his top issue was something known as on-call pay, and after that, the wage scale, because he felt undercompensated for his skill level and years of experience. We decided I should invite him to the union hall to sit down with me in my "big negotiator" office.

When Sean walked in it was immediately apparent that he did not suffer fools easily. I figured maybe we could bond over that, because neither do I. We engaged in some chitchat. We discovered we both loved to ski, party, and travel. We had skied some of the same mountains and travelled to some of the same countries. So far, so good. We moved on to the contract issues, on which his views were very much those of a nurse from the cath lab. These workers are super skilled, and they don't confront the same staffing issues as other nurses. They care for only one patient at a time: one heart, one line, one nurse, and a doctor. Many of the worst aspects of nursing pass them by, like the frenetic scene on the medical surgical floors where every patient is buzzing for help at once. But Sean knew nurses in other states, and he knew they got paid a lot more for being put "on call." And because cath lab nurses were in great demand, they were put on call a lot. This was his central issue.

Morgan had informed me that Sean was on a first-name basis with the Desert Springs chief financial officer, and now he was dropping names of other managers at the hospital to give me a measure of his importance. This was my entry point.

"So Sean, have you gone to ask your manager for an increase in on-call pay, and has he said yes?" And again later, "Sean, sorry, I know you know these guys, but why don't they just solve the problem and give you a raise?"

"Jane, the CEO told me if it weren't for the contract he could already have given the cath lab a big raise because we deserve it. It's because we have a union contract that we are getting screwed."

"Sean, would it make sense for a union to turn down fair improvements that a boss offered to make mid-contract?"

"No, I suppose not."

"Well, you go tell the boss tomorrow that we would happily accept moving up fair raises right away during negotiations."

You could see light bulbs going off in Sean's head. I told him that in my view the only way he was going to get the raise he deserved would be to join up with his coworkers and get into negotiations. In fact, I wanted *him* to be the one to present this terrible abuse to the management team at the bargaining table. At the end of the meeting, Sean signed his membership card. I thought Morgan was going to have a heart attack, and it would have been a good time to do it, with a super skilled heart procedure nurse right there in the room.

Over the next few days our membership numbers jumped to 60 percent. Then came the next bargaining session and Sean's presentation about the stresses of living your life on mandatory on-call status. You couldn't make plans, you couldn't go out, you couldn't drink (in Vegas), you couldn't do lots of things if you might be called to the hospital at any moment's notice. Sean spoke well. He sat next to me at the table, usually a spot reserved for leaders so we could whisper important stuff back and forth. And when he walked out of bargaining that day, it was all over for Desert Springs management. They had lost him.

Sean had begun taking assignments. He signed up the entire cath lab, then moved on to the emergency room. The Morgan-and-Sean team was rolling up the hospital.

Something similar was happening at Valley. This was the big hospital, what everyone in Vegas, including the nurses, called the inner city (as a New Yorker I always found this funny). Teresa had been doing the same highly disciplined organizing there that Morgan was doing at Desert Springs: refusing to get distracted by anything, identifying the right leaders and then seriously engaging them to move them over to the union. Teresa's particular obstacle was that Valley had a lot of Filipina nurses, and the behavior of some visible longtime union nurses—white ones—toward them was horribly racist. The problem was a constant challenge throughout my time in Vegas. This country is rattled by racism every day, and every smart boss knows how to play that card. At Valley hospital I had to repeatedly take on white nurses about the racist comments they would make about the large and growing number of their Filipina colleagues.

"Why do you think the boss is hiring all these Filipinas into nursing jobs here?"

"To pay them less than us."

"So, if you don't talk to the Filipina nurses, then your pay is just going to go down?"

Fortunately, at Valley Teresa had ID'd a Filipina named Aurora Delacruz as a leader of leaders, much like Sean at Desert Springs. Aurora was a tough ICU nurse with twenty-five years' experience. She was deeply religious and her faith often spilled over into discussions about negotiations. She had impeccable fashion sense. And she understood who we had to move at Valley. She also understood the informal Filipino family connections throughout all of Las Vegas.

We wanted to get the workers from both Desert Springs and Valley meeting together and seeing this as one big campaign against the Universal Health Services corporation, so we asked that the bargaining session for the two hospitals' tables be combined. UHS absolutely refused. Rick Albert and his team might have been slow on some of the curve balls we had been throwing at them, but any idiot bargaining for a boss knows that the name of the game is Divide and Conquer, and merging bargaining tables that are already established as separate obviously doesn't fit that game plan. So we did a "majority petition" demanding that we bargain as one union at one table.

A majority petition, a formal demand signed by a majority of workers at a shop, is a very particular tool in the organizer's kit. If done right, it advances the demand, puts the boss on notice that the union has a majority, and provides an accurate bench test of the organizing that has been done. Petitioning for a joint bargaining table also provides an educational opportunity and ups the ante on the organizing evaluation, because the petition you are asking people to sign requires considerable explanation for workers unaccustomed to thinking about the details of union strategy. Beyond just getting your majority, another key metric is how *fast* you get it. Once bargaining starts to get intense, things can change very quickly, and a strong union has to respond at the same pace. So a majority petition is a test of your structure, both numbers and overall organization per unit. Our members got their majorities at both hospitals in five days. Taking into account that not all workers were there every day—half are always off, some are weekend-only, then you have all the shifts to chase—that was pretty good—but not good enough. We declared that two days would be our holy grail. A union that can turn around a majority petition in a large shop with multiple shifts in two days is ready for battle.

So, "Good work everyone, but too slow. You need a two-day turnaround in your organization inside the hospital. Let's find out where the system is weak and fix it." We made a big blow-up version of the petition with all the signatures, and the workers marched it all around the hospital on their way to deliver it to the top management. We photographed them and made a flyer with the photos. This is the nuts-and-bolts of real fights: testing and retesting your organization, using everything as a tool for education, empowerment, leadership ID, organization, and mobilization.

The Desert Springs contract had now expired. This was a big deal. Under US labor law, when a contract expires, four dangerous things happen: workers can strike; the employer can lock workers out; the employer can stop collecting union membership dues from the workers' paychecks; and the "permanent window" period for decertifying the union begins. In short, everything escalates. Shutting down dues collection is a major escalation and creates an immediate crisis. It rarely happens. Unions have to fight for contracts that stipulate that the employer deduct union dues from the paychecks of the union members and forward the money to the union. This is the money that keeps things running, and a union can find itself suddenly bankrupt if a large employer stops collecting dues. And a strike, well, a strike is another order of magnitude entirely. And a strike in a hospital, well, that had never happened in the history of Las Vegas.

So when UHS offered a contract extension at Desert Springs, there were compelling reasons to accept. The bargaining, however, was going nowhere. We had lots of workers at negotiations, and they had made detailed proposals. These proposals certainly were not going to make UHS *happy*, but they were worthy of serious consideration: We had shown that they would improve patient care and that the hospital could afford them. And still, UHS wouldn't budge. In union-busting literature this is called "creating futility." On the other hand, we were at 70 percent membership at Desert Springs and 65 percent at Valley, we were building a tight organization, and all the excitement and buzz was in our favor. We rejected the contract extension. It was time to put the workers' new power into play.

I gave the go-ahead for our first sticker-up, even though I thought the numbers were still a little weak (another one of those moments of not knowing how lame normal labor organizing is). A sticker-up sounds simple: Everyone wears a sticker today. Well, good luck. A sticker-up is a major operation that tests every aspect of union organization. The idea is to demonstrate to the boss and to the workers themselves that the workers are standing together and the union is in charge. But if the sticker-up fails to reach critical mass, you end up demonstrating exactly the opposite, and the boss will be laughing all the way to the bank. Here is a little run-down of what you need:

- Stickers that say something everyone has agreed on and is excited about.
- Staffing schedules for every unit on every floor in every department of the hospital. Not last month's or last week's or today's, but the schedules for the planned day of the sticker-up.
- A high functioning committee formed of every worker-leader in the hospital, unit by unit.
- A detailed plan for getting stickers to every leader.
- Finally, a plan for the leaders to personally stick them on everybody, and then go back through every unit two hours later to make sure the stickers are still on, and then repeat this all day long as management will be trying to pull them off the workers or scare them into removing the stickers themselves.

For a worker on the job, putting on a sticker is a bigger deal than you might think: It tells her supervisor, once and for all and to his face, "We are the union." And then she has to stick to her guns when the supervisor threatens her and orders her to remove it.

As always, the leaders are the key. This would be a good time to revisit what I said earlier about a skilled organizer's definition of a leader: the one the workers on the shift turn to when they have a question or need support. And when the supervisor says take off your stickers or else, they are going to need big-time support. If a real leader has been identified for each unit and the sticker-up has been well-organized, someone is going to be there, ready with a smile, some encouraging words, and another sticker if the first one didn't make it through the confrontation with the boss.

Our members chose stickers that simply said "65 percent," at Valley, and "70 percent," at Desert. A sticker like that gets everyone asking questions about it. When someone looks at yours and says, "What's that mean?" then we have what we wanted: people talking about what it means to have a strong union. We did role-playing rehearsals with workers to help them collect their thoughts. Just two months earlier their shop had had union membership in the 30 percent range, but the only ones at the hospital who knew this were the bosses. Now was our members' chance to explain to everyone who had not yet joined that the union's numbers were real and growing. We were shooting for the tipping point when an organizing drive becomes a movement.

We timed the sticker-up to coincide with a bargaining session. By now the sessions were packed with workers coming to see this new thing the union was doing, something they spontaneously christened "*big* bargaining." The nurses in both hospitals were nervous and ready. Dozens got up early to stand in the parking lots at morning shift change to sticker up the other nurses as they arrived at work. At the bargaining session that day, two hundred nurses squeezed into the room. When we got the 10 am reports from all the leaders on all the units, we knew those stickers weren't coming off the scrubs no matter what the supervisors did. The leaders were walking the floors doing checks. If a member said her sticker had fallen off, the leader would put a new one on. Some workers were having so much fun, one sticker wasn't enough—their entire bodies were covered.

The management was clearly getting the same reports we were; the situation was spinning out of their control. Finally, the bosses cracked. Their negotiating team came in with new proposals on floating and a few other small items. But the workers could smell opportunity now. The boss wasn't moving on money or staffing or health care, but the boss was moving. In late May, at the final Valley Hospital bargaining session before that hospital's contract expired too, Rick Albert came in and meekly said, "I don't suppose you want to extend this contract either, do you?" And having already discussed this with the workers, I was empowered to give the best possible answer: "No!" When we went into our caucus, the workers were clapping and screaming and high-fiving. They just loved saying No! to their boss; it's something a worker so rarely gets to do.

Now we had two contracts expired, and though we were having a hell of a good time, all we had moved at the bargaining table was an inadequate proposal on floating. On the phone Jerry kept telling me, "Don't worry, you're fine. Keep reminding the workers it's always like this. Don't worry about the table, just keep being an organizer. Get them ready, get them stronger, do what you know how to do, throw the boss off, get him scared and confused."

Within a few days of the first sticker-up, we had hit 75 percent membership at Desert and 70 percent at Valley and were ready for the next one. We stickered up with the new numbers. Overnight we hit 80 percent at Desert Springs and 75 percent at Valley. We stickered up again. It was like a drug. The workers wanted more and more sticker-ups. We had to move off the numbers theme because we were pretty much there. The workers' organization was a well-oiled machine now. We did another majority petition, I can't even remember on what, and it was finished in two days. It was a real union now, because the workers were in constant conversation with one another about everything going on.

Then Morgan came into my office one day to say we had hit 85 percent at Desert Springs. "Jeeezuz Christ, McAlevey, I thought you were out of your fucking mind." And off she went in search of more members.

We had held off contacting the media until we had huge majorities, and now we were there. We decided it was time to make the fight public. Furthermore, the workers needed something to do. That might sound flippant, but it's not. We had created a real sense of movement. Once you cross that threshold you have to keep the sense of forward motion going or the whole thing can fizzle. There always has to be something to do that is meaningful, social, and fun. We decided to hold our first rally.

There's a special set of laws that govern labor activities at health-care facilities. The bosses sold these laws to the public by playing on a legitimate concern for maintaining patient care. The laws are completely unnecessary, because no one is more concerned about patient care than nurses, but as usual, management logic carried the day. Health-care workers only got the right to unionize in 1974, and it came packaged with an overwhelming amount of regulation. To hold a simple informational picket outside a hospital, you must give the boss a "ten-day notice to picket" stating the exact time and place of the event. Our members took a vote and agreed that if the boss came to negotiations with nothing much to put on the table, the workers would hand the legal ten-day notification across it. It turned out Rick Albert was being a jerk that day so we just handed it across the table and ended the day's session.

We set the picket for high noon on the day of the next bargaining session. I remembered that way back in March, when I first discussed strategy with D Taylor from the casino workers union, he'd warned me, "Your contracts expire in early summer. That's bad, McAlevey. You're new here. Do you know how hot it is in Vegas in June? Your workers will die picketing then." Oh, boy.

We were still demanding that the bargaining tables at the two hospitals be merged, and UHS was still refusing. We wanted everyone to understand that our adversary was not a hospital named Desert Springs or Valley, but a huge corporation named Universal Health Services, and that the real boss sitting on his throne at the top of the whole empire was a man named Alan Miller who made $20 million a year. Someone had pointed out that UHS was headquartered in a rich suburb outside Philadelphia called King of Prussia, PA—no kidding—and we had already blanketed the hospitals with flyers showing the King of Prussia on horseback. We had a weekend sign-making party with lots of workers, music, kids, balloons, 400 paper crowns, and 400 fake-rhinestone tiaras. We made sashes that looked like the one the King of Prussia wears in the history books, and the kids covered them with glitter. Delegations of nurses went to all the other unions in town, explaining what was happening and asking for support. We had nurses calling politicians, briefing them, and asking them to attend the rally. Statements from our nurse spokespeople were popping up in the press, and wow, were they good.

On the big day, we began the morning bargaining session as usual. The room was so packed, there's no way a fire marshal would have allowed it, but no one was there to stop us. Tensions were high. At the lunch break we all went out to picket. We had 300 nurses out there, and the casino workers and carpenters had sent members to support us. The men wore paper crowns, the women wore tiaras, and everyone wore sashes. The press was all over it. Everything was working. But D Taylor had been right about the weather: it was hot as hell. We brought loads of water bottles, but even so, after an hour some picketers seemed on the verge of passing out. I knew in my bones that a full-scale strike in June in Nevada would not be an option.

By the time we went back inside to resume negotiations, we were already getting reports, from nurses calling nurses calling nurses, that we were all over the TV. They were interrupting regular programming; we were the breaking news. "Nurses are standing up for patient care at Desert Springs Hospital…" "Hundreds of angry nurses took to the streets today…" The nurses asked me to please keep my tiara on. A suit, a set of pearls, a poker face, and a tiara. They were in stitches. From that moment forward, usually in the presence of the employer, the nurses mostly referred to me as the Queen of Prussia. Rick Albert came in steaming mad, red in the face, like a cartoon character with smoke coming out of both ears. He conveyed the distinct impression that he had just come from a meeting with his superiors that he had found exceedingly unpleasant.

By now there was a federal mediator in the room at all times.[*] Jerry had repeatedly warned me not to trust mediators, not because they were anti-union but simply because often they were not too bright. I would go on to work with quite a few and it was true that many of them were a few fries short of a Happy Meal. But by pure luck (yes, there is an element

---

[*] Generally speaking, in the case of health-care disputes, as soon as a contract expires the Federal Mediation and Conciliation Services becomes a potential player. Once a ten-day notice has been sent notifying them of a pending job action, the FMCS will insert itself into the bargaining process.

of luck to bargaining after all) we got Lavonne Ritter, seventy-five years old and sharp as a tack. Heeding Jerry's advice, I was trying to keep her at bay, but she soon began to assert herself. In his rage, Albert wasted no time in making a big mistake: He pointed at my head and screeched out that I still had my tiara on. I looked up and calmly asked if he had anything else to say aside from commenting on my wardrobe? He blew up. Then out they stormed, the entire management team. I knew this meant we were in for more escalation, but really that was the only place to go.

Throughout the whole bargaining circus I was calling Jerry at least twice a day—from my office, my car, my bed, the women's bathroom outside the bargaining room—going over contract language. This requires a kind of attention to minutiae that is hard to describe to someone who has not had the misfortune of having to negotiate it. A word here or there can mean everything. Get tired and type "if" instead of "but" and you can blow $10,000 a year in pay for every nurse. Jerry was such an old hand at this he didn't even have to see it on paper. He could just listen to me on the phone and correct a word here and there.

The contract campaigns at the UHS hospitals were not the only ball we had rolling in Vegas. We were also beating the decert at the ambulance company. Ambulance drivers have extensive interaction with emergency room nurses, and now our tightly organized ER nurses were keeping the drivers in the union. Viral. Our public service workers were walking precincts for our County Commission candidate three days a week. Our government workers were excited by the political campaign, and we were getting press from that endorsement.

But even though we were building a great public image and drawing in individual activists, there was essentially no institutional support to be tapped in that dry desert town. That is just a fact of life in the tourist-dominated, transient-filled, gambling-crazy city of Las Vegas. Beyond the casino workers and carpenters there was no union support, and the only church with any real presence in town was the Mormons, and they sure weren't going to help out a union. This contract campaign was going to be won or lost by the workers inside the hospitals.

So here we were. The contracts had expired and UHS wasn't budging at the tables. The situation was roughly similar to the moment before the gunfight in a western, with two gunslingers facing each other in the middle of Main Street. Jerry and I decided to recommend a strike vote at both hospitals. I didn't think we were ready to really go on strike. I had a team of young organizers who had never, not one of them, even seen one. But a strike vote doesn't actually mean there will be a strike. A strike vote authorizes someone, in this case the bargaining team, to call one at a future time. Knowing that we didn't really want a strike, calling the vote was pure brinksmanship. And it was also the next test of the workers' organization.

The workers were starting to get scared, and for good reason. A strike is an explosive thing, and a strike at a hospital is an explosive thing squared. A strike at two hospitals is an explosive thing cubed. We were practically living in each other's pockets by this time: the members, the organizers, and me.

Like everything else about organizing at this level of intensity, the strike vote was intended to be both a public escalation and an internal test of our organization. I was reporting daily structure tests and numbers to Jerry, and I knew the vote would pass. The crucial question was how many members would turn out for it. And in fact the authorization to strike passed by an overwhelming margin of 98 percent of votes cast, but as I'd expected, we hadn't got the turnout we needed to actually win a strike. The turnout in an internal vote is one of the few key pieces of information a union is not required to share with the employer, and I made absolutely certain that this number didn't leak. Our public stance was that a strike had been authorized by a nearly unanimous vote, and it was now our job to follow through on our members' wishes.

Both newspapers ran big headlines in our favor the next day. The TV coverage never stopped. Nurses in Las Vegas had never held a picket line before, let alone voted to strike. Our union had been a joke, and suddenly we were everywhere. Back at national SEIU headquarters in Washington, Larry Fox was thrilled but nervous. He reminded me that almost no one in the national headquarters except for him really believed in strikes anymore, and most certainly not in hospital strikes. Andy Stern was taking SEIU in the opposite direction. In Stern's view, the long battle on the shop floor between boss and worker was over and the boss had won. Workplace struggle was out; political deal-making was in. Hey, good to know. I'm out in the Wild West trying to get a decent contract for poorly paid nurses at two for-profit scumbag hospitals, and the head of the national union doesn't believe in strikes. Truth was, I didn't care. These horses were long out of the barn. Plus, Jerry was teaching me the fine arts of negotiating and power and risk-taking and more, and I was *soaking it up*. There wasn't a better teacher for bargaining to the brink.

The day after the vote, we stickered up with "98 percent." By now we were 80 percent membership at Valley and 88 percent at Desert Springs, the highest figures we would ever hit during my time in Las Vegas. In the press there simply wasn't anything else happening in Nevada. The TV news started running a regular "Nurse Strike Count Down" banner. When nurses are united and angry, they are formidable opponents in the court of public opinion for even the most astute corporate PR flacks. Everyone loves nurses. When you are laid up in the hospital, you might rarely see your doctor. Your nurse will be the human face of the care that may save your life. And this was local nurses versus out-of-state, for-profit, money-grubbing Easterners. Even the laziest journalist could make some hay with that story.

One of the most important skills for an organizer is knowing when you have hit your moment of maximum power. Once you do, if you just keep pressing the pedal to the metal, your engine will stop revving and begin to die. We decided we were going for it. If Rick Albert came back into negotiations again without anything to offer, we'd hand him another ten-day notice, this time to strike. And so it happened. Back in caucus all the high-fiving and back-slapping stopped right then and there. We were as ready as we were ever going to be, but this was serious, scary stuff, and I was scared right along with everyone else.

The federal mediator was now trying to get actively involved, but I wasn't letting her do much. Jerry had been adamant about never letting a mediator into your private caucus, or run "shuttle diplomacy," meaning the mediator floats a proposal to the workers and then walks down the hall to see if management will agree. As much as I liked Lavonne Ritter, Jerry's argument that you have to make the boss face the workers rang true. I talked it over with the nurses and everyone agreed to refuse her services. Negotiations were suspended, and we were ten days from the first hospital strike in Vegas history.

Then we did what we do best: we organized. We acted as if we were going on strike. We sent nurses out to the other unions asking for support. The workers were having strike parties in the breakrooms at lunchtime. They made countdown stickers, and just about everyone in every unit of the two hospitals wore them. The whole point of legally requiring the ten-day notice to strike is to push the sides to settle, but the days and the stickers were ticking by: 10, 9, 8, 7… I kept waiting for the call from Rick Albert, but my phone didn't ring. Jerry kept saying, "Trust me, McAlevey, you have them by the balls. They're scared. Your level of worker engagement is great. The press in on your side. Just keep doing what you know how to do, and the boss will be calling soon."

And then it happened. Rick Albert was on the phone. "We'd like to meet for negotiations the day after tomorrow. We think we are ready to propose the framework for a total settlement."

"At a joint table?"

"Yes, Jane, the two hospitals can bargain together."

I got Morgan in and she began to scream. Every worker was calling every other. The press was announcing that bargaining was to resume. Our stickers read "6" when we walked into our first joint bargaining session with all the workers from both hospitals together. Victory number one! We had nurses hanging from the rafters. For the first time, I was in *real* negotiations—not posturing, but the end-game chess moves that would determine which of our demands we actually went home with. Jerry warned me that this would be the hardest part for me, because at the very end there would have to be real compromise, and compromise was not one of my better sports. After spending months raising worker expectations, somehow I was now supposed to set them to reality. And I was so exhausted I could barely keep my eyes focused.

The first thing management passed across the table was fully employer-paid health care for the nurses and their families. I had a hard time not crying right then and there. Not one health-care worker in all of Nevada had fully employer-paid individual health care, let alone employer-paid family health care. Poker face. Poker face. Next came new floating rules that were pretty much exactly what we had asked for. The UHS proposal was real and comprehensive. It must have taken them the whole three days just to type it up. And they were costing it, meaning the boss was actually doing the math on what it would cost to implement the agreement. By the end of that day we were seriously bargaining, but we got stuck on the costing. We disagreed on the math of what a few things would cost to the tune of millions of dollars. Furthermore, management was refusing to agree to a two-year contract. The nurses weren't leaving the table without a two-year deal. This was serious.

Management knew our demand for a two-year contract was the beginning of our plan to strategically align the market for 2006. Our local had a number of contracts set to expire in 2006: one at another big private-sector hospital, another at the public hospital, and a third with the county civil service. If we could get our other contracts to expire in that same year, we could align the market and organize the mother of all contract campaigns. We had said over and over in every bargaining session that we could not and would not settle for anything other than an expiration in 2006. It was what we called a strike issue, meaning if we didn't win it in negotiations we would win it in a strike (and yes, that was a bluff, but it was so important that the workers understand the power of common expirations, we talked about as much as any single issue). The management clearly hoped that the workers would trade this long-term investment in union power for all the other goodies they were offering in the here and now. But we were the new Las Vegas SEIU, we had done our homework, and this just wasn't going to fly with our members.

After an excruciatingly long day there was a proposal to take a day off from bargaining and have the federal mediator, the UHS money people, and the union money people sit down and see if they could make apples equal apples and oranges equal oranges. Of course, the management's money people were the top financial guys at one of the largest health-care corporations in the world. The union "money people" was twentysomething Sara Rothstein! Did someone say "pressure"? By this point Sara also couldn't see straight, and now she was confronted with huge spreadsheets with more numbers than I could ever handle while wide awake. I called Jerry from the bathroom to ask for advice. The fact was, we really didn't understand what management was doing with the math. Jerry thought we should accept the proposal, provided that first I explain the idea to the members and actually have them vote to authorize the idea. We stipulated that one worker leader attend the meeting along with Sara so that the workers would know for certain that the union wasn't cutting a last-minute deal behind their backs. I added that I didn't even have to be in the meeting, which was another signal that this was not going to be a secret deal. This didn't make Sara happy at all, but it was the right thing to do, and anyway I had a ridiculous amount of language in the management proposals to wade through. The members agreed, management agreed, and negotiations were suspended.

Sara went to the meeting, reporting to me by phone many times throughout the day. It turned out the UHS team was using two different sets of baseline numbers, which can really change the amounts involved when you are talking about a thousand workers. Inside the hospitals, the workers were wearing their Day 5 stickers. Everyone was tense. All three local TV stations had set up camp outside the bargaining site, all news, all the time: "Can the Nurses' Strike Be Averted?" There was press waiting for me outside the office. The whole thing was nuts.

The next day, bargaining resumed. A couple of hundred nurses were there, all wearing Day 4 stickers. We had teams of workers in every corner of the room reading the counterproposals I had written the day before. And then, for the first time in the campaign, divisions began to emerge among the nurses. Sure enough, just as Jerry had warned me during our first conversations about bargaining, the source of tension was the wage scale. At 10 pm we were still in session. We took a caucus. I realized that the everyone-welcome "big bargaining" style we had developed might be coming back to haunt us. Now it was a madhouse, with nurses from the two hospitals who didn't know each other fighting over stuff that was really pretty minor in the scheme of things. Eventually, the only issue the workers hadn't settled on was the wage scale, but that discussion was going nowhere. At close to midnight, Cathy Stoddard, a nurse from Pittsburgh who had come all the way to Vegas to help, called me aside and asked if she could have the floor. People like her are invaluable to campaigns like this. Cathy was not union staff, she was a real nurse. Her commitment to nurses and unions was of the sort that would bring her far from home to support nurses she had never met. She had real experience as a worker leader. In short, she spoke with a unique authority, and when she spoke, people listened. Now she let out a yell to get everyone's attention, then slammed the contract proposals on the table. She screamed as loud as she could, "*Ten percent!*" Everyone was staring at her, baffled. Then she continued.

"Hey, you know me, I am Cathy from Pittsburgh. I have been a union nurse for a really long time. I have never in my life been offered a 10 percent raise in each year of a contract. Jane has explained that the way the wage scale works, every one of you will get a raise of no less than 10 percent each for the next two years, and that's just your wages. Your on-call pay just doubled. Your health care is now free. I think you should *shut up and settle*. I'm sorry, I don't mean to offend any of you. I know I'm from out of town, but the nurses in my hospital would die for this contract. *Put the wage scale down and start celebrating.*" When she sat down, it was over.

It was midnight. The workers took off the "4" stickers they were wearing and put on the "3" stickers. Teams went out to get the night shift to do the same. I called management back in and handed them a comprehensive counterproposal, telling them not to come back until they were ready to give us everything in the proposal and a contract that expired in 2006. They left. An hour later they returned, and it was done. We had won everything.

I remembered back to that very first pathetic meeting of seven nurses, and how when I asked what they most wanted to change in the contract they had replied, "Everything." Everything was exactly what they had got.

We packed up, shook hands with management, and said good-night. And then came the bedlam. Some nurses went running—and I mean *running*—around the night shift with news of the settlement. Others went to Valley Hospital to tell the night shift there. Still others were insisting we go drinking because this was Las Vegas and there was a 24-hour bar across the street. I remember sitting in that bar at 2:30 am watching nurses in curlers walk in. They were getting out of their beds and coming to the bar. Some had their husbands with them. Tequila shots were going around, who knows who was buying. There was no news in Las Vegas the next day except our victory.

I actually didn't yet comprehend how much we had won. We had set a new standard for nurses in almost every aspect of the contract. Right there in the bar the nurses decided to run one more sticker-up the next day, another simple sticker with just a number: "673"—the number of days until their new contract would expire, in 2006.

Weeks later our candidate won the Democratic county commissioner primary, and everyone in the Nevada power elite was wondering, What the hell is going on over at the SEIU?

CHAPTER FIVE

Laying the Foundation: At Catholic Healthcare West, an Enlightened CEO; at SEIU, an Unenlightened President

It took the rest of July to turn the hundreds of pages of proposals approved in the negotiations at Desert Springs and Valley hospitals into actual written contracts. I spent my "free time" walking precincts for the county commission primary and encouraging others to do the same. Finally, I had some time to get to know Tom Collins, our candidate. He was a Mormon. (Was this for real? Not only was I living in Las Vegas, but I was also pounding the pavement to elect a Mormon to public office?) But when it comes to electoral politics, Las Vegas is a Mormon town. They used to say Vegas was run by the five M's: mob, military, media, mining and Mormons. By the time I got to town, some of these had been eclipsed, leaving the Mormons the biggest show going. It seems incongruous, the Mormons running Sin City. But if you remember that the Church of Latter Day Saints is really a highly efficient capitalist enterprise, it makes all kinds of sense, because there is a ton of money to be made in Las Vegas.

Tom was what people in Nevada call a "Jack Mormon," meaning he was born and raised in the church but didn't really follow its teachings anymore. He was also populist to the core; a Democrat who believed in unions; anti-choice (ouch); a cowboy who had ridden rodeo back in the day; and just plain interesting.

Right off the bat we bonded over horses, riding, roping and rodeos. He made fun of my cowboy boots and constantly needled me about being a vegetarian from New York who couldn't possibly know anything about roping and riding. I put up with a year of that until he finally invited me—no, *dared* me—to come to his ranch for a day of herding, branding, antibiotic dosing, and calves. When I jumped on a horse and effectively moved a herd of cattle, my relationship with Tom hit a new high. It turned out that my life of owning, riding and training horses, considered an odd and useless personal quirk back east, would come in handy again and again in my dealings with the Nevada power structure. There was even a moment when we were organizing a rural hospital in the northeastern part of the state, which is sheep country complete with immigrant Basque shepherds moving huge herds around the Ruby Mountains, that my month of sheep farming in New Zealand would prove useful.

When Tom won the August primary, in a district with overwhelmingly Democratic registration, we had essentially won the seat. After that, I took a long nap. When I woke up, it was time to get back to trying to rebuild the local. I finally had time to dive into sorting out the money and organizational structure and recruiting good staff. The wonderful organizers we had borrowed, Tobin and Stoddard, returned home, and the national SEIU had officially reassigned Morgan back to the dormant campaign at the two hospitals she had been tending to before I had arrived in Vegas. Not surprisingly, the nurses at these hospitals suddenly wanted the SEIU. Not only had our victory been all over the news, but in Vegas it is common for nurses who work a main job in one hospital to have a part-time job in another, which makes for a very effective grapevine. Nurses in Nevada had never heard of 10 percent raises or fully employer-paid health care. Good contracts were spawning new organizing opportunities, just as Larry Fox had said they would, convincing me beyond any shadow of a doubt that the firewall the national union had erected between organizing campaigns and contract campaigns made no sense at all.

The obvious first move for building the Nevada staff was to bring Morgan into it permanently. It was clear to both Morgan and me that with all the momentum we had built in the UHS campaigns, the right place for her was not with the national union but with our local. I also knew that her exit from the national staff would do nothing to ease my rather problematic relationship with Washington. Soon Morgan called headquarters to resign from her national post and make it known she was signing on to be the first real organizing director of the revitalized Nevada local.

Morgan had initially come to Vegas in the fall of 2003 to try to capitalize on an election procedure agreement, or EPA. These are typically made between a national union and a large corporation. The corporation agrees to set aside some portion of the weaponry in its union-busting arsenal, and in return the union offers something like, for example, limiting its organizing efforts to a specified list of states or particular facilities. Not all EPAs are created equal. The best ones commit the employer to lay down its arms and allow the workers to vote on whether to form a union in a neutral context. This, by the way, is what the law is supposed to do but doesn't—let workers decide to form a union in a neutral context! The worst EPAs commit the employer to nothing of the kind. They give away the store for very little, and as we would learn later, they are often negotiated with no worker participation at all.

The EPA reached between the national SEIU and Catholic Healthcare West was one of the best the union ever achieved during my years in labor. In northern California, SEIU Local 250, headed by Sal Rosselli had been fighting a full-on war with CHW, the largest hospital chain in California and the eighth-largest in the country, and Local 250 had run them so ragged that its corporate headquarters had finally signed a peace treaty, technically a neutrality agreement—one of many terms for an EPA—with the national SEIU. Negotiated by Mary Kay Henry and Sal Rosselli, the unprecedented accord committed CHW to allowing union efforts to organize CHW hospitals without interference from the boss. It even provided for meetings of hospital workers at which the terms of the deal would be jointly explained to employees by the hospital CEO and a union rep, so that management couldn't later misrepresent the agreement at meetings from which the union was barred. In exchange, Rosselli's team agreed to an immediate cease-fire in their war of attrition against CHW. CHW had two hospitals in Vegas that were covered by the agreement, but when the old local tried to run elections, in 2003, even with the advantage of boss neutrality conferred by the agreement worker enthusiasm was so low they couldn't pull off the election. Now there was a new SEIU in town, coming off big contract wins at Desert Springs and Valley. The CHW workers had heard all about it, and now *they* were calling *us* asking for help in forming a union.

It turned out that the CEO of these hospitals was another Mormon cowboy into rodeos, and he and I now shared county commissioner-elect Tom Collins as a political ally. Beyond that, Rod David was rather unique among hospital CEOs. I called his office to set up a meeting to discuss the neutrality agreement and how we would implement it in Vegas, and he invited me to breakfast. I had never heard of a CEO doing such a thing. At breakfast he was genuinely polite. As we were getting up from the table he smiled warmly and said, "It was nice to meet you. Hopefully I will see you again somewhere else, because my workers, and certainly my nurses, will *never* vote for a union."

Two months later, in two separate elections, one for the nurses and one for the ancillary staff, the workers voted decisively to form a union with SEIU. The victory margin was nearly 2-to-1. Rod phoned me at 8 am sharp the next morning to congratulate me: "Great campaign. Really shocked me. Obviously you have something to teach me about my nurses." This was the single most unusual employer phone call I received in ten years in labor, and I suspect it would have been for almost anyone else in the movement, however long they'd been there. I suggested to Rod that we meet and "figure out how to build the highest-quality hospitals in Nevada, because among other things, that's what your nurses want," and he agreed. Had I somehow fallen into a parallel universe? We had just added 1,600 new members to the union and the boss was OK with it?

In early August I had a meeting with Vicky Hedderman, the president of the Vegas local, and proposed that we hold a three-day retreat for the executive board and all the staff. As a former staffer at the Highlander Center in Tennessee, I knew that the simple act of getting people out of their comfort zone and throwing them together for a few days of bonding and meals could go a long way toward building bridges among groups accustomed to functioning as islands. Vicky agreed, and in mid-September board and staff headed off to the Oasis Hotel and Casino in the little town of Mesquite, Nevada.

One of the beautiful things about a three-day retreat is that you can step back from the immediate tasks at hand and think about big-picture ideas, like putting your day-to-day battles in historical context. This can be particularly helpful in the United States, where the long and rich history of the labor movement is completely absent from the public discourse and almost never part of anyone's civics class. We spent a good deal of time on this. We reviewed how the private sector unions had set the best contract standards in the country, at a time when government workers didn't even have the right to organize. And how the big corporations, headed by the Business Roundtable in the 1970s had decided to crush unions in the private sector, and they would be coming for the public sector next. In the case of these workers, we were taking the education further, positing a two-step dance of labor history and tax history. We had slide shows with graphs and pie charts showing how much taxpayer money actually goes into so-called private sector hospitals. Medicaid and Medicare actually paid most of the salaries of "private sector" nurses. Once the smoke and mirrors were cleared away, there really wasn't much difference between public and private sector hospitals, and whatever happened to private sector nurses today was going to happen to public sector ones tomorrow.

We also made extensive changes to the formal structure of the local, creating actual job descriptions for the elected officers, to which the officer would be held accountable. These changes were driven by Maryanne Salm, the one truly outstanding staff member I found upon arriving in Vegas. Maryanne was comparable to Morgan in terms of sheer talent, but their talents were different. Morgan was an organizer; Maryanne was a radical educator.* She had a knack for thinking about systems, and she was a team player. In many ways, Maryanne's talent and dedication had been holding the Vegas local together for years prior to my arrival. She was calm, measured in manner, and thought before she voiced opinions. And she could not voice opinions in the same way the rest of us could. She had had a tracheotomy to correct a congenital birth defect. The fact that she could be a highly effective union staff person in spite of such a severe handicap should give you an initial sense of her extraordinary abilities.

During the three days of the retreat we "buddied up" the private

---

* A good organizer has to be a radical educator. But a good organizer *also* understands and helps to drive strategy, knows how to assess the status of thousands of workers in a campaign, how to design the action-learning progression for each leader, has a grasp of matters like "framing," momentum, and critical mass, can identify who the organic leaders are and be capable of much, much more.

and public sector workers at each meal, rotating everyone to a carefully assigned meal partner and having the partners tell each other something about their contracts. The Clark County workers seemed to learn for the first time just what garbage their old union had negotiated for everyone else. These workers had been kept apart for years, and now they were at last becoming people to each other. Three years later Hedderman would stir this very division right back in, but that's later. For now, we were building "union" instead of "division."

Having been convinced by experience that winning great contracts for one set of workers led to organizing victories with other workers, Morgan and I dove into the first contract campaign at the two newly organized CHW hospitals. We did not expect that Rod Davis would fight his own workers the way the Universal Health Services corporation had fought theirs, but we planned a serious campaign nonetheless, because we saw this as an opportunity to set a high standard we could hold up to other hospitals in the market. Plus, we needed to use the contract campaign to continue building the workers' organization at these hospitals. The longer we worked in Vegas, the more we realized that in a city where nurses regularly rotated from one hospital to another, our union's reputation in one would be carried to all the others. This was true of the kudos the revitalized local had won in the last few months, and true of the contempt in which many people obviously held the old one. To our utter dismay, we discovered that it was well known among nurses that the old leadership had repeatedly negotiated contracts with the public hospital in which the nurses got less than the ancillary workers. In the rest of the country this just doesn't happen, since nurses are the more skilled group. But Hedderman was a unit secretary, not a nurse.

With no urgent crisis to deal with, I finally had a minute to try to get a handle on our local's finances. We had just begun serious discussions with the executive board about raising the dues, but before we could move on the future budget we needed to understand the current one. By this time I had participated in five meetings of the executive board and I knew that the old board hadn't known much about the money. It was sort of amazing to me, but the report about the board meetings I had earlier heard from members who actually went to them was true: Nothing much happened. The "financial report," consisted of the longtime treasurer giving a *verbal* account of how much money was in the bank. That was about it.

Though math always gave me the heebie-jeebies, I had been responsible for a large endowment when I was at the Highlander Center. Later, as a program officer at a progressive foundation, I had routinely reviewed large foundation budgets as well as the financial records of various organizations across the country. Reading financial statements was something I actually could do. I couldn't write them, but I could interpret them. Not surprisingly, the financial statements of the local made absolutely no sense. The books had supposedly been kept by the office manager, but when I sat her down and asked her to explain them to me, she told me they had hired an outside accountant who was *really* doing the books. This accountant was from the same firm that did the audits every three years.

What I thought was, "Holy shit!" What I said was, "Call the guy and get him in here right away, because none of this makes any sense."

I still have the memos that flew back and forth between this accountant and me as I tried to sort out what the hell was going on. Millions of dollars were running through a union that had no approved budget; the bookkeeper claimed to not understand finances, documents that required the signatures of the union's authorized leaders were signed with rubber stamps; and audits were done by the man who was keeping the books.

I immediately fired the accounting firm and brought a package of cleanup recommendations to the executive board, including annual audits by an outside firm (that was not involved in doing the books), budgets approved by the board, which would then receive real monthly financial statements, and creating a new position, financial director, to be filled by a trained professional. All of this was approved at the next board meeting.

What I did not do was demand a full investigation, and that was a tough call indeed. But I was getting along with the new executive board just fine, and Hedderman and the old guard were not getting in the way of anything I was trying to do. And we had multiple campaigns in full swing, all of which stood an excellent chance of making the lives of thousands of real people better in multiple ways, and all of which would have been totally derailed by a big-deal financial investigation. But it was obvious that I was in a very tenuous position. Still, I had taken this job because I wanted to organize workers, and I was doing it. We were doing it. On the phone, Jerry Brown advised me to let the sleeping dog lie and keep pressing forward, and I agreed. The problem with sleeping dogs, however, is that eventually they wake up.

I t was now autumn. We had just won huge contract fights at two hospitals owned by Universal Health Services. We had organized two more hospitals owned by Catholic Healthcare West, where we had not yet even begun to negotiate the first contracts for our new members. We were players in several races in the fall general elections. We were rebuilding the infrastructure of the organization. That felt like a pretty full plate until my staff told me that they had just noticed some language in a research memo that indicated our local had two EPAs, covering two more hospitals, that were about to expire.

Just before we made this discovery, SEIU had held its quadrennial national convention, at which Andy Stern replaced Larry Fox with Mary Kay Henry as his new national head of the hospital division. Disagreement about the sort of EPAs SEIU should approve was one reason for Fox's fall, though at the time no one understood this. This was typical of how Andy Stern operates. When he gives you the boot, it is never clear what was actually going on; you don't really understand what really happened to you until later. Larry told me that Stern had told him not to worry, it was just an organizational restructuring, and he was making Larry special assistant to the president for national employer relations. Everyone assumed that Stern was rewarding Mary Kay for running his successful campaign for national president back in 1996, and on one level he was. It was not until much later that Larry fully realized that "special assistant to the president for national employer relations" really meant "Siberia," where he'd been sent in large part for his insistence that EPAs between huge corporations and the union not be negotiated behind the backs—or worse, *on* the backs—of workers.

The expiring EPA now in question was between the national SEIU and the Hospital Corporation of America. The surprise was that it covered two HCA-owned hospitals in Vegas: Mountain View and Southern Hills. We assume this had been overlooked because when the deal was originally negotiated, neither hospital physically existed (Las Vegas went through an extraordinary growth spurt, as mentioned). I got Larry on the phone and explained the situation. "No, Jane, that can't be right. I am certain you are wrong. Let me look into it and I'll get back to you." Whew, what a relief, until Larry called back to say that somehow in the chaos that can result from frequent changes in leadership, the little detail of an EPA expiring for two hospitals had fallen through the cracks.

We had just run two hospital elections and now we were staring down the barrel of two more. And the clock was ticking. Those elections would have to take place in just three months to be covered by the EPAs. To pull this off would require more good organizers than I had managed to assemble, so once again I'd be dependent on whatever staff I could wrangle out of national headquarters. Larry Fox was out and Mary Kay Henry was in. Mary Kay was smart, witty and conveyed a sense of real concern for workers, but as Kirk Adams would say, she was informally known as the whirling dervish, because caught up as she was in the rush of running a big division of a national union, it was often difficult to get her to focus in a sustained way on a given problem. She was notorious for not returning phone calls. That weird experience I had coming back from New Zealand, being offered the job in California and then never getting the confirmation call? The person who never made that call was Mary Kay Henry. Given the time pressure we were under in Nevada, dealing with her was beyond frustrating. Mary Kay and the staff leadership team she brought with her had just spent a year running smooth elections under the much more favorable CHW agreement. And in Vegas, we had so handily just won the two CHW elections, well, such a busy person might say, what was all the fuss from McAlevey about needing some talented staff?

Back in 1998, years before I came to Nevada, the national SEIU had run a major organizing campaign at Sunrise, HCA's biggest hospital in Vegas. The campaign ended with a victory, but it had taken a monumental effort, including top organizers flown in from around the country, years of resources from the national union, and a criminal indictment against HCA for massive Medicare fraud. And then, as soon as the workers had voted to form a union, just like that all the national talent had left town, rushed off to the next organizing campaign. The campaign to win the crucial first contract for 2,400 new union members was left in the hands of the old Local 1107. You can almost pity them. The national union had parachuted in top organizers and gobs of resources to run an organizing campaign far beyond what the local union could have run, then disappeared in a flash, leaving the follow-up entirely in their hands. (Sort of like what the US military was doing in Afghanistan and Iraq, where highly specialized American units would blast their way through a critical region and then quickly move on, leaving the corrupt and poorly trained local forces to face rapidly regrouping insurgents.) The entirely predictable result was that the first Sunrise contract the local negotiated on behalf of those 2,400 workers was a huge embarrassment.

This was the background. Now we were supposed to try to pick up the pieces and organize HCA's Mountain View and Southern Hills hospitals, in three months. When HCA opened Mountain View, many of the nurses and technicians from Sunrise moved to the shiny new suburban hospital with the beautiful view of Red Rocks State Park. They brought with them the memory of that epic drive to form a union and the resulting disastrous contract their new union had signed on their behalf. And it got worse: The CEO of the new hospital was nobody's fool, and unlike me he had been fully briefed on the fact that an agreement his parent corporation had signed with the national SEIU meant he would be confronting a union election at some point. So he had made sure to give the workers at his new nonunion hospital better pay and working conditions than those same workers had had at the unionized hospital where they'd previously worked. To top it all off, there were also a large number of nurses at Mountain View who had worked at the Clark County hospital, where Local 1107 had accepted those weird contracts that gave ancillary workers a better deal than RNs. Now we were supposed to convince these nurses that they should dive into *another* campaign to join the new, improved SEIU, a campaign that would again involve long hours of work and of ducking the truckloads of slime HCA was certain to throw in their direction. Great.

Most of the organizers Washington eventually sent were so green as to be nearly useless, and some were so bad we sent them back. Thankfully, among them was also one true gem: Jessica Foster. Foster was a walking worker encyclopedia—there was no fact about the whole life of any worker she had ever met that wasn't neatly stored in her brain for instant recall—giving her the best possible understanding of relations among and between workers. She was every bit Morgan's equal as an organizer, and I quickly made her the lead organizer for HCA's Mountain View Hospital. Mary Kay also facilitated an arrangement with Sal Rosselli's local in northern California to send us some organizers. Rosselli was still on decent terms with Andy Stern's leadership team (sometimes at the peril of the values he would later champion in his explosive break with the Stern crowd). Rosselli's very talented organizing director was Glen Goldstein, and Glen was as good as they get. He came from the old national 1199, had spent twenty years helping to build the outstanding local in Washington State, had developed legions of talented organizers using the 1199 model, and he and I had formed a friendly relationship during my time at 1199 New England. Glen understood our situation at Mountain View right away and sent a team of organizers led by Brian McNamara. He thought very highly of Brian, who had already come to Las Vegas once to help us out during the last week of the CHW election in October. We already had confidence in him.

As the local's new organizing director, Morgan understandably wanted to run the HCA campaign. But after much discussion it was agreed that Brian would head that campaign while Morgan and I would jam as fast as humanly possible to win a great contract at the two Catholic Healthcare West hospitals. The goal was to win the new contract with CHW before the workers at Mountain View and Southern Hills voted on whether to form a union. We wanted the hospital workers at the HCA hospitals to see yet more evidence of the kinds of contracts the new SEIU local was winning before they made their decision.

With all of this going on, there had been no time to find a larger home for the local, and now our union hall was overflowing with huge teams running campaigns at four hospitals. It was a 24/7 operation. Charts and diagrams papered the walls. People fell asleep on the floor. It felt like a movement. For me, it felt like home.

Even though we were pressed to the wall with the hospital campaigns, there were political developments in the state we could not ignore. The Club for Growth, a conservative political powerhouse, had targeted Nevada for a property tax initiative that would gut the state's social programs in the same way Prop 13 had wrecked California's. Our local had no choice but to dive headfirst into this campaign too, along with the state-level AFL-CIO. Not only would this initiative be a disaster for our members if it passed, but fighting it was another opportunity to engage the government workers in the union in an educational political battle.

Over the course of this campaign I learned that the casinos are always available as allies against lowering property taxes. Why? Because if property tax revenues went down, there would be pressure to raise taxes on the casinos. In Louisiana, for example, the much smaller casinos are taxed to the tune of 21 percent; in Vegas, casinos make a killing (like hospitals) in part because they were taxed at only 6.75 percent.

And then there was the issue of the unresolved contract for the Clark County government workers, a time bomb whose fuse had now run out. If we didn't fix it, both the local as an organization and I personally as its executive director were going to get blown up with big fat fines and legal charges. And the members themselves still had no idea of the mess the previous leadership had made. I had been careful not to openly criticize the old guard to the workers. With the 20/20 vision of hindsight, I can see now that this was probably a mistake. But the former executive director was long gone, and Hedderman was doing nothing to obstruct the building of the new union. If Hedderman wasn't going to make problems for me, I certainly didn't have the time to make problems for her, and Jerry Brown and Larry Fox both concurred in that assessment.

But now we had no choice but to tell the county workers what was going on with their contract, and that about 4,500 union members weren't getting the raises they had been counting on. I told them straight up they had been handed a pile of horseshit—their pay provision hadn't been settled and I was sorry. There was still a vanishingly small window of time to try to actually fix the problem, but it would require moving the fight beyond the negotiating table, where we were winning nothing. The only way forward was direct political pressure on the county manager, Tom Reilly. The organizer in me saw this as an opportunity to test whether the civil service workers in the new union we were building could handle a shop floor direct action fight. It was our good fortune that Reilly was cocky and regularly gave quotes to the media that couldn't have served our purposes better if we had written them ourselves. He began by announcing, "There isn't any justification for government workers getting higher cost-of-living increases than what everyone else gets out there."† Thank you. I had just spent a year trying to heal the rift

† *Business Las Vegas*, April 5, 2005.

between public and private sector workers in our union by explaining that the employer's side would try to use lower pay in the private sector to drive down wages in the public sector, and here was the county manager reading my lines for me. We immediately distributed flyers and posters quoting Reilly's own words against him.

At the same time, I kept trying to appeal to Reilly directly, because he, along with the county workers, was frustrated by the unresolved pay dispute. I had a large olive branch to extend: the $100,000 we had spent helping to defeat the property tax measures that would have gutted the budget of Reilly's county government. Unfortunately, given his long history with the old 1107, he had no reason to believe that the new SEIU local would deal with him any differently.

In late January of 2005 the executive board and staff took a second three-day retreat, as planned. With everything else we were doing, the pressure to forgo long-term strategic planning in favor of multiple crises-of-the-moment was considerable. But everyone understood that as crazy as things were now, it was all just a prelude to 2006, when the county hospital workers' contract was due to expire. We had fought hard to ensure that the contracts we signed at Desert Springs and Valley hospitals would expire the same year. The bargaining team working on the contracts at the two CHW hospitals had agreed that we wouldn't settle these contracts without getting the same expiration date. And if and when we won the organizing campaigns at the two HCA-owned hospitals, we would demand it for the first contracts there, too. Then a majority of all the hospitals in Vegas would have contracts on the table in 2006. The local was strategically aligning the market. In 2006, Las Vegas was going to see the mother of all contract campaigns.

We had major work to do to prepare for that. We needed more money, more political power, and more talented staff, and we needed the members of our executive board to get much better at managing the day-to-day issues inside their shops, so that the staff could focus on 2006. This was the main topic of discussion at our January retreat.

We also had a long discussion about grievances and worker power that would profoundly change how the union was run. Maryanne Salm led a discussion of a document she had prepared, "From Grievances to Direct Action." Its main point was that if a union was well organized, workers knew which colleagues were screw-ups and which had real grievances. And also because it was organized, real problems could be dealt with right there in the shop instead of through an arcane, legalistic and disempowering series of grievance procedures that not only sucked up lots of staff time but ultimately left the issue in the hands of the boss, unless the union spent a lot of money on a thing called arbitration—which generally didn't happen until two years after the original grievance was filed. Many unions in this country do nothing else but file and handle grievances. The old Nevada SEIU local had been one of those grievance mills; the new one would not be.

To a certain extent this discussion echoed the line coming from Andy Stern and the national leadership in Washington. Stern hated "grievance mill" locals, and he had made it very clear that his priority was growing the union, not handling grievances. But what we were talking about in Nevada was replacing the grievance procedure with direct action on the shop floor, which would require that the level of participation achieved in a real organizing campaign be maintained indefinitely. In my opinion, what Stern meant when he said grievances were beside the point was a reflection of something more general: He thought the day-to-day dealing with "shop floor" issues was a waste of time. We were prioritizing action on the shop floor—direct worker action.

In putting together our bargaining team for the two new CHW hospitals, we followed the model I had learned from District 1199NE: We elected one worker to the team for every twenty-five workers in the larger units and for every fifteen workers in the smaller units, and we did it by unit and shift so that we had every kind of worker input. If anything, we made our teams even bigger, even including workers from units that had fewer than twenty-five workers total, like the GI labs. And we stuck to the "big bargaining" vision of everyone welcome and encouraged to attend negotiations, whether for a day, an hour, or a coffee break. These were totally transparent union negotiations. When the chief negotiator for CHW flew in from San Francisco for her first bargaining session with us in Vegas, she looked around the room with surprise and said, "My goodness! You have more workers on your bargaining team for two hospitals in Las Vegas than Sal Rosselli has on his for the whole state of California and twenty hospitals."

Meanwhile it was clear that the campaigns to organize HCA's Mountain View and Southern Hills hospitals were not going well at all. My idea had been that Morgan and I would race through the contract campaign with CHW and then turn our attention to the HCA hospitals, our CHW contracts setting yet more high new standards in hand. Based on what we knew of the CEO of the CHW hospitals in Vegas, this had seemed realistic. But the national headquarters for CHW, in San Francisco, turned out to be the worst bureaucracy I'd ever encountered in a successful company. It wasn't that they were trying to sabotage our efforts, but they were, as Local 250's negotiator John Borsos would often say, "simply incompetent." We just could not make them bargain fast enough for our timetable.

There was actually a moment, as I recall, when some DC wizard suggested I settle the CHW contracts without all the details that mattered to those workers, so we could at least show big raises to the HCA workers, but I insisted we could not short-change the workers at two newly organized hospitals to boost our campaign at HCA. Beyond that, I wanted the CHW contract to be the first to include the new concepts and language we'd created to enable the workers to maintain a strong organization in the shop once the contract was settled. And those issues had to be very specifically shaped to handle the realities of a right-to-work state.

One example is whether the union gets any time to speak at the orientation the employer runs for new employees. In a right-to-work state, where each employee individually decides whether to join the union, this is crucial. In a union security state, new employees must become union members, so new employee orientation is not even an issue. (Though it would be great if all of the unions in any state decided to meet workers as soon as they were hired!) In the contracts we negotiated at Desert Spring and Valley hospitals, we'd won fifteen minutes to talk to new employees about the union at every orientation. However, we later learned that the head of human resources would sit in the back of the room looking as intimidating as possible, staring at people to see if they took a union card. We also learned that if our fifteen minutes were tacked on at the end of two days of mind-numbingly boring activities like filling in tax forms and learning where the fire extinguishers are, no one would stick around for the union talk. At CHW, therefore, we wanted language that granted the union a full hour, during which the employer's representatives had to leave the room, and we wanted to pick where in the two-day orientation that hour would fall. We also wanted to make sure that the union hour was paid time, like the rest of the two days.

In addition, we wanted good "drop" language. Because a member in a right-to-work state may quit the union at any time, the casino workers had spent years developing very careful contract language that maintained the worker's right to drop the union, but only during one week on each anniversary of the worker's employment. This was brilliant. Since these hiring anniversaries all fell at different times, there was no way the employer could run an annual all-out campaign to get as many workers as possible to drop the union. The SEIU civil service contracts with Clark County included in their terms a uniform drop month, October. It was essential that we win a new contract that secured the best "drop" language—language that would be even easier to negotiate in subsequent contracts, including those we had coming right up in 2006. Finally, we wanted the union access provisions to be the best anywhere. We wanted the right to walk through the hospitals to talk to workers instead of being confined to the cafeteria or having no access at all. At Desert Springs and Valley we had won full hospital access, but we'd had to agree to notify security every time we showed up, which meant that a security guard or some other management representative could just follow us around. In the CHW settlement, we wanted the right to come and go without notifying anyone.

These three provisions may seem like nit-picking, but when we won them they became the cornerstones on which we would build a powerful union with high membership at the CHW hospitals.

Another hang-up was that a lot of the contract language we were proposing in Las Vegas was being modeled on the contracts SEIU had negotiated with CHW hospitals in California. But Sal Rosselli and the national office had cut a deal with another union, the California Nurses Association, that put the CHW nurses there under the jurisdiction of the CNA. That meant we had to negotiate the contract language for nurses from scratch. This work included issues, like floating, that are extremely detailed and hugely important for the workers they affect. Meanwhile CHW wasn't moving on the money or staffing we wanted yet—they were like a supertanker that took forever just to change course by half a degree. And without that new contract to show off, we were missing the key weapon we had been counting on in our organizing campaign at the hospitals owned by HCA.

Brian and Jessica were doing their best, but they just didn't have enough talented organizers on the ground. Mary Kay and the folks in Washington still believed that HCA was actually abiding by the EPA instead of fighting it tooth and nail every step of the way. If a union has a good EPA and an employer who respects it, you really don't need a lot of organizers up front in the campaign cycle: all that's really critical is the last stage leading up to the election. So you run most of the campaign with a skeletal staff, then air-drop in an army of organizers for the last few days for a professional get-out-the-vote operation. And this is the sort of campaign DC seemed to think we had before us.

The elections were held in late February. We won at Southern Hills Hospital, but lost at Mountain View *by seven votes* in the ancillary unit and seventy-one votes in the nursing unit. So much for our last-minute get-out-the-vote operation.

By winning at one out of two HCA hospitals, we still beat the national average. But with a couple more good organizers throughout that campaign we could have won them both. Certainly we could have overcome the seven votes we lost by in Mountain View's ancillary unit. This defeat—especially because it was so narrow—was a bitter pill for me. Once the voting was over, the national office ordered all the staff that had rolled into Vegas for the campaign to roll right back out again. For many of these organizers, however, Vegas had been their first experience of what a labor movement was like. Some of them thought our new union was the place to be, and a few asked me if there might be a place for them on our staff. This would be a huge boost for our local, but I also knew that "stealing" DC's organizers would land me in yet more serious hot water with Washington. In the end I held on to three. Among them was that "worker Wikipedia" named Jessica Foster, who would go on to play a key role in the coming years. A team was now coming together in Vegas that was effective on the ground and socially tight. It was something people wanted to be part of. Labor organizers travel around a lot and have a highly efficient grapevine. Word was out that if you wanted to learn how to organize, and be part of a militant local, you wanted to be in Las Vegas.

By late spring of 2005 we had set new standards for Las Vegas hospital workers in the contracts we'd won at Desert Springs and Valley hospitals, and then topped those standards with the even better contracts at the two CHW hospitals. We had organized workers at three more hospitals into the union, and had forced the county manager to resolve the outstanding issue in the civil service contract in the workers' favor. We had played a key role in a successful county commission race, and in defeating a right-wing effort to gut property taxes in the state. Internally, our local had tripled the size of its staff, built an organizing department, and fundamentally changed the way the union was run. It had been a busy twelve months.

CHAPTER SIX

Government Workers Get Militant: Big, Representative Bargaining Versus Bad Laws and Bullies

It was spring of 2005, but our strategic sights were set firmly on the following year. Our contract with Sunrise, owned by the Hospital Corporation of America and the largest for-profit hospital in Vegas, expired in 2006. So did our two big contracts with Clark County (one for the county hospital and the other for the county civil service). We had fought bloody hard in negotiations with United Health Services, the second largest hospital chain in the world, to win contracts at Desert Springs and Valley hospitals that would also expire in 2006. We had won contracts at the two hospitals owned by Catholic Healthcare West that carried an unusual 15-month term, again, so that they would expire in 2006. We had strategically aligned the market: In 2006, virtually all of the workers in our local would confront their employers together.

In four private-sector hospitals, we had built a tried and tested union led by workers who had risen organically through organized struggle and a membership that knew how to stare down harassment and intimidation from the boss. We had not, however, had a chance to test much of this work in our public-sector units. But now we would have our chance with the Clark County Health District contract expiring in early June 2005.

The Clark County Health District was not the public hospital but rather 480 county public health workers: a mix of public health specialists, nurses, scientists, support staff, secretaries, and so on. These employees had offices but were rarely in them, as much of their work was done out in the community, where their activities ranged from testing the water to testing the food safety of the big casino buffets to administering programs that helped ensure fetal and maternal health among the poor. They had been part of the local for more than a decade, and their contract, the one that would soon expire, stank. Everyone's old contracts stank except for those of the workers who had always been on the political radar of the local's president, Hedderman, and her old guard. The contracts for the Housing Authority, the Las Vegas Convention & Visitors Authority, and the Clark County Health District—they all stank to high heaven. They were nearly as bad as the private-sector contracts I'd encountered when I first arrived in Las Vegas. These poor workers didn't even get the healthcare benefits enjoyed by the more privileged Clark County workers. The only thing that separated them from the worst private-sector contracts was the pension that all government workers had across the board.

Not surprisingly, many Health District employees hated the union, but these were the informed few. When we started to talk to workers about their expiring contract, the majority didn't even know they *had* a union. The stories they told echoed the stories we had heard at Desert Springs and Valley hospitals. Every few years, a notice would circulate about negotiations, and after a while, for reasons they didn't understand, there would be a settlement offer that would then be ratified by a simple majority of whoever showed up to vote.

There was broad skepticism from the local old guard and from SEIU headquarters in Washington, DC, as to whether the militant, movement-oriented organizing model we were creating in the private sector would work with government employees. And there was a real problem here: At our spring 2005 annual membership meeting we had voted to make "big representative bargaining" the official policy of the local, mandating one bargaining team member per twenty-five workers in big shops and one per fifteen in small shops and inviting any worker to stop by and watch. Yet our existing government contracts, which the old guard had negotiated, all had language explicitly limiting the size of union negotiating teams.

When I explained this to Jerry, he didn't believe it.

"Just read it to me, McAlevey."

"OK. *The Union shall be represented during negotiation sessions by a negotiating committee of not more than ten (10) Union members at any given time, designated by the Union. Committee members shall be granted leave from duty with full pay on the day of negotiations sessions with the County for all meetings held for the purpose of renegotiating the terms of this contract when such meetings take place at a time when such members are scheduled to be on duty.* That's, ah, Article 8, Section 8." Long pause.

"Good God, McAlevey, those people should be hung or shot, not sure which."

Jerry could read between the lines of this sort of thing as he did headlines in the morning paper, and he quickly pointed out what this language really accomplished. First, it made negotiations secret: No one was allowed in the room but a tiny bargaining team. Second, it offered full wages to the special few who got to sit in negotiations instead of working, so who wants to settle when the boss is buying lunch? No wonder the Clark County contract had taken almost two years to complete. And no wonder no one outside the ten members of the bargaining team understood that the merit pay system had been left unresolved.

Some in labor will argue that having the boss pay the bargaining team for time spent in negotiations is a victory for the union: The workers get compensated for their time, union work is recognized by the boss as "real" work, and so on. But a union that sees this as a good thing is not built on any sort of notion of the collective power of workers. No boss is going to pay 50, or 100, or 200, or even 300 workers to exercise their collective power across the bargaining table from management. And since in most unions contracts are all the action there is, aside from presidential-year politics, why not make negotiating one the most exciting, transparent, participatory experience possible? When the workers at our annual membership meeting passed the resolution to move to big representative bargaining, one of the old-guard executive board members asked me, "Jane, if we have these big bargaining teams, those of us who are board members will still get paid even if we let others in, right?" I had to excuse myself to the bathroom right then and there. These people had no shame.

Jamie Ware was our organizer assigned to the Health District contract. Jamie had come on board in the spring of 2004, and during the Valley and Desert Springs campaigns had learned the ropes of the worker-centered model of organizing we were developing. One of her first tasks was to figure out just how many members we had in the Health District.

Of course, she couldn't rely on our broken computer database. But even after meeting with quite a few workers and gathering schedules and so on, she still couldn't figure out how many people were actually in the union. This led to the first of what became many membership-card audits: Jamie and our database person would unlock the fireproof vault that held the original copy of every membership card we had and count them all by hand. In November Jamie sat down with me and Morgan and Maryanne (they were known then as the M & M team, and wow were they good) to report the sad fact that only 26 percent of the workers at the Health District were in the union. We did the math. That was 125 members, and most of them hated the union.

So we were at 26 percent membership and the clock was ticking on the contract expiration. Well, we had started at a similar low at Desert Springs and hit 88 percent in just a few months. There were half as many workers in the Health District as at the hospital, and they worked in buildings that were public property. We could walk right in and talk to them without some bastard calling the cops and yelling, "Trespassers!"

Jamie threw herself into the work. She would hold up the four recent hospital contracts we'd won as proof of what the new union was doing. She began to raise these workers' expectations that together they, too, could win a terrific contract. Several times a month I would attend worker meetings with her, backing her up with that special authority that comes from being the actual negotiator. We missed no opportunity to say that every single worker was going to be encouraged to attend negotiations, no matter what the contract said. I cannot overstate the importance of this ironclad commitment to transparency in bargaining to these educated, middle-class workers. And at every meeting I would say, "We won't be opening this negotiating table until you have a supermajority of your coworkers in the union. There's no point otherwise; you would get slaughtered. You keep building the union with your organizer and when you hit 50 percent membership plus one we will hold elections for the bargaining team and start drafting the language."

One thing that struck me over and over in Vegas and almost everywhere else I worked for unions: workers want to make things better so badly that they are willing again and again to set aside frustration and anger stemming from past bad experiences with unions if you offer them a plan to win that makes them the central participants. The ability to bring workers to this sort of expectation is what separates the best organizers from merely good. It isn't easy. The key is that laser-like focus on identifying and developing leaders. Jamie had developed into a solid organizer, and she and the leaders built a hell of a union at the Health District.

The contract expiration date was now breathing hard down our necks. As we had done before, to buy time we gave the Health District boss our detailed information request, a document now infamous among bosses in Vegas. The boss was, ah, not happy. But until he provided all of the information we asked for, which he was required to under the law, our refusal to open negotiations was perfectly legal.

There were lots of terrific workers in the Health District, people who went out to poor communities to do prenatal and mother-baby care or immunize children. Like our hospital nurses, they were saints in the eyes of the public. Our top Health District leader, Diana Daniels, was a secretary, but she actually led everyone, including scientists and nurses, who don't usually accept the leadership of less skilled workers. Diana was Black, in her mid fifties, the pastor of an evangelical church, and a leader's leader. She had been on the local's executive board before I arrived, and had repeated to me the same story I'd heard from other members: She rarely went to board meetings, because they were so awful. She really didn't care for most of the people there. But she had her own faith in the union, which in some way seemed connected to her faith in God, as well as to an unshakeable sense of what fairness meant. Several times Diana took me aside to inquire in private exactly how we were going to encourage everyone to come to the bargaining table when the contract explicitly said we could not. "Imagine this," I replied, "The first thing we do is inform the boss that no one wants to get paid for being there, that you don't want to charge the taxpayer for bargaining your contract. That will be new. And then we will just demand that if the workers don't expect pay, what's wrong with transparency?"

By the time negotiations opened, we had supermajority membership and the workers had successfully run their first sticker-up and majority petition. We had complete contract language for every proposal we wanted. Members of the bargaining team had each selected sections of the contract to adopt as their own throughout negotiations. And we had decided that since this was an odd-sized unit, neither large nor small, they would elect a bargaining team of one team member to every fifteen workers, rather than to the usual twenty-five. The elections ran poor Jamie ragged, as the Health District had eight off-site locations scattered all over town. And we got a good indication of what sort of boss we were dealing with when Jamie was harassed and even thrown out of several locations for conducting a vote on public property—something we hadn't anticipated

On the first day of negotiations, we had more than 100 workers in the room, nearly a quarter of the shop's entire workforce. When the boss, Angus MacEachern, walked into the room with his two assistants, he looked like a heart attack in the making. He literally turned beet red. The contract authorized no more than five workers across the table. And if he was paying attention, which he was, he certainly noticed that among the assembled throngs were the health district's most important employees, including the county's top epidemiologist. I said, "Hello, you must be Angus. My name is Jane. We have a proposed agenda for the session, and if it makes sense to you I am prepared to review it." He proposed that we talk about ground rules instead, and noted that he had with him a copy of the ground rules that had been repeatedly agreed to by my predecessor.

Employers often request ground rules for negotiations. They typically include things like "Both parties agree that neither party shall talk to the media during the life of these negotiations" or "It is understood that each party shall have only one person who speaks during negotiations." Well, none of that makes any sense to a group of workers who are trying to win a contract campaign. In fact, 1199 teaches its negotiators that ground rules are just a way for the boss to control the table, and in Nevada we were forging an approach to bargaining that was even more inclusive and participatory than the norm for 1199. So I replied that the workers had a presentation they would like to make, and then we would like to hand over our proposals and run through them. Once that was done, we would examine and consider his proposed ground rules. Then, without really waiting, the workers launched into their presentation. I watched the management team as the workers rose one by one. Nearly fifty people read at least one sentence on one of the slides, articulating some improvement they collectively wanted to make. And when that was over, they began to present their specific contract proposals.

The boss again requested that I sign his ground rules, "just like every other time we have negotiated with the SEIU." We decided to take a caucus. With 100 workers crowded into the room, the bargaining team members quickly explained to the newcomers why we opposed the ground rules and that we had the legal right to refuse them. When we went back into session I called on Diana, who had rehearsed a line we would teach thousands of workers during my four years in Nevada: "The law clearly states that ground rules are a permissive subject of bargaining, not a mandatory subject. As such, we appreciate your offer and we are happy to discuss them with you. However, we have decided to not accept them, and you cannot hold up further negotiations on this matter." At this point MacEachern's complexion went from beet to fire-engine red. He stood and announced that he was done and led his team out of the room, though not before his assistant made a comment about how it seemed that the workers wanted to eat lobster for dinner every day of their lives.

A week later about 100 workers again showed up for the second session. When we arrived we saw that the boss had instructed his staff to prepare the room with one table in the middle, placing chairs only for him, me, and five workers—the number specified in the contract. The rest of the chairs were shoved back to the very edges of the room. It was totally odd, as if seven of us were sitting down to dinner in front of a hundred spectators. So we rearranged things in a more conventional fashion, with one table for the workers, one for the boss, and a little space in between. This time, MacEachern did explode. He actually shoved his table at me, squarely into my gut, yelling, "What the hell do you think you are doing? This isn't negotiations, this is a zoo! I don't have to sit here and look at all these people and I won't! I am filing bad-faith bargaining charges against you immediately for violating the negotiations clause of the agreement. Come talk to me when you have a committee of five paid workers." And he stormed out.

Out loud I said nothing. In my head I said, "Thanks, idiot. Thanks for being the best organizer we have." When preparing the workers for negotiations, we always made a big deal about the importance of keeping a poker face no matter what the boss did, never making a sound we hadn't planned, keeping totally silent when management entered the room, and passing me notes instead of talking. This was Las Vegas, where people understand the power of a poker face. And here I was, in a sharp blue suit, my hair tidy and tied up, everyone sitting quiet as librarians, and the boss comes in and starts yelling and shoving tables. I have seen bosses do all kinds of things—some much more underhanded—but never anything this childish. When the door closed I turned to everyone and put my finger to my lips, signaling for silence. I got up walked around the table and asked Diana to go look out the door and be sure they were not out in the hall. When she confirmed that they were indeed gone, the room broke out into applause, high fives, and a lot of "Can you *believe* that?" Standing up to this jerk was a new experience for everyone in the room. This is something I would see over and over, and it is a big part of why I believe every worker should attend contract negotiations at least once. That's the only time in their lives when workers sit with their employer as legal equals. These workers weren't poor, but they were cogs in a giant government bureaucracy that dehumanized them in too many ways. To anyone who hasn't had a job doing shift work in a government office, where you punch a timestamp to enter and again when you leave, and quitting is not an option for any number of reasons, it's hard to explain how much standing up to your employer means. I learned. Any union can choose to open up negotiations so that their workers can have such an experience. So why don't they?

Naturally, the workers soon began asking questions about what had just happened.

"Gee Jane, is it really legal what we did?"

"Maybe we shouldn't have had so many of us."

As always in such situations, I just facilitated the conversation for some time before I spoke. This was crucial. A big piece of my job was helping workers think this stuff through on their own, and often when it would come to my turn I would have little to add. This time, I simply asked, "If we can't get the boss to agree to sit in the room with you when you are acting respectful and professional, no matter how many of you there are, do you really think we can win the improvements you want in the contract?"

This incident proved to be the first of a series of major fights over the awful language in our public sector contracts. And oftentimes the first and toughest battle was getting the boss to come into the room on the workers' terms. The bosses had the law on their side, but only because of rotten contract language. I would often say to the workers, "Sometimes if you want to change a bad law, you have to break it first."

Some nasty back-and-forth correspondence ensued. My letters to employers during negotiations always included a "cc: the workers," and I always had the organizers staple copies of them together with the employer's and hand them out all over the workplace. You would think that once a boss saw his first nasty, stupid letter generally distributed he would wise up about his writing style, but not Angus MacEachern. His first letter stated that he wouldn't come to any more negotiations unless I cleared the room of workers. Thanks again, Angus. In my response, I ignored the contract language we had inherited and referred instead to key provisions of Nevada labor law, which roughly states that management has the right to choose its team and the workers have the right to choose theirs:

> Your attempt to dictate to the Union who or who is not a member of the bargaining team is clearly an attempt to interfere, restrain or coerce the employees in the exercise of their legal rights to choose their bargaining representative (NRS 288.270(1)(a)). You are prohibited from dominating, interfering or assisting in the administration of any employee organization, as your attempt to say "who" from the employee members of our Union can be at the negotiation sessions (NRS 288.270(1)(b)).

When the next scheduled session arrived, we showed up in full force, but management never even walked into the room. Perfect.

Strategically, we figured that if we were going to win, we would have to get the contract decision making out of the hands of Angus MacEachern, who was a Human Resources guy, and into the hands of the county's Public Health District Board. We began explaining this to the workers, and how they needed to see themselves as part of a constellation of power that extended far beyond their workplace. Once they could see how pushing MacEachern to the side was a step in the right direction, MacEachern's ridiculous refusal to attend bargaining sessions came to have precisely the opposite effect he intended: Instead of disempowering the workers, it gave them greater confidence in their ultimate victory, and really pissed them off to boot. At this point we introduced the idea of the power structure analysis. We'd do one focusing on who the members of the Public Health District Board were, who had appointed them to the board, how long their terms were, and what our researcher knew about each of them. And we also asked all 480 of the workers what they already knew about each board member.

Serving on the Public Health District Board was none other than the newest member of the Clark County Commission, Tom Collins, who had just been elected with substantial help from our union. We broke out the workers who lived in his district and they began meeting with him. We formed a similar group of members who lived in the electoral district of Lawrence Weekly, a new member of the City Council who had recently been appointed to the District Board. The chair of the board was another county commissioner named Rory Reid, son of Harry Reid, who was then the minority leader of the US Senate. The Reid family essentially runs the Democratic Party in Nevada. We had no real relationship with Rory at that point, but we assigned a group of workers who were his constituents to approach him. As soon as Tom Collins understood the issues, we asked him to also brief Rory on how absurdly management was behaving. Finally, we did educationals with the workers on which committees in the state legislature had approval of budgeting monies to the Public Health District Board, widening the targets for member action and engagement.

In Stamford I had learned that the people who were leaders in the workplace were often also leaders in the community, and we now discovered this was true in Vegas as well. Diana Daniels was deeply connected to the African American power structure. Diana not only knew Weekly, she was close to his assistant at the City Council, and knew a long list of people who also knew him. Diana led the delegation to brief Weekly. To all the politicians we sent one simple request: Get the management team to show up for negotiations.

It is always a good idea for the workers themselves to approach elected officials and educate them on the issues; for one thing, it very effectively develops their leadership skills. In this case it became even more important when the Public Health District issued a memo to its board members stating that they were legally prohibited from discussing with the union all issues that were the subject of negotiations. We put SEIU attorneys to work developing a counterargument to the district's position, but also made it clear to the members that they needed to approach the politicians as their constituents, with constituent concerns, not as union members. And if the district wanted to tell the elected officials on their board that it was illegal to speak with their own constituents, well, if they were that dumb they would again be doing our work for us.

As the next meeting of the Public Health District Board approached, we prepared our members to request speaking time during the public comment section of the agenda. None of the workers had ever spoken at a public meeting. The members were getting nervous, but good nervous— not the kind that paralyzes you, but the kind that develops strong leaders.

This would not be a meeting with a boss but with our own elected officials, and we didn't want to start by being too pushy. So we sent just twenty workers to back up the three leaders who would take the microphone and explain that we were the ones being reasonable and that we had filed legal charges against the district for refusal to bargain, charges we were confident we would eventually win. Now, these kinds of charges take forever to resolve, which is why workers should *never* place all their eggs in that basket. We hadn't filed them thinking we would win anything through them directly, but because they would give the workers a sense of moral authority. They also gave our allies on the board a basis on which to talk with management about the risks their behavior was creating for the district in terms of legal fees, fines, and embarrassment. And finally, the charges brought us the media.

The meeting was a key moment in the campaign. All the Public Health managers sat watching their workers challenge their boss. The workers delivered terrific speeches, which the nervous quiver in their voices did not spoil in the least. The board members listened with poker faces. When the speeches were done, the board asked just one question in response: "Did you say the only thing you are asking for is that management start to negotiate?" A closed session was called, during which the board instructed management to get off its ass and back to the table. That week our membership grew to nearly 75 percent. We knew a central strategy was to overcome the rap the management had tried to pin on us, that the union was creating a zoo-like atmosphere by packing so many workers into the bargaining room. So at some point we had the constituents of Tom Collins ask him to show up at the proceedings without

warning and sit in the back to bear witness to the fact that when we negotiated you could hear a pin drop.

It was at that first Public Health District Board meeting that we laid
the groundwork for "big, representative bargaining" for all of our public
sector workers. Our three wonderful leaders explained our principles for
all to hear: In exchange for the right to have large, inclusive and transparent bargaining teams we were ready to immediately surrender the pay
they were contractually owed for our bargaining time. They explained
that as public servants who wanted to provide the best possible client
services, they needed every type of worker present at the bargaining sessions. And they asked that negotiations start late in the day and run into
the evening so that the citizens of the county could still get their kids vac-
cinated, their water tested, their food inspected, and so on. This approach
absolutely infuriated every public management team we would go on to
negotiate with because there was simply no way they could disagree with
it in public. And since the nine-to-five mentality is so deeply ingrained
in these bureaucrats, the fact that they were going to have to work late
(for pay) because their workers now wanted to participate in bargaining
(for no pay) added insult to their injury.

Negotiations resumed but went nowhere. MacEachern may have been
ordered back to the table, but he had not been ordered to yield to any
of our demands. We slowed down as well. There is nowhere in the country
where August is a good time to try to pull workers together for action,
and I had learned from the previous year that when you add the heat of
the Las Vegas summer to the normal rhythm of August, big mobilizing
is simply not viable. We decided that since bargaining was not moving
much anyway, we would begin to space the bargaining sessions further
apart and turn our focus to systematically building relationships between
the members of the union and the members of the Public Health District
Board. Our members spoke at every board meeting that summer, taking
up more and more time with more and more speakers, and generally
driving everyone crazy reporting over and over that though management
was now at the table, they were not bargaining.

Some members of the Public Health District Board were not elected
officials but "private members" appointed to the board for one reason
or another. The district was taking the position that board members

were not allowed to talk to the union, so workers were approaching them as constituents, not unionists. This approach didn't work for the private members, as they were unelected and thus had no constituents. Hmmm. A legal memo says we can't talk to them? We decided that didn't mean we couldn't *communicate* with them, so we decided to write them letters. *Lots* of letters. With the scorching desert heat outside, writing letters seemed like a good summer activity. The workers who attended the board meetings, and thus had some idea who these private members were, handwrote the first ones, all about how much they loved working in public health, how awful the boss was, and how impossible it was to do their jobs to the best of their abilities. They brought their letters to Jamie and we made twelve photocopies of each, inserted them in hand-addressed envelopes the workers had filled in when they wrote their letter, mailed them out, and kept the originals. We then made packets to distribute to our health district members, each containing twelve blank envelopes (the worker had to be willing to use their own return addresses and sign their names clearly, another test of members' willingness to be identified as stepping up in a union campaign), a blank sheet of paper, a sample letter, and the addresses of each of the twelve Public Health District Board members. Like everything else we did, this was also a test of organization. We decided to shoot for ten letters a day, five days a week, until every union member had written one. And we did it: For months on end, every single day the mail brought each board member at least ten handwritten letters appealing to him or her to move the boss in negotiations.

The August meeting of the Public Health District Board began with Lawrence Weekly announcing that he wanted to have a conversation in executive session about the mail he was receiving. At which point he picked up a pillow case sitting behind him and dumped hundreds of letters onto the floor. The workers struggled to keep their poker faces. Even Rory Reid was a little ruffled. It so happened that we had a little drama of our own planned for that meeting. When the public comment period arrived, about fifty workers stood and began unfurling a banner made from copies of all the letters that had been mailed. The banner was so large it wrapped twice around the entire board room.

While we churned through the motions of the heath district nego-tiations in the summer of 2005, the local's finances remained a disaster, and no matter how hard I tried I could not seem to find a finance manager who was right for the job. I even turned to hiring firms for this one position. The local was a multimillion-dollar operation with complex and legally separate political funds. The laws that regulate union finances were allegedly intended to slow or stop corruption, and on that their record is mixed, but there's no doubt they made managing the local's finances more difficult. At the June 2005 executive board meeting we put forward a real budget for the local union that was reviewed, debated, and approved. Remarkably, this had never happened before.

The local's treasurer had held his post for two decades, and was com-pletely in fear of, as he put it, "the members ever seeing the finances. They just won't understand, Jane, what it takes to run an organization. We can't show them." It took constant pushing at board meetings month after month to get him in particular and the old guard in general to slowly let the finances become more transparent. My prod was that if the workers were going to approve an increase in their dues at some point in the future, they needed to understand where the money would go and why.

Having won such good contracts at Desert Springs and Valley, we began a campaign to organize the nurses at Vegas's other two United Health Services hospitals, Spring Valley and Summerlin. It was slow going, and it was months before we realized why. UHS management in Vegas was not stupid, and during our contract campaigns at Desert Springs and Valley they had monitored all the talk among the nurses about how great it would be to have the workers at all the UHS hospi-tals in Vegas bargaining together in 2006. So management had quietly brought in a union-busting consultant and put him to work in the two unorganized hospitals, intimidating the employees. By midsummer we had abandoned the Summerlin drive in order to concentrate our efforts on Spring Valley.

That summer saw the height of the Las Vegas real estate boom, with the prices of houses, condos and casinos shooting up at an astounding rate. Word broke in the press that the developers were making a move to privatize some 350 residential building inspectors who worked for the county and were in our union. I called D Taylor at the casino workers' union for advice. (I tried to never, ever call him for help, just advice.) "Jane," he told me, "don't even bother. You can't beat the developers. They own the commission." Two months later, after the same tried methods of intense member-to-member organizing, rebuilding the unit of building inspectors with one public action after another and editorials in our favor, we won that campaign too. That was probably the first time that the shadowy power structure that really runs Las Vegas began to see me personally as a problem and the growing strength of our union as something to watch. We had, in fact, beat the developers on an issue that mattered greatly to them.

In September, the summer heat and the Public Health District Board broke at the same time: the board announced that they were removing Angus MacEachern as the lead contract negotiator and hiring outside counsel to get the negotiations moving. Nothing could have empowered the workers more at that point. Their nemesis, the boss who had originally seemed so untouchable, had been thrown out on his ass. The attorney who replaced him called to introduce himself to me, and from his tone I knew a completed contract was just a matter of time. Our membership was peaking, worker organization was strong, and we would now be across the table from someone who essentially had been brought in to settle. By the end of the first session with the new negotiator, we had signed off on one third of the contract.

The next issues on the bargaining table would be harder, as they involved precedent and money. At the outset of the campaign, one of the first things the workers agreed to was that under no circumstances would they accept a two-tiered contract, that is, one in which current workers secure their own level of wages and benefits in exchange for reduced wages and benefits for future hires. It's easy for a union faced with a tough fight to accept two-tiering because it protects the current members, the people who will soon vote on whether to re-elect the union leaders who negotiated the contract. But two-tiering is the beginning of the end for them too, since selling out the newest and often younger members to keep the older members secure is no way to build a strong union.

Two-tiering had been agreed to several times by the old-guard leadership of the local, and even by the Las Vegas police and firefighters, who generally have the strongest unions around. Conventional wisdom held that there was no way the county civil service workers could win where the cops and firefighters had lost, just as conventional wisdom held that there was no way we could take the mobilized and militant big-bargaining approach we had developed at private-sector hospitals and make it fly with the workers who sat at the rows of desks in the county bureaucracy. The latter was something I heard regularly even from my own national headquarters, but I believed that good organizing was about raising expectations, and wanted to put this idea that public-sector workers can't get militant to the test. We knew that two-tiering would be a key bone of contention in the much larger negotiation with the county coming up in 2006, and we wanted to show workers and bosses alike that we could buck conventional wisdom in the current negotiations for the much smaller Public Health District workforce. And having banished the old boss from the tables, the workers were ready for anything—they were gaining a sense of the power of collective action.

The Public Health District workers organized a great picket line outside the October meeting of the PHD board, and all of the local media covered it. We took photos of every member and assembled them into 4' x 3' color posters, which the workers hand-delivered to each member of the board. And inside the workplace there were actions every single day. Squads of workers showed up at work early every day and waited outside the building for the two top district officials, and then walked them from their car to their office, explaining why the workers deserved, and the Public Health District needed, a good settlement. And every day at noon a delegation of different workers would march down the hall on their lunch break and demand to see the same two men. And at the end of the day, yet another group would wait and walk them back to their cars.

We called it "running an internal strike." In Nevada, as in most of the country, government workers are prohibited by law from striking. So we shifted the concept of what a "strike" was, and the workers got it: If they couldn't walk out, they would create a crisis inside. It worked beautifully. In early December the contract was settled, with the workers winning nearly every demand they had made: no two-tiering of any benefit in the contract, a much improved human resources management system, a fair and transparent promotion process, bilingual pay, and more.

The summer and fall had seen six straight months of public-sector victories: we'd got the favorable resolution of the civil service contract pay issue, defeated the privatization effort of the building inspectors, and won the Public Health District contract. In the private sector, however, we hit the first real roadblock in our campaign to unionize the two remaining unorganized hospitals owned by Universal Health Services in Vegas. We had abandoned the effort at Summerlin in order to concentrate our efforts on Spring Valley. Now in October we had to postpone the election at Spring Valley just days before the voting, when it became clear that we were headed for defeat. Not for nothing had UHS located all the hospitals in second-largest hospital chain in the world in right-to-work states and then shut out unions. They'd done it to make money. Lots of money. Naturally they were not at all pleased when the upstart members of the rinky-dink SEIU local in, of all places, Las Vegas took them to the cleaners with big contract wins at Desert Springs and Valley.

I would have loved to be a fly on the wall when the corporate leadership read the riot act to whichever of their suits they held responsible for our victories. Desert Springs and Valley had been the only organized UHS hospitals to begin with, and that was because the unions were already there when the company bought them. Hospitals in Vegas were so profitable that a corporation like UHS couldn't resist snapping them up, even if they came with a union. And that union hadn't given them much trouble—before the new SEIU came to town.

Well, now UHS had had enough of us. It was obvious they intended to shut this whole union thing right down, and they were doing it at Spring Valley Hospital. An intense fear campaign was being waged inside the hospital, and the workers were crumbling. Morgan, Jessica and I pulled the plug on the election by filing legal charges against UHS for intimidation and harassment of workers. Filing these charges gives you the right to suspend an election on the grounds that the employer has been illegally bullying the workers to the point where the election would be unfair. This bought us some time. We decided that a realistic objective was to put off the union elections at Spring Valley and Summerlin until 2006.

We knew that UHS had brought in someone from the outside to run an "A-level boss fight." This someone had produced a DVD about our union, calling us thugs and featuring, well, us. The whole thing was slickly contrived to make us seem like corrupt union bosses rather than the hyperdemocratic movement types we were. A DVD was mailed to every single nurse who would have voted in the election. And when even that was judged insufficient they started running what are called mandatory captive audience meetings, in which small groups of workers were forced to watch the DVD in the presence of management, who made sure they paid attention. It was then that we learned who was running their whole dog-and-pony show: an infamous union buster named Brent Yessin. And he hadn't come just for the election at Spring Valley. UHS clearly understood what we were trying to bring off by lining up all our contracts, and after the Spring Valley vote was suspended, Yessin stayed put in Las Vegas and became the UHS field general for the battle of 2006.

But suspending the election meant that we, too, could throw ourselves into preparations for the coming year. We had already made a 23-month calendar, taking every opportunity to discuss what preparations we had to make to win in 2006. We removed the last vestige of the firewall between organizing new workers and servicing old ones, and collapsed our "external" and "internal" organizing teams into one. This was totally against the rules that the national SEIU insisted its locals play by. If SEIU locals wanted big subsidies for organizing drives (and we certainly did), they were supposed to reinforce that firewall, not tear it down. Fortunately, we had Eliseo Medina, SEIU's executive vice president for the Southwestern region, and his right arm, Sheila Velazco, running interference for us with the national union. Eliseo had promised this to me when recruiting me for the Vegas job, and now he came through. Having him going to bat for us from Los Angeles wasn't the same as having Larry Fox watching our back on the ground in Washington, but Eliseo and Sheila spent a lot of time and energy defending our unconventional approach, for which we were *very* grateful.

Our position was that these firewall rules had been made by a national union whose power, numbers and experience had come overwhelmingly from union security states. In a right-to-work state, where you have to struggle constantly to hold your membership, the organizing that is required to keep your existing members in the union is not that different from the organizing you do to bring workers on the outside in. And we were based in Las Vegas, with its extremely high turnover, which meant that thousands of new hires had to be organized into our existing shops, orientation by orientation. It also meant that in addition to the normal attrition one expects from employer harassment, there were always bus-loads of members who simply picked up and left town. Just maintaining our existing shops in this kind of environment meant thinking way outside of the box.

How was a local in our position to make sense of the national SEIU's demand that our best organizers should be out bringing in new members, working in isolation from our B-team people, who were supposed to have the "easy" job of running the union? We couldn't, and in fact we did the opposite. We put the entire existing union into the same mode of organizing we had used for external campaigns to bring in new members. Every single shop was charted with big wall charts. We collected schedules for every facility. We ran nonstop worker trainings on how to chart, how to get schedules systematically, how to talk to coworkers about the coming contract campaigns, and how to grow their membership high and their worksite structures tight. Veterans of previous campaigns taught newbies. "Leader ID" became a term that rank-and-file workers in Nevada understood, not just our professional organizers.

Our chapters shifted from stewards-only to all-workers-welcome meetings. We began monthly sector-wide meetings, bringing together all our public-sector or private-sector members across facilities. We had moved to much larger offices and finally had a hall that could accommodate the dizzying succession of meetings large and small. We began to put together what became known as our war room. We had night-shift teams. We were ramping up our political program. We built our "healthy chapter" goals into the day-to-day work of the organizing teams. Every staff organizer and worker leader had to be ready at any moment to answer three questions: How many new members did they need to hit whatever their next goal was; how many did they need to hit 90 percent; and how many members needed to contribute to the political program to achieve 50 percent of all members donating extra money to politics? These quizzes took place in the coffee room, the parking lot outside the hall, or even in a bar if we ran into each other. The organizers knew they were in real trouble if they couldn't answer those three questions about their shops without looking at a piece of paper or a wall chart.

One real test of whether we were on track for 2006 was whether we could pass a planned dues increase. This became almost as contentious with the national union as our merging of internal and external organizing. In the fall of 2005 I was asked to make a presentation to the full national health-care division board, a body made up of local leaders like myself from across the country. I showed them essentially the same slide presentation we were using with the members in Vegas, outlining our big vision and goals for 2006 and walking them through the steps of our plan to win. The year would begin with us running concurrent bargaining team elections to choose 1,000 workers to represent 15,000 others from across the union. These bargaining team members would be the foot soldiers in the battles to come. Their first challenge would be winning the vote to raise the dues, and the higher dues would pay for everything else. We were also asking for a major subsidy from the national union, which we would no longer need once we had passed a dues increase that would double the amount each worker contributed each month. In a sense, the dues increase was our local's way of saying that although we needed one more year of big subsidies from the national union, we were preparing for financial independence. At the same time, the dues vote would give us a measure of how the members felt about their union after two years of new leadership, as well as send a message to employers about the collective strength of their employees.

After my presentation, both Sal Rosselli and Andy Stern approached me separately to tell me nicely that they thought I was insane. Stern got to me first. He said I was asking the members to raise their dues too high too fast. Yes, we were on a roll in Vegas, but that didn't mean we could take a union that had been so awful just eighteen months ago and double its dues. When Stern was done with me, Sal and his lieutenant, John Borsos, buttonholed me to say basically the same thing. They insisted that I should run the dues vote *after* winning big in 2006, not before. So here were the president of the national SEIU from the east coast, and the head of its west coast powerhouse local, speaking nearly the same words in the same tone of voice. They even looked the same: same age, same smooth come-on, same same.

Hmmm. I had a plan to make the Nevada local financially self-sufficient and now Andy Stern and Sal Rosselli were separately counseling me to wait. It almost sounded as if they didn't *want* the Nevada local to be financially self-sufficient.

Here I should explain a particular dynamic that is common among unions, actually sort of a twin pair of dynamics. National unions are often dominated by a few powerful locals that generate lots of money, which enables them to put their loyalists in positions of power at national headquarters. The national then subsidizes the smaller locals. The subsidies undercut the power of the smaller locals to stand up to the national union when they need to. This was one dynamic, and it was why I would tell the core leaders in Vegas that our dues increase would be our declaration of independence from Washington. The other dynamic pertains not to the national union but to the powerful locals. If you are the head of one of those powerhouses and you want to lay claim to greater power inside the national union, the way to do it is to grow your local. And the easiest way to grow your local is not to organize new workers, which is time-consuming and difficult, but to merge nearby little locals into yours. And Sal Rosselli was pursuing this route to power big-time.

In those days Rosselli was on reasonably good terms with Stern and the Washington leadership and had recently cut a deal with them that merged SEIU Local 399 in Los Angeles into 250, the outfit Rosselli ran out of Oakland. In that one acquisition of an underperforming local, Sal had doubled the size of his jurisdiction. Yet he would soon be leveling blistering criticism against Stern for, you guessed it, consolidating power through mergers and acquisitions. After having devoured Los Angeles, Sal had his sights firmly set on Nevada. Now, the Nevada health-care market was simply not big enough to support a local that would ever be the same sort of powerhouse as SEIU's locals in New York and California, but if we passed our dues increase we could no longer be considered "underperforming" in any way, which would make it far less likely that Washington would sign us over to anyone.

But Sal was relentless in his desire for our union to merge with his. He was envious that the New York City local under Dennis Rivera had recently been granted many of the health-care unions in the Northeast, and he wanted parity. And in that sense, he was right—there was a double standard taking place. He began to systematically work on persuading the SEIU health-care unions in Oregon and Washington, as well as our entire Nevada local, to merge with his newly renamed United Healthcare Workers West. It wasn't just for himself. Sal believed that if all the health-care workers on the west coast united into one local, the workers would be better served, especially in negotiations with regional corporate players who operated from Arizona to Washington State.

When I first got to Nevada, Sal had told me in very direct and clear language that he would support keeping the Nevada local independent as long as we were doing good work. Here we were, on such a roll that the national union couldn't help but sit up and take notice, and Sal was relentlessly doing the opposite of what he had promised. Sal invited me for dinner at his house, and to a San Francisco 49ers game, all to persuade me that the Nevada members would be better off if they were part of Local 250, and that I could become a vice president in his new power-house union if I facilitated the deal.

My interest, however, was not in acquiring titles but in social movements and whether New Labor could become a force for social change. And I was convinced that the way to build a real labor movement in a right-to-work state was necessarily different from how you would do it in a union security state. The smaller locals that had been merged into the New York powerhouse didn't have these issues, since the states neighboring New York are union security. And if anyone needed evidence in support of this argument, then my fight with the national union over the separation of internal and external organizing was Exhibit A. So sorry, Sal, I thought, but merging the California and Nevada locals doesn't make *sense*.

I pushed back against both Stern's and Rosselli's opposition to the dues increase and moved ahead. I was confident we had the necessary support from the members. You could see it in the stream of overflowing meetings of workers packing into our new union hall to prepare for the year ahead. But more than that, we knew it from everything we were doing: the workplace charting, the schedule collecting, everything. Stern responded by suggesting that I work with Steve Trossman, one of the communications staffers in the national union, to hire an outside polling firm to gauge the members. I thought this was a waste of the members' hard-earned money but I couldn't really refuse when Stern said he was willing to pay for it. Polls cost big money. A credible poll costs about $50,000, and that's for a sample size as low as 600. We had thousands of these workers in conversation, so a poll seemed silly.

Steve Trossman was one of the best communications people I had ever met. At the time he was leading the communications team at Eliseo

Medina's South-Southwest regional office in Los Angeles, which had jurisdiction over Nevada. A couple of months later, Steve called me with the results of the poll. "Jesus Christ, Jane, we have never really seen numbers like this. The workers love their new union." Trossman had framed the questions in the poll to make it as useful as it could possibly be for organizing. There were specific questions that tested how workers felt about the old union versus the new. Across the board the workers gave their new union high approval ratings.

In late December I gave the entire staff two weeks' vacation just to take a nap, telling them to sleep while they could, because there would be no more time off, vacations, breaks, or really much other sleep until 2007.

CHAPTER SEVEN

Launching the 2006 Las Vegas Labor Offensive

January brought our first big test of 2006: electing bargaining teams for all those contract negotiations. Electing a bargaining team is usually pretty routine, but our commitment to big, representative bargaining meant that we would have to mobilize 15,000 workers spread all over the city to elect 1,000 representatives. And to stay on our timeline, which because of the expiration dates of the various contracts included no wiggle room whatsoever, the elections had to be completed in the space of a week. The logistical challenge of pulling this off was, shall we say, not trivial. But it was also exhilarating: Elect one bargaining team for one hospital and everyone feels like part of a real organization; elect 1,000 team members across the city from a multitude of employers and professions and everyone feels like part of something much bigger—a labor movement.

Beginning in October of 2005, our organizers had begun to identify leaders for every shop in every unit that hadn't already been charted. This was a time-consuming process with no shortcuts. The walls of our war room were covered top to bottom with charts showing our progress in each shop or unit: leadership identified, nominations in, nominee accepted, nominee said no, and so on. Staff and leaders were getting dizzy from this process, but it worked. By the third week of January the voting was concluded, and before the month was out we had mailed letters to just over 900 workers inviting them to their first mass bargaining team meeting, in two weeks.

At the same time, we were wrapping up our first negotiations at Southern Hills, the HCA-owned hospital where we had eked out an election victory by the slimmest of margins less than a year before. The campaign at Southern Hills had been organized in a mad rush to beat the expiration date of an Election Procedure Agreement, and though we had won, we had by no means built the sort of union there that we had at other hospitals. That's part of what's wrong with these types of agreements. After the election, we assigned a young organizer named Pete Reilly to build up the new Southern Hills union—increase membership, identify leaders, the works. As was always our policy, he was told that when he had majority membership in all the units in the hospital we would put together our bargaining team elections and prepare for negotiations.

Pete was green, but he also seemed hip. He projected a cool image and talked a really good line in staff meetings. And he methodically reported his growing membership numbers to Morgan, our organizing director. She then walked him through holding the bargaining team elections. In early September Morgan forwarded to me Pete's list of the newly elected Southern Hills bargaining team. With that in hand, I sent a letter to the employer stating who had been elected to the bargaining committee and asking for bargaining dates. It wasn't until the employer called me a week later that I had any idea what had really happened, which was nothing. Everything Pete had turned in was fake—he had never even been to the hospital. We immediately fired him, but our union at Southern Hills never fully recovered.

It did help that all around Nevada, the SEIU was winning and worker engagement was high. When we told the workers at Southern Hills that the debacle with their fake organizer was not the way our union usually worked, they could see we were being truthful.

The issue galvanizing the workers at Southern Hills Hospital was management's "call-off" policy: The boss could—and frequently did—send employees home if the number of patients in the hospital did not require a full staff. These were workers who supposedly had full-time jobs, and they were going broke. We had won good language on this issue at our other hospitals, so we invited the Southern Hills leaders to the big kickoff to 2006 bargaining so they could talk to those workers and get a sense of what the union was doing elsewhere in the city.

On the second Tuesday in February, the line of workers waiting to get into the hall for the first mass meeting of private-sector workers snaked out the door and down the street. If they weren't yet donating to the union political fund, we took them aside to discuss its importance. This was partly why we came to have the third-highest percentage of members donating to our political funds in the entire national SEIU healthcare division, just behind the two powerhouse locals in California and New York City.

I kicked off the meeting with a slide presentation on our core vision and strategy for the year. First, we would seek universal standards for wages, benefits, and work conditions across all the hospitals in the region. We wanted employers to compete for workers through the quality of the work inside the hospital rather than with sign-on bonuses and other goodies. At a minimum, these standards would include a uniform wage scale, so that all hospital workers in the greater Las Vegas area who did the same kind of work would get the same pay;* fully employer-paid family health care; the same nurse-to-patient ratios prevalent in California; worker-patient ratios for all the other workers in the hospital, something that California did not have; and the "right to retire"—and we didn't care whether this took the form of a 401K or a defined benefit pension, as long as every employer in the region contributed the same amount, 10 percent of the worker's salary. Beyond the contract standards, we would fight for improvements in patient care in the hospitals and improved client service at the County. Finally, we would go all out to elect Chris Giunculiani ("Chris G" for short) to the County Commission, and thus swing the commission decisively in our favor.

As for the strategy to win all this, we proposed what is called pattern bargaining. We would open our negotiations first with the employer from whom we thought we could get the best deal. All other negotiations would open only after that gold standard was established. In Vegas, that meant starting with Catholic Healthcare West. "If it's good enough for the Catholics, it's good enough for the capitalists," became a running joke.

---

* The public hospital was the exception here, given the excellent pension, vacation and sick leave package the workers there already had. All of the county employees had the same benefits package, which was one reason we had the public-hospital bargaining teams meet with the other county workers instead of with workers from the private-sector hospitals.

"Pattern bargaining" is not without risks—we could end up setting a low standard to which all the other employers would try to sink. And by delaying the start of negotiations at the other hospitals, we risked having the contracts there expire, opening a legal window for management to run a decert campaign. We talked about all this at length, and decided that our chances of setting a high standard at CHW's hospitals were good. And with at least 70 percent membership at each of the other hospitals, "decerts" were not a serious concern.

We also talked about the message it would send to employers if at the start of our market-wide negotiations the union members voted to increase their dues. We discussed how to use the dues vote as yet another test of how the workers felt about their union, how strong our organization was in each facility, and how capable our new bargaining team members were in moving their units.

After voting a nearly unanimous approval of the goals and strategy, we broke into subgroups representing the individual hospitals, each with its assigned staff organizer. By the end of the night everyone was feeling totally high. All the days and months of planning were bearing fruit. The 2006 Las Vegas labor offensive was in gear. It was working, it was fun, and we were sure we were going to win.

Two days later we were back at the union hall for the mass meeting of public-sector workers. By now we had the check-in process down. As the new bargaining team members arrived, a rank-and-file member would sit them down and check whether they were registered to vote, if they knew their election district and precinct, and if they were eligible to vote in Democratic primaries. If they weren't registered to vote, we registered them; if they were Republican and willing to switch parties to help Chris G win the Democratic primary, we had them re-register. Then we asked how much they'd contributed to the union political funds. If they were already giving, we asked if they could give more. If they weren't giving, the member-to-member teams would sit them down and discuss what it meant to be a leader in the union, and specifically to be a leader in a government workers' union where their ability to win had everything to do with the balance of power in the Clark County Commission. They were asked what the membership percentages were in their units. Finally, we took their photos to make posters for the dues and contract campaigns.

When we finally announced that it was time to begin the meeting, more than 300 people burst out in applause and cheers. It was like shackles coming off, the toppling of a monument to secret negotiations and divided workers. And a good thing, too, because we were going to need all that good energy to carry us through what we knew would be a difficult discussion. We began with an overall vision-and-strategy presentation, just as we had at the previous meeting, but the goals we presented were quite different: Hold on to everything we had in terms of wages and percentage increases; reject two-tiering; and win increased job security, which meant beating back threats of privatization and subcontracting and also helping the growing contingent of part-time workers form a union with us.

Selling these public-sector workers on the idea that they were not even going to *ask* for any additional money, when our private-sector members had fought pitched battles the previous year that had won unprecedented raises, was not easy. Jerry Brown's motto, Trust the workers and treat them like grown-ups, was my guide.

We began by walking everyone through an analysis of the forces arrayed against them. They were already better paid than their private-sector counterparts in the Las Vegas area, and the public was generally not supportive of government workers having big contract fights. The city's main newspaper, the *Las Vegas Review Journal*; the Chamber of Commerce; and the Nevada Taxpayer Association were acting in concert with the county manager to beat the drum against them. The police—almost always the strongest public-sector union—had recently signed contracts far short of their demands. If the county commissioners could strong-arm the cops, how were civil service workers like tax collectors or property assessors going to fare better?

The only recent bright spot for workers in the public sector was the big victory we had just pulled off with the Public Health District. We asked some of those Public Health District workers to take the floor to tell the story of how they had engaged in a multifaceted campaign that extended beyond the workplace to sway the Public Health District Board, ultimately creating a crisis so large that the board had had to surrender. We described the balance of power in the Clark County Commission, and particularly the important role of Tom Collins, the commissioner our union had worked so hard to elect.

We had been running this rap with the county workers all fall in one-on-one discussions. Big meetings have more potential than private discussions for both excitement and enthusiasm on the one hand and anger and resentment on the other. This meeting included some classic angry white guys who were adamant about going for big raises. But cooler heads carried the day, and our proposed goals passed with nearly unanimous support.

Achieving these goals would require fundamentally changing the balance of power on the County Commission. Our strategy would be throwing our hundreds of newly elected bargaining team members into a pell-mell drive to elect Chris G. To say that this notion of what it means to be on a bargaining team was outside the box wouldn't begin to do it justice. And this was a substantial force to commit to a primary election in August. But if they could carry Chris G through the primary (which would essentially elect her, as her district was heavily Democratic), and work with the police and firefighters unions to carry an additional seat in November, it would swing us the four votes we needed to override the county manager.

Part of being a good organizer is to think like the boss. Not only could I imagine the boss analyzing this same scenario, I was sure that of the hundreds of people in that room at least one had been sent by the boss to take notes. This was an unavoidable side effect of running a democratic union by mass meetings. There's a very real tension here, and it gives undemocratic unions an excuse to hide behind a veil of secrecy.

We could bet the boss knew of our plans for the coming elections. And we were fairly confident that we knew what his counter-strategy would be. He would sit on his ass for a while, let bargaining come to a deadlock, and then invoke mandatory binding arbitration to force a settlement. This is a legal mechanism in which an allegedly neutral arbitrator arrives at a final contract based on the "last best offers" of both sides. Like judges in the court system, arbitrators rely heavily on recent precedent. And the most recent precedent here was the park police (separate from the larger police force) and the big police contract. The county manager had extracted some key concessions from both units—and done it through mandatory binding arbitration.

Now, the old SEIU local had often embraced binding arbitration—in my opinion because it covered up the fact that their organizing was not strong enough to win at the bargaining table. That meant our members were not accustomed to looking on arbitration as something to avoid, and in fact there are many contracts with good standards in this country that have been won that way. But settling a contract in arbitration takes the workers out of the equation altogether, as it moves the settlement into a remote and opaque legal terrain. Even if arbitration might win you something, it does nothing to build the union or the power of the workers. And our local was all about building long-term worker power.

The problem was that Nevada law sets a final date by which either the union or management can invoke binding arbitration. It was now mid-February. Arbitration could be invoked as early as July 5, and the County Commission general elections were not until November. Tactically, we were going to have to throw everything and the kitchen sink into keeping the contracts out of arbitration until then.

Almost every piece of this strategic mosaic was completely alien to the way our public sector members were accustomed to thinking. When the leaders left the mass meeting, they would have to be able to in turn explain everything to their coworkers, so every point had to be carefully gone over. The police union defeat had been covered extensively in the press, and those articles made excellent handouts. We used those articles to illustrate the county manager's strategy for bringing down the public-sector standards: take down the cops, set precedents, then force us into arbitration and invoke them. The guy knew what he was doing.

Two weeks later, we settled the first contract with HCA's Southern Hills hospital, including a series of "me too" clauses stipulating that workers at Southern Hills would benefit from whatever the workers at HCA's much larger Sunrise Hospital might win at their upcoming negotiations. Although the Southern Hills workers wouldn't technically be at the table, we'd effectively added them to the huge pool of workers that would be mobilized in the coming battles.

CHAPTER EIGHT

The Gloves Come Off: Union Busters, the NLRB, and a Purple RV

To the Universal Health Services corporation, Las Vegas was like a freak oil well that never ran dry. In 2005, their Vegas hospitals generated 20 percent of corporate revenue, though they constituted a tiny fraction of UHS facilities around the country. From 2001 to 2005, the UHS hospitals in Vegas generated profits of $105 million, nearly as much as all the other Vegas-area hospitals' profits combined. And that was just the figure they reported. There was another $85 million that they hid through an accounting maneuver called home office allocations: a corporation bills itself in one location and pays itself in another, so it can siphon money out of one region and stash it back home. Add that money back in, and the UHS hospitals in Las Vegas sent profits of $190 million out of the Nevada desert and off to King of Prussia, PA. UHS's second most profitable regional operation was in New Orleans. Like Vegas, New Orleans was full of tourists (and thus of lucrative out-of-network health insurance billing), known for corruption, and located in a right-to-work state. This was the sort of business model one could expect from a cutthroat for-profit hospital corporation.

"*Nothing less than depraved indifference*," was how Dr. Paul Verrette described the evacuation of Chalmette Medical Center, the UHS hospital in St. Bernard Parish during Hurricane Katrina. Verrette was medical director of St. Bernard's emergency preparedness office. The Chalmette staff was left alone as power failed, water rose, and patients died. As nurse Charlene Gonzalez told the national press, "They left me to die and now nobody's even called to say, 'Thank you.' " Then, just a few weeks after the flood, UHS sent a message to its 2,800 hospital workers in New Orleans that everyone definitely heard: With the hospitals out of commission, their pay and medical benefits would be cut off in two weeks.[*]

The CEO who signed off on these decisions was Alan Miller, whose own pay had made him a multi millionaire. Miller was a personal friend of, and large donor to, President George W. Bush, and was closely aligned with him on issues like taxes, government regulation and unions. Presumably, Miller was not at all pleased when his employees at Desert Springs and Valley hospitals won contracts that set standards for pay, working conditions and patient care far above the prevailing Las Vegas norm. He hadn't located four facilities out in a right-to-work desert to get pushed around by some upstart SEIU local, and now he decided to pull out all the stops. Soon the nurses at two UHS hospitals in California, members of the California Nurses Association, lost their unions after a ferocious corporate decertification campaign. We learned about the CNA's defeat when flyers started showing up at the UHS hospitals in Las Vegas that read, "*California UHS Nurses Take Decisive Action, Throw Out Their Union. You Can Too!*"

Mr. Miller sent us Larry Arnold, a roaming gunslinger of a union buster who was just about the meanest, nastiest son of a bitch any of us had ever seen. "Cancer in the system," was how he described our union, "and my job is to wipe it out." Nice one, Larry, clever thing to say to a bunch of nurses. Rick Albert, the charmer UHS had sent to run their bargaining last time around, was coming, too, but as Arnold's sidekick. I didn't know much about Larry Arnold, so I called our attorney, Bill Sokol, at his San Francisco office.

"Yo, Sokol, it's McAlevey. Do you know anything about Larry Arnold from…"

"Oh, McAlevey, they are out to kill you. He's who they send in to *kill* unions. That's his only job, nothing else. Don't know if he's ever completed a contract, because that's who you bring in to make sure there is no contract. Call Dana Simon and ask him about Arnold. Arnold has had Dana locked in a no-win first contract fight in a hospital up in Chico for two years."

---

[*] Nicholas Riccardi and Ellen Barry, "Hospital Staff Endures Storm, Faces Layoffs," *Los Angeles Times*, September 20, 2005.

Dana Simon was the talented organizer I had worked closely with back in 2003, in the Fresno Homecare workers' struggle.

"Dana, hey, it's Jane McAlevey. Listen, Sokol says you know Larry Arnold…"

"That bastard? Oh, that's bad, Jane, bad. This guy is going to try to shred you. It's going to be a long fight, Jane, really long. He's the worst, the most awful asshole I have ever had to deal with. Let me tell you a few Larry Arnold stories. Better yet, we should send a worker or two from our Chico hospital to come talk to your workers there about what this schmuck is going to do."

And Dana began to tell me about Larry Arnold. The hospital workers in Chico had been trying to get a first contract from Arnold for two years. The workers were tiring. But that's exactly what happened with Arnold advising the hospital. I figured that the problem in Chico was probably that in the world of California unions, nurses were organized by the CNA while the rest of the hospital workers were organized by the SEIU. So when the SEIU called a strike at a hospital, only half of the workforce participated, and the easier-to-replace half at that. Maybe what was happening in Chico was less an example of what a badass Arnold was and more an example of why it didn't make sense to have the nurses in one union and everyone else at a hospital in another.

We got our first taste of what Alan Miller, Larry Arnold, and Universal Health Services had in mind for Las Vegas when the security staff at Valley Hospital called the police on Jessica Foster, our rock star organizer running the bargaining team elections there. "Shit, McAlevey," she told me, "they just called the cops on me for sitting quietly in the corner of the cafeteria with a ballot box for the workers to vote in the bargaining team elections. We've been voting everywhere. What's their problem? Anyway, I have almost every worker's vote in the box already—the day shift came in on their way into work—so I should have this election wrapped up before the cops get here."

The next canary keeled over in February, when management barred one of our organizers from entering Desert Springs. This was straight up illegal. Those great contracts we had won from UHS at Desert Springs and Valley hospitals had been the first in Las Vegas to include the right for our organizers to freely walk the hospital floors and to enter all break rooms to meet with workers. At Sunrise, the union had access to the cafeteria only. That was considered a big victory at the time the contract was signed, but management would send security to the cafeteria to watch every interaction between organizer and the worker, which was intimidating, to say the least. And more importantly, most workers and certainly most nurses never leave their unit for lunch anyway—so getting access to hospital breakrooms was key. When we negotiated the UHS contracts at Desert Springs and Valley, we made hospital access a "strike issue," along with an expiration date in 2006.

Jerry Brown had come up with the key language to winning breakroom access in those first negotiations at UHS: In return for hospital-wide access, we would give management the power to use the grievance and arbitration clause if we ever violated terms of the access clause. When I suggested this to the workers, they thought I was nuts.

"No way, Jane, why would we want to enable the boss to be able to use *our* grievance process against *us*?"

"Look, you know as well as I do that grievances take forever. If we work that system like management does, it will be years before they make the process work in their favor, just like it takes years for you to make it work for you. But it's going to *seem* fair. How is the boss going to say no to the very process he wants you to use when you think management has acted unjustly?"

Everyone got it right away. To this day I have never seen another contract with that access language. If the boss wanted to file an access grievance against us, he would have to start at the bottom with a union organizer, who would handle the first step. He could then appeal the organizer's decision to me. And if he didn't agree with my assessment of whether we had violated the contract's access provision, he could take it to arbitration, where, years later, he would get a ruling.

And now the boss at UHS had just *banned* our organizer from the hospital. When Morgan sent back an email stating that management couldn't just kick an organizer out, but had to file a grievance per the contract, management replied stating that if this organizer ever returned to the hospital the security there would call the police.

Not long after that Morgan came flying down the hall with the news that there was a decertification petition filed against us at Desert Springs. Huh? The nurses had a real union at Desert and would never vote to decertify. What was she talking about? "It's the techs, Jane. This is really clever. They got to the techs."

As I mentioned earlier, when I first arrived in Nevada, the techs and LPNs at Desert Springs had one of those horrendous contracts negotiated by the local's old guard. The really good contract that had been the revitalized union's first big victory was for the nurses. We'd engaged whatever techs we could in the effort, and some had come to negotiations, to see what was going on with the crazy open-invitation bargaining the new union was running, but we had not built their union as we could have if we had gone through a contract with them. From the moment I landed in Vegas there were already so many urgent campaigns to run on short deadlines, the unions at the center of those crises had got all the attention of our overstretched staff. As a result, our efforts that January and February to ramp up every shop in the union for the 2006 contract campaigns included the first real attention we had given to the Desert Springs techs. And while we were busy electing and training their bargaining team members, the boss at UHS had been very quietly working to get 30 percent of the techs unit to sign a petition, for an election to decertify the union. Legally, a boss cannot run such a petition himself, but it is a simple matter to dress one up to look as if it legally originated with disgruntled workers. In almost any workplace, 30 percent of the employees are grumpy about something or other and receptive to promises about how much more management will give the workers if they throw out the union. The Desert Springs technical unit contract expired on May 31, so the boss—oops, I mean the allegedly unhappy technical workers—had until the last day of February to file the decertification petition, and that was the very day it was filed.

Welcome to the Las Vegas labor war of 2006, I thought. You could smell the opening rounds of an "A-level boss fight" coming. UHS had figured out the weakest link in the union, calculated the decert window, and filed a decert petition on the very last day of the window. And while pursuing their legal options so cleverly, they had illegally banned one organizer from the hospital and called the cops on another. Once again I phoned our lawyer.

"Yo, Sokol, um, decert at UHS, there's going to be a hearing, can we jam them somehow and delay it?"

"It's Larry Arnold. Jane, meet Larry."

The most immediate consequence of the petition was that we had to pull our organizers off the work we had so carefully scheduled for them and reassign them to the decertification election. The first step in a decert election is a formal National Labor Relations Board hearing. UHS was expecting us to come into that hearing and make any number of the technical challenges that unions typically use to buy time before the workers vote on whether to decertify. Our assessment, however, was that we were going to win, and given everything else on our plate, it was in our interest to get it over with as quickly as possible. So we surprised everyone at the hearing by cooperating fully, even urging the NLRB to move the process quickly ahead. The NLRB set the election date for May 4. We knew it would be a terrible distraction and major drain on resources, but Morgan and I were feeling cocky from all our recent victories. Fact was, we had no idea what was coming.

The workers were reporting big changes inside the UHS hospitals: new and more security staff, plus big unidentified men in fancy suits running around like they owned the place. Could this be Larry Arnold, who was tall, wore fancy suits, and was arrogant? "No, there's more than one" came back the report. Soon we learned that the UHS operation was actually being run by a Brent Yessin, a figure even more sinister than Arnold, the guy we'd heard described as the union assassin, who worked under him. Rick Albert, the UHS heavy from the last contract negotiations, was under Arnold. An unholy trinity for sure.

It took us a while to get a line on Yessin. He had first appeared on our radar as part of the Burke Group, a California law firm whose main purpose was to beat back the CNA. Yessin had recently split off from Burke to set up his own union-busting consulting firm, Yessin and Associates, that specialized in busting nurses' unions. But Yessin kept a low profile. Our researcher found just one story about him, from New Jersey. The New York State Nurses Association had started a hospital organizing campaign with majorities of nurses in favor of the union, then lost the union election by a landslide. We also knew this guy had just beat the CNA in California and decertified two of its unions.

We tried to figure out how much money UHS was spending on these guys in suits and on the new security guards. Before the year was over, UHS would spend over *$5 million* fighting their own employees in Las Vegas. Or as Larry Arnold would say at negotiations, "To get the cancer out." This is the hallmark of an A-level boss fight: the employer makes a strategic assessment that beating the union in a given fight will be worth far more to the corporation in the long run than the actual cost of giving the workers in question a good contract. And when a corporation the size of UHS, whose CEO has the political inclinations of Alan Miller, makes this assessment, the sky is the limit.

I called Jerry Brown.

"Get the workers ready, Jane. Just get off the phone and stop worrying. No one is going to help you. Get the workers ready like you know how, and call when you need help with something you don't know how to do."

Um, thanks, Jerry. Every now and then just a morsel of sympathy would have come in handy. What's wrong with, "Whoa there, whoo-eee you are in for a big fight, yes indeed." But that wouldn't have been the Jerry Brown I had picked to be my mentor.

In early March, we received two letters from Clark County that showed us how tough they wanted to play in the public-sector negotiations. They arrived on the very same day, one from John Espinoza, the head of HR at the public hospital, and the other from Ray Visconti, Espinoza's counterpart in the main Clark County offices. We had received some funny letters from bosses before, but these took the cake. Both stated that the county had "evidence of ulterior motives on the part of SEIU." What these ulterior motives might be was left unstated, but the bulk of the letter dealt with "rumors" that we had planned to "import outside groups into negotiations." I was informed this was illegal, since the contract limited the bargaining team to ten members. More would not be tolerated, and they would happily file government charges against us if any of these rumors were true. Gee whiz, we had been running the nominations for our bargaining teams for two months. There was literature spread around every break room and posted on union bulletin boards stating the exact number of team members we were electing—hardly a "rumor." When I read the letters to some of the workers, we laughed so hard we couldn't speak. We inferred that someone who had attended the mass meetings and so was a member of one of our bargaining teams had reported the details of our discussions to the boss. But that's life; we had known that was going to happen.

After consulting with the key worker leaders, I sent a reply covering all the legal issues HR had raised. As always, I included a "CC: the workers." We then made 5,000 copies each of management's letters and my answer, which the organizers distributed to everyone in the county buildings and public hospital. I kept asking myself, "Don't these guys pick up the phone and talk to each other the way we do, about how we work these things?" Very soon our fax machine was spitting out another letter from the same guys, this time threatening me about the "confidential" and "sensitive" nature of employer-to-union communications. I wrote back explaining that I understood their letter was sensitive and related to bargaining, but we had a very large bargaining team, and really as far as we were concerned the real bargaining team included every worker in the shop, and since we were a democratic union I had to consult my team. I concluded by asking for access to their employee email system so that we could save paper and therefore trees. We immediately put out thousands of copies of this second exchange.

I had heard enough about John Espinoza from the University Medical Center workers to know that he and I were not going to get along. Over at the main Clark County government building, however, Ray Visconti was well known and respected among the workers as a decent person and a fair Human Resources director. I wanted my relationship with Visconti to reflect the views of the members, and I also wanted to demonstrate that we were always more than happy to work with decent bosses. Shortly after publishing the second set of letters, I phoned Visconti to break the ice.

"Hi, Ray, it's Jane McAlevey. I know you've heard a lot about me, and I know we have never met, but honestly, if you just stop all this silliness the lawyers are coaching you to do in these letters, we will be fine in negotiations. We share the same goals: high-quality, well-run public services. To get there we need a well-run human resources system that respects the expertise of the workers. That's all we want." Silence.

It would take months of this before he would realize that I was sincere.

All through March and April and into mid-May, the public-sector worker leaders tested their organization and the militancy of the members. They attempted their first majority petition demanding that management stop obstructing and meet them at the negotiations table. To do this, people had to drive from one end of town to the other and back: from Building Inspections to Social Services to Roads Crew to the main county seat to Parks and Recreation to Real Property Management (the workers who cleaned all the other buildings). After six weeks the petition still hadn't quite hit majority, which confirmed what Jessica, Morgan, Maryanne and I suspected: The organizers we had running the public-sector work were not fully up to speed. But we had no reinforcements to spare, thanks to the decert battle over at Desert Springs, so we called it quits on gathering signatures even though we were shy of 51 percent. Even at less than half, there were thousands of workers' names on their first big petition to management.

We made big blowups of the petition, and the workers held the first "march on the boss" in Clark County. They were nervous, trembling, in fact—a scene witnessed many times in the life of an organizer. The ones who led the march and confronted Tom Reilly in the hallway were top performers with nothing but high marks in every work evaluation they'd ever had. Reilly was flabbergasted and furious. The buzz quickly spread throughout the county labor force that the workers had marched on the liberal county manager, who was digging his heels in hard enough to bore a hole to China. Reilly wouldn't budge on bargaining dates until we agreed to come to negotiations with only ten people.

We made a giant calendar (Kinko's did well by our union in 2006) to take to the next County Commission meeting. The workers piled into the meeting, and when it came time for the public comment period (really my favorite law in America), they got up, uncovered their giant calendar, and handed a red marker to Tom Reilly saying, "We will take any date, a Saturday, a Sunday, or the middle of the night. Just circle any date and we are ready for negotiations." The commission sat silent and squirming, except for our one ally, Tom Collins, who was smiling from ear to ear. The workers who spoke were public hospital nurses, who came in their scrubs, and top child-welfare advocates. The next day's press could not have made Reilly happy. The commission went into private session, where they agreed to ask the chief federal mediator in town, Lavonne Ritter, whom we knew, to convene a meeting with Reilly and me to "make a plan for negotiations." Once again, the workers were learning about their own power.

At the meeting Reilly yelled at me about how we had been hurting his feelings and his reputation and were breaking our contract and on and on. But when the session was over we had a date to open the first "master" negotiations Clark County had ever seen, at which 120 workers representing both the public hospital and the civil service would jointly negotiate their next contract. The union's only concession was to a cap of no more than 120 workers in the room at one time. From 10 to 120? Deal! I had learned by now how to think strategically about language, and had added "in the room at one time." We would soon be parading in 120 workers for the morning sessions, then swapping them out for another 120 in the afternoon, and so on.

Just as important, the agreement also stipulated that neither party could invoke mandatory binding arbitration for at least six months, to give the bargaining process time to work. I honestly think Reilly missed what I was doing here. It was already late May. The first bargaining date for the county units was in June, so neither party would be able to invoke arbitration until mid-November, after the County Commission elections.

In late March the management at Desert Springs hospital had begun sending workers to mandatory captive audience meetings. In a clear sign that UHS was targeting the whole union, nurses were required to attend even though the decertification petition was only for the technical workers. A nurse would literally be in the middle of a procedure with a patient and her manager would show up and say, "Stop what you are doing and get downstairs and report to meeting room A." If she was one of the tougher ones, she'd say, "When I am finished," which would win her about one minute, and then the manager would be back, threatening, "You will be fired for gross insubordination if you refuse to take this assignment. You must go down to the conference room, now."

Brent Yessin probably thought he was playing good offense by forcing the nurses to attend the meetings, but he may have had second thoughts when he discovered just how staunchly pro-union they were. They would go to the meetings wearing their union buttons and immediately raise their hands and start asking all sorts of disruptive questions. They would clap at inappropriate times, pretend to fall asleep and snore as a group, and constantly interrupt to ask if they could go back to their patients.

For their next series of forced two-hour meetings, the Yessin team produced a scary video about SEIU Nevada. We dispatched organizers to buy hundreds of microwave popcorn packets and distribute them to all the workers as fast as they could. The break rooms at the hospital were all equipped with microwaves, and for the entire week workers walked into the screenings ready for the horror flick with popcorn in hand. In organizer shoptalk this is called cutting the tension.

By the end of April the average worker in that hospital had been through *ten hours* of mandatory captive audience meetings. Then management replaced the meetings with mandatory one-on-ones, working every intimidation angle they could. Evidently it had dawned on them that when you put workers who are organized and united together in the same room, even as a captive audience, the result is not exactly union-busting. Maybe their message would be more convincing in an isolation cell, er, a private office.

By this point union access to the hospital had been severely curtailed. Our organizers had to notify management whenever they were coming. They would be given special badges on arrival and were restricted to three-hour visits, clocked by security. After a few weeks of this we knew we had to shake up the dynamic. We called the national union and requested one of SEIU's giant purple recreational vehicles, and Sal Rosselli's California local sent one. If the boss was going to essentially kick us out of the hospital, we were going to set up a new satellite office right outside the front door, with staff living in it round the clock ready to talk to workers from each shift as they took their breaks or came and left work.

That RV was emblematic of the overall tension-cutting strategy that Yessin's campaign required 24/7. Yessin had no right to limit our hospital access in the manner they were, but instead of trying to fight him through a legal challenge that would disappear into some mysterious government cubicle in the sky for a judgment from on high, we seized the opportunity to build more community, to build enough worker power that the restriction of our organizer's access became irrelevant. Nothing raised the spirit of the workers quite like the day the big purple RV pulled up directly across from the hospital, covered with banners and balloons. We moved our entire operation out of the union hall and into the RV. And, partly because we needed to talk to every worker and to be able to react quickly to changes in the situation, and partly because some thug might vandalize the RV in a New York minute, the staff moved in, too.

We brainstormed with the worker leaders on how to get their more timid coworkers out to our new headquarters. Just approaching the RV was an act of bravery, as Yessin had put it under surveillance. There were always at least three security guards there; they made a show of taking photos of every worker who crossed the street from the hospital to the RV. Our leaders thought that food might do the trick. The hospital cafeteria served hospital food. It seems like every hospital cafeteria is run by the same grumpy British guy with no taste buds. We stocked the RV with energy snack bars, quality candy, fruit, and drinks. At lunch and dinner we would cater in good local food and also held Mexican and Chinese nights.

That RV became the place to be. It developed its own microculture. The staff had lawn chairs spread out around it. The workers would walk up to the security men and do little skits for them, posing for their photos. "Wait, I need my lipstick, oh, and I want Sally with me, no wait, let me get some more people in the shot!" This was all great fun and serious organizing. Nevertheless, Morgan and I knew that although just about every Desert Springs nurse was visiting the RV, we weren't hitting our goals with the technical workers who had the upcoming decert vote.

Around this time, flyers began circulating saying that the reason UHS negotiations hadn't started was because "JANE is too busy with GOVERNMENT workers, while you just sit around like a second-class hospital team." It really was amazing how crassly they played on the image of the lazy government worker; even so, Yessin's effort to blame the union for delaying the start of bargaining, was beginning to get traction among the techs. The "pattern bargaining" strategy we had adopted at the mass meetings in February called for delaying negotiations at Desert Springs and Valley until we had won a contract at the Catholic Healthcare West hospitals. But in the face of Yessin's counteroffensive, it was time to zig and zag.

Though Yessin was Larry Arnold's superior in the union-busting hierarchy, Arnold was formally the head of the UHS negotiating team. As we had anticipated, he refused to agree to joint negotiations for Desert Springs and Valley. But he went beyond that and refused to even let the workers from Desert Springs sit down together, demanding that nurses and techs have separate tables, citing federal labor law about distinct bargaining units—the sort of thing union busters with an essentially unlimited budget can dish out endlessly. Also, management had clearly learned from their first encounter with big, representative bargaining that it was not in their interest to hold the sessions in the hospitals, where workers could just drop in. The Desert Springs negotiations opened April 13 for the nurses and April 17 for the techs; the Valley negotiations for nurses opened April 19. Though we had acceded to separate tables, we made sure delegations of workers from each table would rotate at all three negotiations. So that even though technically the tables were separate, the workers would be treating them as one. When the first nurse's session opened, on April 13, everyone was there.

Arnold walked in and got right down to the business of doing our work for us. He chomped on gum with his mouth wide open. The workers made bets about how many pieces he had in his mouth at once—at least enough to make him nearly unintelligible. Health-care workers tend not to like behavior that needlessly promotes the spread of germs, and no one in the room could understand what he was saying. If we asked for clarification, he would look up, say, "I said it already," and just proceed. I responded each time by interrupting him mid-sentence and exercising my right to call a private caucus, informing him that when he was ready to stop yelling at the workers he could knock on the door and we might let him back in. With every break, Arnold's behavior got increasingly out of control; meanwhile our caucuses became more lighthearted. The nurses loved it; they were on a high. Hey, you could actually do this. In fact, it was fun.

When you have a union, you don't have to take bullshit from the boss. You can just send him to his room and tell him he can come out when he's ready to behave. The negotiations wrapped up early that day; it was obvious they were going nowhere.

In one caucus, the nurses had talked about how the tech workers didn't know me as well as they did, and suggested that to really move the organizing on the tech side forward, I should just come to the hospital, walk around and say hi. They would walk me through the break rooms and introduce me to the many tech workers I didn't know. This was a difficult call. Management had been illegally blocking the access of other organizers. Would they risk harassing me? And if they did, would it demonstrate to the workers just how nasty these people were, or would it ratchet up their fear by demonstrating that these union-busters could run roughshod even over the head of the union? Morgan and I talked it over, and decided to follow the lead of the nurses themselves, and they thought it was a great idea.

I was literally a minute from the front door when four security guards came around the corner and surrounded us. I asked them to move aside, and they refused. One nervous guy was talking loudly on his walkie-talkie:

"Yes, she's here."

"It's actually her, yes."

"Do what, verify her name?"

"Are you Jane McAlevey?"

I just smiled and wriggled past them, then continued down the hall. I told the nurses they didn't all have to stay with me—I would be fine. They agreed to drop me off at the first break room. The security guys trailed behind, like the wake of a boat.

The first break room belonged to the radiology technicians, the most anti-union unit in the hospital, and Morgan had advised me to start with them. We had heard that management was promising them fat raises if they threw out the union. Just as I entered the room I heard a voice behind me.

"Well now, is this *the* Jane McAlevey?"

"Oh, and you must be Brent Yessin?"

And when I turned around, there was the devil himself, with grey hair coiffed like a movie star's, and one of those perfect tans that looks as if it came from a bottle. The situation was tricky. Some part of me knew I should get out of the hospital. Walking around with goons trailing me would accomplish nothing good. But the nurses had phoned ahead to Tower 3, telling all the workers there to gather in the break room because I was on my way. The techs were already a little scared, and it would hardly help them to see their leader buckled under one application of pressure they had to deal with at work every day. I had an organizer with me named Karen who had been staff at the hospital but had "come out" to work with the union. Karen called Morgan and we all agreed I should get to the Tower 3 break room and then make my way out. There was no point walking around the hospital with eight security guys with radios crackling behind me and Brent Yessin in my face. As we passed a nurses' station, Yessin started yelling, "Hey everyone, this is the big union boss. She is illegally in your hospital and so we are thinking we have to arrest her for trespassing!"

I was trying to speed the whole thing up and arrived at the Tower 3 break room sooner than planned—meaning sooner than the workers were going to get there. One tech worker was there, quietly eating her dinner. Yessin was carrying on belligerently. He was good. He was saying smart things. Karen knew the worker and made subtle hand motions to me that meant "This one is still undecided." Yessin addressed her by name (yeah, he was doing his homework, too). He said,

"Don't you think Jane should leave *your* break room so *you* can eat?"

She stood up, and looking him square in the eyes she said, "Actually, you've just persuaded me to join up with my coworkers in the union. You are being impossible, while Jane is just trying to update me on the facts about the negotiations." And she walked out, leaving both Yessin and me momentarily speechless. By now, no one could get in or out of the room—the security guards had blocked the doors. Karen and I went into the women's bathroom inside of the breakroom just to get away from Yessin for a minute and think about what to do. We phoned Morgan at the RV and agreed that I would leave the hospital and Karen would continue through the rest of the building. It was clear that all the security was going to stick with me, so she would have free rein.

When we came out of the bathroom the break room was empty, but it was the calm before the storm. We gathered our nerve. I opened the door and immediately Yessin began to push me back in again while loudly baiting me.

"We know you have decided already to take all the workers out *on strike, Jane.*"

"*When is the strike, Jane?*"

I was pretty sure I looked calm, but inside I was definitely getting flustered. So flustered that as I left the break room I walked right past the elevator I wanted and on to where the hallway ended. *Shit.* I was cornered. I turned around and they were right on me. The confrontation was becoming physical. I pushed through them back to the elevators. Of course, as fate would have it, it was a long wait. When the elevator doors finally opened, Yessin and all eight security guards followed me in. I immediately realized how dangerous this was and put my arm out to stop the doors from closing. Yessin knocked my arm away and I was trapped. I started frantically hitting the Open button, but he pushed my arm down again, and the doors closed. He turned to me and pinned me to the elevator wall with his six-foot-plus body, literally pressing his cock against me. That was it. I began to scream, really scream. *"Get your body off me, you cocksucking motherfucker."* My adrenalin was pumping so hard I could barely see straight. His security guys had all closed in behind him while he held me pinned to the elevator wall so that his penis rubbed up against me. I was completely alone. Shit, had any workers seen me go in here? When the doors finally opened on the ground floor they revealed still more security goons, waiting. Yessin again began loudly baiting me:

"When will you stop beating your husband?"

"Jane, when will *you* order the strike and make all these workers get fired?"

"Jane, can you tell all these people why you just used a four-letter word in the hospital?"

I was heading for the door. I could see Morgan and some nurses pacing outside looking for me. The one thing I wanted out of the experience was this guy's picture. Even with all our research on him, we hadn't found anyone who had a photo of the infamous Brent Yessin. Morgan ran up to me as soon as I was out, and I whispered, "I can hold him. Run get the camera from the RV and get his picture. *Run.*"

Yessin was still behind me. Much calmer now that I was out of the hospital, I turned to him and said something like, "Thanks so much for that personal escorted tour of the hospital. Can I count on this every time I come?" And he began to chat, as if that whole scene inside hadn't happened. It was psychotic. Morgan ran up and started snapping photos, which finally got him out of my face and back inside the hospital.

Shortly after this, Desert Springs and Valley both notified us that every single staff person from the union was "indefinitely banned" from setting foot on hospital property. The nurses were furious.

"But we *won* that. They can't do it; it's not legal. We fought so hard for that."

"Yes, I know, and now the boss wants to take back every shred of what you won. Good thing you are all so strong and your organization on the inside is so tight."

I believed it, but my belief was partly bravado. In the pit of my stomach I knew we were in for the fight of our lives. In the morning I called the head of the police union and told him the story of being pinned in the elevator by Yessin.

"Jane, that's called assault and battery. When he hit your arm, that's assault and battery. Get down to the station and file a report."

And I did.

CHAPTER NINE

The Gold Standard: What a Good Contract Looks Like, and How It Relates to Patient Care

While the intimidation campaign at the for-profit Universal Health Services (UHS) hospitals escalated to outright goonery, contract negotiations with the Catholic Healthcare West hospitals proceeded in a remarkably civilized way. The result was a new contract that not only gave the workers a good deal but also set new standards for improving patient care in Nevada and opened the door for management and the union to work together in innovative ways to do what everyone in a hospital really wants to do: heal the sick. The details of the contract are worth going into, because they speak volumes about the sorry state of health care in the country, demonstrate that the fight for better working conditions for nurses and all hospital workers and the fight for better patient care are one and the same, and show how an enlightened management can work with unions to achieve both.

Let's look at the wage scale first. Before our reinvigorated SEIU local got to work, there was no wage scale for hospital workers in Las Vegas that credited them for their experience in the industry.* Instead, there were signing bonuses. These were significant—$10,000 was not uncommon—but were paid in installments over a period of two years. That is, a hospital would dangle the signing bonus as bait to get an experienced nurse to tolerate two years of crappy working conditions. Often, two years to the day from the beginning of her employment, the nurse

---

* The Sunrise Hospital workers had won a rudimentary wage scale based on years of service at their hospital, not on years of experience in the industry.

would collect the final installment, quit her job and go to work at another hospital, for another bonus.

Signing bonuses are great for a for-profit hospital's bottom line and terrible for the workers, because they are nonrecurring and add nothing to a nurse's base pay. In other words, if you fill a position for thirty years with a series of nurses who rotate in and out every two years, you can pay the last nurse no more than you paid the first. But if instead of signing bonuses you have a wage scale that rewards the same nurse for good work over many years, at the end of thirty years that nurse will be costing management significantly more.

The system was also a disaster for the quality of patient care. The best way to deliver health care is through team building over a series of years. Nurses need to get to know the doctors they are working with, and vice versa. They also need to get to know the technicians and dieticians and nursing aids. High-quality healthcare is a team effort. In a well-managed hospital with a well-planned wage scale, workers are paid based on their skill and experience, and have an incentive to stay. In the Las Vegas system, a deeply experienced nurse who had worked for two decades in the same hospital would make *less* money than a new hire straight out of nursing school who could add a signing bonus to the low regular wage. Pop quiz #1: When your appendix bursts, who do you want in the emergency room, a two-year-rotating nurse or a nurse who's worked there twenty years?

Once some hospitals have instituted signing bonuses, all the other hospitals come under pressure to do the same. In short, the Wild West, bottom-line, bottom-feeder hospitals re-created the surrounding casino culture, with a transient staff, that never gelled into well-functioning teams, seeking a transient prosperity in a system where the least competent could make as much as or more than the most highly skilled. The nurses hated it. The patients suffered.

In bargaining for the contracts we won in 2004 at Desert Springs and Valley Hospitals, we had negotiated away the heart and the retention bonuses for a good wage scale with real money in it to reward experience and skill. We had wanted an outright ban on the whole bonus concept, but UHS had made the credible argument that if their hospitals dropped it entirely, they would be at a competitive disadvantage. We settled for eliminating all bonuses except the signing bonuses, incorporated the bonus money into their base wages, and told UHS straight up that we intended to eliminate signing bonuses across the entire market in 2006. When all of the contracts in the market are on the table, negotiations really can become a race to the top.

The whole issue of signing bonuses versus wage scales was just one of many ways that good conditions for nurses was tied to good patient care. Every time our nurses ended up in front of TV cameras, they'd get right to that point, and they meant it. People who put money first get MBAs and go to work for the sort of firms that in 2008 brought down the world economy. People who want to nurse sick people back to health become RNs and hospital workers of all kinds. Every proposal we advanced in our first contract negotiations in 2004—for example, ending mandatory overtime for nurses and limiting how many hours they can work in a given time period—would make any hospital better for patients too. Some nurses were going straight from a twelve-hour shift to on-call status. Another of our key demands had been fully employer-paid family health care. Many nurses in Vegas opted out of the expensive health-care plans their employers offered because they couldn't afford them, and more still opted out of the even more expensive plans that included their families. Pop quiz #2: When you are sick in the hospital, do you want to be cared for by a sick nurse or a healthy one? How about one who comes to work wearing her sick child's germs on her twentieth hour straight?

The nurses didn't even have a real sick leave program. The hospitals had converted what used to be sick leave and vacation time into a concept called Paid Time Off. PTO was sold to nonunion workers as a way to get longer vacations. You combine sick and vacation days into one pot and spend them as you like. Hooray. Except in practice it's a special kind of math in which the whole is almost always less than the sum of the parts. And if the nurse actually gets sick, there goes a year's worth of vacation.

The management used PTO to split young nurses from older ones whose aging bodies got sick or injured more often. Most people have no idea that the on-the-job injury rate for nurses in this country is higher than for construction workers. Nursing is a silent body destroyer, with the most common career-ending and life-altering injury being spinal damage from lifting too many patients with too little help. The numbers are shocking. In the short time I spent in Vegas, there were six career-ending spinal injuries among our top nurse leaders alone. We were often asked to help negotiate individual agreements to force an employer to move an injured nurse from the ICU to, say, a quality inspection team where she no longer had to lift patients. The US Bureau of Labor Statistics reported the incidence rate per 100 full-time workers for nonfatal occupational injuries and illnesses for 1993 as 11.8 for hospital establishments and 17.3 for nursing and personal care facilities. The private-industry rate in 1994 was just 8.5 percent (BLS, 1994b). Certified nurses' aides were second only to truck drivers in total number of cases of disabling injury and illness, with an estimated 145,900 cases for truck drivers and 111,100 for certified nurses' aides.

When the sorry state of patient care in this country is being discussed, legal regulation is brought up as a possible solution far more often than strong unions. But one look at the political quagmire surrounding health-care reform dumps a big bucket of cold water on all that. The most workable solution is the most obviously local: patient care issues can be solved on the spot by a strong union that sees these problems as shop floor issues. If the organization of workers in a hospital is weak, nurses will go on working to exhaustion, and patients will go on lying in pain, pressing call buttons that no one answers because one worker is frantically tending to three other call buttons. Even if we could pass laws regulating this sort of thing, the only appropriate enforcers would be the workers in the hospital. This is a problem that has plagued all kinds of efforts at social change, from labor to civil rights to the environment and more: we fight so hard to get the right policy or law, then forget that the only way to enforce it is through ongoing organizing and mobilizing at the base. The only way to stop unfair and dangerous hospital practices is for nurses and hospital workers to build strong organizations. Period. Nurses are the most highly skilled workers in the hospital, which means they have the most power with the boss. So nurses are the key.

The biggest expense on the balance sheet of any hospital is the payroll, and the biggest item in the payroll is the nurses. So employers are going to fight long and hard before any meaningful reform makes it to nurse level, which also happens to be the patient level. Here again, nurses are the key. In this sense, hospitals are no different from factories or steel works. The most powerful workers are the most skilled. And it is in the boss's interest to divide the most skilled workers from all the rest, just as much as it is in the interests of the workers to stand together, one big union wall-to-wall. Any college undergrad who has taken Introduction to Labor History knows this, which is why it is so crazy for the California Nurses Association to package itself as a progressive union when what they do is skim the cream off the top of the shop, divide the workers and leave those with less skill to fend for themselves.

Another issue we wanted to completely reframe in the CHW negotiations was how the hospital and the union handle labor-management conflict. The norm in this regard is the grievance and arbitration process. In many unions, including the old Las Vegas SEIU local, the filing and managing of grievances is nearly the only thing the union actually does for its members. This means a lot of the union budget goes to lawyers' fees, often with no real gain for the workers. A grievance that is pursued to full-blown arbitration costs *at least* $10,000 in legal fees and often much more. The grievance process is designed to put control of the outcome into the hands of the boss at every step. As each boss up the hierarchy defends the decisions of his or her immediate subordinate, months and sometimes years crawl by.

Eventually the union will do its other thing: file for arbitration. If you're lucky, that will get you a response two years later. The only workers' power involved is the power to pay the dues with which the union finances the whole charade. The system is bad for the workers and even bad for management. If the industry in question is health care, the system is also bad for patients. The only ones who benefit are a cottage industry of lawyers and arbitrators, and the sort of union leaders for whom these cases are bread and butter.

And frankly, there are workers whom the boss has good reason for disciplining. Always have been, always will be. We've all met them. But in a shop with a well-organized union that is on top of things day to day and not just when it is time to renegotiate the contract, everyone knows which workers have legitimate complaints and which ones are bullshitting. If worker organization is ongoing, the worst of the grievance quagmire, unions endlessly defending the indefensible, can be pretty much avoided. A shop like that very rarely needs to file a grievance, because management gets it that people are working conscientiously and that the union is ready to step forward when the boss is truly unfair. Yet most unions teach their members and staff that the way to defend the contract is to pursue *every* worker complaint from grievance all the way to arbitration.

The only way to take on this culture of grievance is to challenge it from within the union. This is hard, but attacking it from the outside plays right into the hands of corporate power, and corporations already have plenty of power in this country. Our local began such a challenge from the inside with our new union-wide policy "From Grievances to Direct Action," which I discussed in an earlier chapter. The old guard of the local, however, had maintained control of the union by trading their attentiveness to individual grievances for the votes of the workers who filed them, and they were not about to let this go. As a result, our members would try to implement the direct-action approach the new leadership was advocating but would often file a grievance at the same time, in case the direct action didn't work.

In the first UHS contracts we signed in 2004, at Desert Springs and Valley hospitals, we had enough power to win a "short-timeline two-step grievance process," which condensed the process prior to arbitration. We negotiated a similar process in our first contracts with the CHW hospitals in 2005. But we knew this wasn't a real solution, and we invited the CHW workers to come up with better ideas for resolving contract violations affecting individual workers.

It is hard to convey to someone outside the very particular culture of labor unions just how deeply against the grain this initiative went. Traditional union leaders get returned to office over and over again in elections in which most workers don't bother to vote and the few who do are those whose grievances the union leaders handled and "won." In our new 2006 negotiations, we proposed that the management and union hire—and management pay for—an outside consultant, Restructuring Associates, Inc. RAI specialized in redesigning work systems in what are called high-performance workplaces, with a reservation: They would work only for shops with unions. I had been introduced to RAI through Larry Fox, and I had been impressed with Tom Schneider, RAI's principle staff person. SEIU's only complaint about RAI was that they were expensive, which was true. But since the expense of restructuring work systems to make them more efficient was properly the burden of management, we asked management to bring in RAI to help redesign not only the grievance process but also many other work structures. Though bringing in an outside consultant to "redesign work systems" sounds deathly boring, in fact it was anything but. The idea was not only to blow to bits the decrepit old labor-management conflict resolution system but also to reexamine the structure of work in the hospital from the ground up, and to involve the workers, outside experts, and the supportive members of management in the process. We wanted to give hospital workers what they wanted most: a high-quality work environment where they could deliver high-quality health care. That is the dream of every health-care worker. In the final analysis, this was where we got to engage our most radical impulses, even more than we did in more obviously militant struggles.

One final angle in our strategic approach to the CHW contract negotiations was to see if we could demonstrate that an innovative CEO who listened to his workers could pay for a very expensive contract by building a reputation for having the best hospitals in the area and thereby drawing in the most patients. We talked about this with the CEO, Rod Davis, and the workers. We had a handful of simple proposals for the negotiations, and each one was expensive. We assured Davis over and over that he would be able to pay for the contract expenses by having hospitals full of patients drawn in by good care. We also sold him on the idea that our proposals would help him prepare for the day when the federal government restructured the Medicare and Medicaid reimbursement system to reward hospitals with better patient outcomes. Everyone knew such a system was coming—the only questions were when and how. Davis understood the concept. He also understood that we were trying to set a high standard in our contract with him that we would then use to win similar contracts at the other hospitals in the market. If that worked, his expenses wouldn't be dramatically out of line with those of his competitors, and if he settled smartly and quickly he could improve not only the care his hospital provided but also its public image, by avoiding the sort of labor wars that were brewing at the for-profits. Rod Davis was a savvy CEO, way ahead of his time.

The CHW contract was settled in just three bargaining sessions, and included everything the workers had asked for: the best wages in Nevada; an improved wage scale that rewarded experience and skill; the best on-call pay system in the region; a health care plan that continued after they retired (a first for any Nevada hospital); nurse-patient ratios equal to those in California (along with a commitment to develop similar ratios for all the other workers in the hospital); and the hiring of RAI so the workers themselves could begin to redesign the patient care process.

As usual, it was 4 am when the last paper was signed and we headed off to the nearest bar. But now there was time for only one drink, for at 5:30 am the polls were to open for our local's union-wide voting on whether to increase the dues. By the time the clock struck midnight of the following day, we had set the highest standard for patient care and health-care worker compensation in Nevada, and our members had voted to double their dues with 77 percent voting yes to the increase.

CHAPTER TEN

The CEO, the Union Buster, and the Gunrunner

As a result of my brief harrowing visit to Desert Springs hospital, we now had a picture of Brent Yessin, literally and figuratively. The platoon of union busters under his command, however, remained hidden. All the new security personnel were out in plain view, and of course we already knew the two negotiators from California, Rick Albert and Larry Arnold. But as for Yessin's lieutenants, the suits who were really running the operation, all we had were their first names. Worker reports on the mandatory captive audience meetings at Desert Springs noted at least five full-time people on his core team—and this is in addition to the countless security guards watching every move the workers made. Yessin's gang included a couple of well-dressed women who were the "good cops," sent to talk nicely to the nurses and techs; a guy named Byron, who said he was a behavioral psychologist; and Jose. Jose was clearly the "bad cop." At the captive audience meetings he would get right in everyone's face, asking over and over (completely illegally), "Are you going to do the right thing and stand with your unit manager and your patients and keep your job, or betray your patients and employer?" This was 2006, just before the dawn of the age of cell phone cameras, and photographing everyone everywhere anytime was not the bizarre social norm it would so soon become. We decided it was high time to unmask these goons.

The plan was to send Morgan Levi to crash a mandatory captive. Of course she would be kicked out, but, we hoped, not before she had eye-balled and photographed the union-buster general command. Morgan was totally up for this sort of thing—she wasn't a body builder for nothing. Our core new leadership—Morgan, Jessica, and Maryanne—was cut from the same mold of tough-as-nails women. This had become so normal at our local it was easy to forget that most union locals in this country are run by men. And it really worked for one that represented so many nurses, a profession that draws tough—and smart and socially conscious—women.

We had to pick the right captive meeting, one in which all the workers attending were solidly with the union; we didn't want to alienate anyone. The big day came. Surrounded by a group of nurses, Morgan navigated undetected through the back halls of the hospital to the conference room behind the cafeteria where the meeting was under way. The nurses opened the doors and in walked the well-known star union organizer. CEO Sam Kaufman was personally addressing some techs, and at the sight of Morgan he stood up and began to belch orders about this being a private meeting. You could always count on Sam losing his cool, and making him do it was fun. The process of getting Morgan thrown out began almost instantly, but she got the photos we wanted, plus a good look at the whole setup of the suits in the room.

Beyond Yessin himself, this Jose character was clearly a real problem, as he was actually beginning to scare the workers. Choosing Morgan to crash that meeting was real serendipity because she discovered, much to her surprise, that she *knew* this man. His full name was Jose Salgado. He had joined one of SEIU's organizer-training programs several years earlier, in another state, and it had been Morgan herself who had fired him. Now either this guy was here because he had a crazy thing for getting back at Morgan, which seemed unlikely, or he had gone as a spy to get the SEIU organizer training manual, or maybe being fired had pissed him off and instead of going postal, he'd done the next best thing and gone rabidly anti-union. Whatever the reason, he was working for Yessin, and if he hadn't lost his notes and manual, they now had some sense of our playbook—though ours in Nevada was a bit different from Washington's.

Luck further had it that Morgan's father was a private investigator, and she asked him to do some PI-level background research on both Yessin and Salgado. The dirt he turned up on Salgado was a mother lode. Jose had been convicted of running guns. *Lots* of guns, the sort that could arm a drug gang. We could never have made up something like this guy's arrest record. So that was the sort of operation Brent Yessin ran, infiltrating unions with convicted gunrunners. Here were all our fresh-out-of-college idealistic twentysomething organizers, plus nurses themselves who had become our organizers, illegally banned from a hospital where they admitted a convicted gunrunner, who had clearly been brought in to scare the workers. Blowing this jerk out of the water was going to be a pleasure.

We called the national communications team in DC to get advice on how best to break this news. My mistake: I forgot this would trigger a review by the SEIU legal department, which told us that we couldn't use the information because we couldn't say where we had obtained it. I was mentally kicking myself: I should have known better than to call DC. Now that they had discussed it with me, I would be directly disobeying legal counsel if I broke the story. I could have acted first and talked to our lawyers second. I already had a reputation among them for this sort of thing, and I readily admit it was well founded. Lawyers, not surprisingly, get very caught up in the law. But the laws regulating unions in the country are pathetic, and the amount of attention that unions pay to them is one reason (among many) that the labor movement in this country is dying. It was legalized to death.

Don't get me wrong here. The SEIU does have some excellent lawyers who are devoted to the labor movement. If some day I actually wind up in legal trouble I would be delighted to have a lawyer as good as them. The problem is that lawyers wake up each day and think about how labor leaders can get their work done inside a legal framework that is deadly to unions. I woke up every day and thought about how to disrupt that system. I respected and appreciated them—I just didn't listen to them as often as they wanted.

Knowing when to listen to lawyers and when to ignore them is a key for an organizer. My own rule of thumb is this: If something I want to do might get me in trouble, I do it; if it might get the workers or staff in trouble, I don't. Really good labor lawyers help people like me with militant impulses understand when to cut the crap. The very best also know that sometimes, ignoring them is part of the organizer's job. When an action needs to be taken right away or the union will lose, you take it and resolve the legal issue later. We were fighting a decertification effort with enormous stakes. If we lost, UHS could kick the legs out from under a plan that had taken thousands of hours to assemble. If we won, we could create unprecedented standards for workers and patients in a right-to-work state, and a presidential swing state to boot. What drives me absolutely crazy is how so often over the recent history of the movement, labor leaders have followed the letter of the law when confronting the boss while throwing the book out the window when confronting each other.

After hanging up with our legal department, I called D Taylor over at the casino workers' union. D said, "Get a copy of the complete arrest record with the gun list over to my office right away." I had no doubt that very soon all of Las Vegas would know who Universal Health Services had brought into town.

We ran a sticker-up at Desert Springs hospital with a big round sticker like a shooting-range target, and across it the words "NO WAY JOSE!" The workers had never had so much fun with a sticker. In a matter of hours Jose's power over them was in the hospital's toxic refuse bins. People would shout at him in the halls. "Hey! It's the *gun runner*; don't shoot me!" Very quickly Jose vanished from Las Vegas.

Yes, there was a legal issue to resolve—after we had won. The hospital filed a racial discrimination suit against me, claiming that "No way Jose" was a racial slur. And they distributed a flyer declaring that I personally had "maligned an innocent Hispanic man with a racial slur by using a common phrase with Jose in it and linking a Hispanic man to guns to attack his integrity." Just as we had with the boss's letters, we made copies of these charges for all the workers. Now even the lawyers in DC were laughing on the phone with me.

The decert vote among the techs at Desert Springs was now just a few days away. The walls of the RV were covered with charts and assessments, papers strewn everywhere, food scattered all over. I would stop in to clean the place up at night and remind our young organizers that the much older techs and nurses didn't live like twentysomethings. But the RV was fantastic. The hospital management had tried many times to get the cops to tow it away on one pretext or another, but they weren't interested. We had supported the police union when they had been blindsided with awful arbitration, and we were currently campaigning together for the same County Commission candidates. And anyway, cops don't like convicted felons in general, and gunrunners in particular. Neither do politicians, news editors, or pretty much anyone.

In public, Morgan and Jessica and I were brimming with confidence about the decert vote but privately we were in panic mode. We had scored a major victory running Salgado out of the hospital, but it was still a tough campaign. Hell, we had been banned from the hospital for nearly the entire fight, while the workers were locked up inside with Yessin's gang. UHS had run the most expensive A-level boss fight any of us had ever seen. By now we'd moved every good organizer we had to this campaign. In the final days, they house-called every single tech worker, and more than once.

I am not sure whether Morgan, Jessica or I slept at all during the last three days. Our get-out-the-vote operation was tight. We had individual plans for each worker we were certain would vote union. If we could get every one of them to the polls, we would win. The boss's campaign at that point was just to get the workers to shut down, stay home, stay away, not vote. The voting was at the hospital, and on any given day half the workers are not on shift. That afternoon our organizers and worker leaders chased down workers in shopping malls, casinos, wherever the people who answered their door at home told us they might be. We had drilled in the Mountain View story over the previous weeks: "The workers lost by *seven* votes."

When the polls closed, we headed to the official NLRB counting room inside the hospital. Yessin was there, smiling. Rick Albert was there from Foley and Lardner, smiling. Some of the rad techs who had been promised big raises for destroying their own union were there, and so was the CEO himself. It was clear that they thought they had won. You don't send all the big guys to a vote count if you think you are going to lose. *Shit.*

The count began. Vote counts are seriously high drama. Everything slows to a crawl. The NLRB officials have to read all sorts of laws out loud. Then there is a whole protocol for the unsealing of the ballot boxes. No one makes a sound. When the paper ballots finally come out, the NLRB agents carefully unfold each one, iron out the crease at the fold, and place it face down on the table. After all the ballots have been prepared, they pick them up one by one and call out "yes" or "no." Everyone in the room knows the magic number that means they have won, and a running tally is kept. In this case, the boss needed a yes vote: Did workers want to decertify the union?

The first few ballots came. "Yes. Yes. Yes."

What? We were keeping poker faces but inside I felt ready to crack. And then it started.

"No. No. No. No. No. No. No. Yes. No. No. No. No."

At the exact "no" we needed to win, we exploded. Yessin and the CEO dashed out of the room. The final tally showed the workers voted by better than 2 to 1 to keep their union. I am pretty sure I got drunk that night in the bar across the street. We all did. It was a repeat of the contract victory from 2004, with everyone phoning everyone else, spouses piling in, no makeup, hair in rollers, and everyone ready to party. I was so tired I couldn't move, but still happy. Never had we seen such ferocious intimidation. We had a great time trying to imagine what Brent Yessin was saying on the phone to UHS CEO Alan Miller back in his corporate palace in King of Prussia, Pennsylvania, about the millions that had been spent on his losing effort to drive out the union.

The count was on a Thursday. The hospitals throughout the weekend and into the next week were quiet. We knew the union busting operation wasn't finished—we just didn't know what their next move would be. Then our fax machine spit out their announcement that they would stop deducting union dues from paychecks. Remember what I said about how the law favors the boss? The workers had just reaffirmed, by an overwhelming margin and in the face of serious intimidation and wage bribery, their desire to have a union. And here was the boss responding with a financial frontal attack. Perfectly legal. Welcome to labor organizing in America. Assuming UHS was going to do the same at Valley hospital when that contract expired, we would suddenly be out $20,000 per month. We scrambled to set up our own dues collection system. What our financial team came up with was a system in which workers could sign up to have their monthly union dues automatically moved from their personal checking accounts to a new union account we would set up for this purpose. The catch was that each individual worker had to provide us with a blank check from his or her personal checking account for us to present to the bank. It was an irony any union organizer would appreciate, because the bosses' most overused slogan against labor is

"Don't give the union a blank check!" This would be yet another test: What percentage of the workers would give us a blank check and access to their personal checking account to keep their union going?

To make matters worse, six days after we won the decertification vote, the fax machine sprang to life again. UHS had filed a legal objection to the decertification vote, alleging that the union had intimidated workers in the tech unit. More slime, and gimme a break. *Which* side of the campaign had repeatedly locked workers in a room with a convicted gunrunner who did his level best to scare the daylights of them? After losing by such a wide margin, I didn't think Yessin actually believed he could win if the election was re-run, but it would be a huge expense for us at the very time he had shut down our dues collection. More than that, he knew it would keep a cloud of tension hanging over the workers. In short, he wanted *futility* to set in.

This is always what union busters go for in the end. If they can't win by any single tactic, they can still create an endless barrage of garbage until the workers decide that unless the union goes away their lives will simply never return to normal. Besides, now the union would have to leap into preparing for the trial instead of preparing to negotiate. We had every second of our time and penny of our money for all of 2006 budgeted on organizing and bargaining campaigns even before Yessin had forced us to fight the decertification campaign. Now he was making us fight a decertification of the (non)decertification.

Keep in mind that Alan Miller had decided that breaking the union was of greater long-term value to Universal Health Services than the dollar amount he spent doing it, and UHS was a Fortune 500 company and one of the largest hospital chains in the world. When it came to stretching, the CEO's budget was a lot more flexible than ours.

Yessin's complaint alleged that Jane McAlevey and Morgan Levi had personally and individually threatened every member of the tech unit with...well, it wasn't really clear with what. With healthy snacks at the RV?

Even though his case was ludicrous, filing it was a smart move. Yessin, it seemed to me, understood the law not as an impartial framework of justice but as one of many tools in his corporate arsenal—an understanding I wish more people on the union side of the fence shared. Not only did we have to go to work gathering evidence and witnesses and preparing the case, but Yessin added to our burdens by feeding loads of crap to the media. Suddenly calls were coming in from the press asking if we "wanted to comment on the legal charges of intimidation of the workers." Morgan and I kept away from the cameras and the press. There was no question that the best way to combat the accusations was to let the workers do the talking. A lot of tech people and nurses stepped up and did exactly that before we got the media back on the real story of who was intimidating whom.

Two weeks into May, the Yessin gang seemed to surrender Desert Springs hospital. The next week we got the first calls from the nurses at UHS's bigger hospital, Valley, saying the union busters were setting up shop there. Within weeks, their entire operation was starting to roll at Valley Hospital. But Yessin's cover had been blown. The Valley union leaders were keenly aware of everything that had gone down at Desert and had already begun to prepare their coworkers for the fight to come.

At the UHS bargaining table, however, nothing, not one thing, nada, was happening.

In early May we had opened negotiations with the Hospital Corporation of America's (HCA) biggest hospital in Las Vegas, Sunrise, right after winning the contract with Catholic Healthcare West. So far those negotiations hadn't gone much beyond perfunctory exchanges of priorities. It was now nearing the end of May and we were about to open additional negotiations with the county hospital and civil service. We had to face the fact that UHS's strategy of making us fight the decert wars had left the union in general and me in particular overstretched. The only fix was for fresh blood to come to Vegas and take over the lead at one of the bargaining tables.

The question of which negotiation to hand off to an outsider wasn't simple. We had three separate tables open with UHS (Desert Springs nurses, Desert Springs techs, and Valley nurses) and the unresolved charges of intimidation at Desert Valley to handle. The public-sector situation was equally complex, involving the first-ever joint negotiations with the public hospital and Clark County, with the old-guard leadership of our local constantly sniping about my alleged lack of concern for public-sector workers. And our B-team organizers had been assigned the public sector because there was no way the public-sector bosses would ever fight as hard as private-sector CEOs. That left the negotiations at Sunrise, HCA's giant hospital.

The question of whom to invite to negotiate was equally delicate. The one person I trusted to parachute in and lead a table in the style of the new Nevada local was Jerry Brown. He had retired just a few months earlier, after thirty years of leading the workers in Connecticut and Rhode Island. Jerry said if we could schedule the negotiations for two consecutive days every three weeks he could do it. Some retirement.

I knew this would cause some disappointment among our leaders at Sunrise. The various legal charges and complaints that bosses had filed against me had made me a sort of minor celebrity in the sordid pantheon of Las Vegas. Plus, some of our members at Sunrise had been attending negotiations at the other tables. They wanted to bring what they saw to their hospital, and they *thought* that meant me personally.

There was one Sunrise nurse in particular whose reaction stood out as something beyond mere disappointment. This was Melanie Sisson, a member of the old executive board of the local. As soon as I sat down to explain I simply couldn't do seven different negotiations simultaneously and run the union, she told me in no uncertain terms that I wasn't treating her with enough respect and that it was going to be a "real problem with the workers that you won't respect us like you respect the workers at UHS and CHW." Wow. This was just the sort of thinking that was typical among the old-guard people. She was repeating the very message that Yessin's union-busting team had been pushing: that the amount of time I personally spent at "her" negotiations showed that the Sunrise workers were somehow unimportant to me. This was wrong on so many levels it was hard to know where to begin to answer her. But since Melanie was the executive board member from that hospital, I sat with her for a long time explaining the situation. I was working eighteen-hour days, three more new tables were about to open, and we were bringing in the one and only Jerry Brown.

At Desert Springs and Valley, we had deliberately slowed negotiations down to a crawl. Given everything that had happened with UHS, it looked as though we were not going to get the contracts we wanted without a strike, or at the very least a credible threat of a strike. If it came to a full strike, it would be the first nurses' strike in Las Vegas history.

It was currently 100 degrees outside. We couldn't even think about a picket until the summer heat had passed. I met with the worker leaders from the UHS hospitals, and explained how important it was for a strike threat to be *credible*. Otherwise, the boss might read it as the last-ditch bluff of a collapsing union. Everyone understood there was no credibility to threatening to walk picket lines in the Las Vegas summer. We brainstormed about what we might do to keep the workers strong through a three-month lull. We were still high from our victory in the decert at Desert Springs and cooling our heels for three months was far from ideal, but we had no choice.

I was focusing on getting the big county civil service and hospital bargaining teams ready for their opening day on June 12, when 120 of them would speak and present proposals. The second round of negotiations at Sunrise was set for the June 10 and 11. Jerry Brown, who would lead our Sunrise bargaining team, was flying in June 9. That afternoon, my cell phone rang and the screen displayed Jerry's phone number, which made no sense at all, because he was supposed to be on a plane.

A very quiet voice came through. "Jane? Jane, it's Jerry. Listen, I am in an ambulance. I just had a heart attack. They grounded the airplane in Pittsburgh to get me off. It's pretty bad. I can't talk. Call my wife …"

So I called Kathy, Jerry's wonderful wife, to tell her that on his way to help me during his "retirement," her husband had had a heart attack. My next call was to alert SEIU's leaders in Pennsylvania that Jerry Brown was in their hands and to get someone over to the hospital to find out what the hell was happening. The report came back that Jerry was alive but definitely out of the picture for Vegas. And my third call was to Larry Fox, to try to figure out how the hell we were going to get all this negotiating done. We decided on the spot that with negotiations the next day and no Jerry Brown, I would have to take the lead at the Sunrise table. We'd find someone else to hold the fort at the Desert Springs and Valley tables. Since we'd decided we didn't want those tables to move during the hot summer months anyway, this seemed the most workable of our very limited options. We would explain to the UHS workers that I would come back as "closer" at the UHS negotiations once we had won at Sunrise. Luckily, these workers were more than capable of understanding the full game plan, including a deliberately slowed-down summer and temporary negotiator. The challenge would be finding someone to take the

UHS assignment—and someone I trusted to stick with the program we were driving, not someone who might listen to headquarters.

The problem was this Larry Arnold character sitting across the table from us. The guy was beyond obnoxious. My substitute would have to have the temperament to take the words of a guy like Arnold and shove them right back down his throat or up his other bodily orifice, as I had made a habit of doing. When an intimidation specialist like Arnold is running the show for the boss, leading the union team is as much a matter of tension-cutting as actual negotiating. Though my techniques for this are certainly not the only way to go, these workers and I had already been through months of bitter struggle with Arnold, Yessin, and UHS. They understood my style, and I understood what they wanted from me. They needed the repeated experience of seeing their side dishing it back and demanding respect.

I wouldn't take shit from Arnold even for a moment, and I'd use the caucus system all day on him if I had to. We would open negotiations in the morning and if he acted like an asshole, which was pretty much guaranteed, I'd call a caucus for several hours before even letting him back in the room. Every time he made some obnoxious comment about nurses I would make a nastier one right back about low-life attorneys. Whatever it took. Each day I let him set the pattern. I always opened pleasantly, because it was important to the workers that we were always ready to be grown-ups. But if Arnold was going to treat them like dirt, I was going to honor them by saying to his face everything they'd always wanted to say in the shop and couldn't. Now I needed someone who'd step in for me and do the same thing.

The opening of the public-sector master table was a tremendous experience for the workers. The County human resource teams walked in and were confronted by a room packed with all of our bargaining team members, seated around enormous tables. The opening presentation was our best ever.

Even at this late date I was still grappling with trying to get the civil service employees to understand how their fates were tied in with the hospital workers' and why it was so important to stand with them as a united front against their common boss. At our final preparations a few days earlier, I was still hearing divisive comments from some of the old-guard members from Clark County, questioning why they were negotiating together with hospital workers. In part this was a reflection of how relentlessly the County had been driving a divisive message. But the fact that it was now five months after the big bargaining-team kick-off meetings and these workers were still not in as good shape internally as the rest of our union was also a reflection of how stretched our organizers were. This was a downside of the strategy of aligning the entire market to negotiate all the contracts at once. By this time we had hired and trained some really terrific organizers (who would go on to become one of the only local organizing teams in the national SEIU that could win hospital union drives without assistance brought in from the national hospital division), but we still didn't have enough high quality organizers to cover all of our shops.

The flip side of this coin was that the public-sector employees rarely worked with our best organizers. That meant I was still organizing the bargaining team members the day the master negotiations with the County opened. It also meant that the complexities of the negotiations were less fully understood by the majority of the workers. As is nearly always the case in such situations, the root of our weakness lay in the failure of our organizers to correctly identify the shop floor leaders. Our lead civil service organizer was a compelling activist who relied on her considerable charisma, which carried her a long way but was no sub-stitute for good leadership identification, knowing how to frame hard questions, and much more. Our lead organizer at the public hospital also had plenty of talent, but was undisciplined to the point of being lazy. And below the level of lead organizers the quality of our people dropped off considerably. So I arrived at the opening day of the joint master negotia-tions still engaged in Labor Pedagogy 101 with the workers.

In spite of everything, that opening day was a big success. This was the battle in which the boss had been sending all manner of letters (which I had forwarded to the workers) claiming that bringing such a large team to the negotiations would create a roaring chaos. In fact, the room was so large that we needed portable microphones just to hear each other, yet at the end of the day Ray Visconti, the HR guy we considered the fair one, remarked how surprised he was that he "really could hear a pin drop all day long."

Our presentation led with a discussion of our plan to defeat some really bad anti-tax measures that would hurt not only the workers but also the managers and, eventually, the entire population the workers served. Then we went on to detail what we wanted from the negotiations:

- "Safe staffing." Under this rubric, we wanted to frame staffing levels in departments such as the (grossly understaffed) child welfare department in the same terms that framed staffing levels at the hospital.
- "Right to Retire." Here we took advantage of our recent victories in the private sector to show that the bar had changed for private sector hospital workers in the region since the last time government workers had negotiated a contract.
- "Fairness and Respect." We wanted a revamping of evaluation and promotion policies. There was far too much favoritism and too many who-knows-who deals in government employment settings, a level of corruption that had sent some Clark County commissioners to jail.
- "Accessible Quality Health Care." Here again, we built on our recent victories in the private sector where our members had won fully employer-paid family health care.
- "Job Security." The focus here was subcontracting rules, and in particular an organizing-rights agreement for some 3,000 part-time and contingent workers countywide.

At the private caucus that followed the opening session, we held a global catch-up session on the status of our big 2006 plans. I explained once again how, in that context, we didn't really want these negotiations to move until after the November elections, when we hoped to pull off a couple of big upsets to get the kind of worker-friendly County Commission we needed to win a really good contract.

CHAPTER ELEVEN

Full Court Press

Over at Sunrise, the workers were in terrific shape. This was a reflection of the talents of Jessica Foster, our lead organizer, and another wonderful young organizer named Jonah McGreevey, who was learning fast under her tutelage. What complicated things at Sunrise was that the rock-solid on-the-ground work done by Jessica and Jonah was caught in a web of deals and alliances both within the national SEIU and between the SEIU and the Hospital Corporation of America, the parent corporation of Sunrise. The issues involved here go right to the core of the problems that would soon wreak havoc in several locals in the national SEIU and drive me out of the union, so they merit explanation.

During the previous four years, the health-care and hospital division of our national union had signed agreements with three major hospital chains that facilitated organizing large numbers of hospital workers: the HCA, Catholic Healthcare West (at whose Vegas hospitals we had just won our gold-standard contracts), and Tenet. Big corporations don't go around handing out agreements like these for nothing. These were big victories that resulted from multifaceted campaigns waged primarily under the leadership of Larry Fox. The national SEIU now had members in different local unions in different states who worked for the same corporation, which could give us vastly greater clout at the bargaining table with hospitals owned by these corporations. This was part of the reason SEIU wanted me in Vegas: to extend the union's national power into the heart of right-to-work, for-profit, cash cow–hospital land. To realize the potential of these agreements, however, would require far better coordination between the various local negotiations, and the national union and its locals.

The 2004 national SEIU convention had voted to form "unity councils," with one for each national employer. One of many goals of these councils was to encourage locals to line up their contracts so that contracts in different parts of the country but with the same parent corporation expired at the same time. So there was also an obvious potential for tension here between local and national priorities, particularly for locals like ours, which had just spent an enormous effort to line up all of the contracts in one region, rather than with others around the country. This was not an insurmountable problem, but the councils were key.

For both CHW and the HCA, the primary locals were the California local, headed by Sal Rosselli, and ours in Nevada. For CHW, the Nevada local was the junior partner, as we had the workers from three hospitals, and the California local had workers from more than twenty. For the HCA, we carried equal weight, with having roughly the same number in both states. If anything, the Nevada local was the senior partner, because the HCA hospitals in Las Vegas produced much more profit than those in California.

All of this meant that in both the CHW and HCA unity councils, the key players were Sal Rosselli from California, Larry Fox from DC, and me. The three of us worked together well enough and got our unity councils up and functioning. I imagine it had to be nerve-wracking for Stern, because suddenly two leaders who were committed to a more militant union tradition and who still believed in the power of the strike—Rosselli and McAlevey—were heading these potentially powerful governance structures.

Stern unleashed the first power grab to wrest control from us back in 2005 when he added Monica Russo of the Florida union and Mitch Ackerman from our Colorado local to the HCA unity council. Neither of them had any members from HCA hospitals, but their addition was justified on the grounds that the national union wanted to expand our agreement with HCA into Florida and Colorado. Stern quickly elevated Monica to chair of the council, although hers was a nursing-home union and the HCA empire includes no nursing homes. Moreover, the Florida local under her leadership never reached even a bare majority of dues-paying members in a single facility during the entire time I was in SEIU, whereas in Las Vegas, our revitalized local had taken membership to 70 percent overall, with every facility above majority. There were many other differences favoring the Nevada local, but the only difference that mattered was that Monica Russo was unquestioning in her loyalty to Andy Stern, and I was not. And unlike me, Stern knew full well what power plays he had in the works, and it was crucial to him to have Monica in charge.

I n 2005 Larry Fox was negotiating with HCA for a new national accord. As always, Larry did everything in close consultation with local union leaders. He was so trusted that we authorized him to meet with HCA alone, knowing that he would constantly brief us. The 2005 HCA accord was the last time anything like that ever happened.

In the accord, the union came up far short of what we had wanted. We simply hadn't had enough power going in. The HCA unity council held extensive strategy discussions about whether to go ahead with an accord at all, or stall it until our HCA contracts in California and Nevada expired. This latter option carried the possibility that we could strike HCA in two states, but whether we had the strength to actually do that was a close call. HCA was essentially telling Fox, "Take a deal now, and we will throw you a few bones in exchange for assurances that Rosselli and McAlevey won't do anything crazy in California or Nevada six months from now when their contracts expire." The union was in a tricky position. Each side was playing hardball in December 2005, and frankly, SEIU was the weak party at the table. In the end the union decided to sign a limited accord.

In it, the HCA promised the SEIU what are called fair election procedures in organizing campaigns at five hospitals in southern Florida.* What the corporation had wanted in return was for Rosselli and me to sign a peace accord that would tie our hands in our upcoming negotiations. And they wanted our local to stay out of HCA's Mountain View hospital in Las Vegas.

---

* Fair election procedures are negotiated processes between unions and employers to conduct elections outside of the NLRB structure. Typical procedures include access to the worksite for the union, a designated and short election timeline, and an agreement that the employer shall not campaign against the union. These agreements vary enormously in strength and specificity.

There was no way the Nevada local was going to agree to that. Remember, this was the hospital where earlier that year we had lost an election by seventy-one votes in the nurse unit and by just seven votes in the ancillary units, and that was before we had begun to put together our track record of winning standard-setting contracts. Our plan was to extend this record with a great new contract at HCA Sunrise, then use that as the launching pad for a return engagement with Mountain View. Eight out of every ten nurses in Las Vegas were in the SEIU local at that point, and with Mountain View we would have nine of ten. This would give us a power in the regional market unmatched anywhere else in the country. We argued that the national union could not trade away the rights of its members in Nevada without their consent, and suggested they should push for an accord that committed HCA to fair election procedures at four Florida hospitals in instead of five, and not compromise the rights of the workers at Mountain View.

HCA was equally adamant in demanding a commitment from the national SEIU to stay out of Mountain View. They knew they would be under enormous pressure to match the excellent contracts our local had won at other hospitals in the Las Vegas market. They also knew that the Florida local was weak, and they thought they stood a good chance of beating SEIU in Florida despite the so-called fair election procedures. Even if the workers in Florida succeeded in forming a union, the HCA would be negotiating with a weaker local for a cheaper contract.

For his part, Stern clearly wanted to raise SEIU's ante in the game of national political power in Washington, DC, and this was Florida. Florida politics was national politics. The nation was just one presidential cycle on from the Bush coup in the 2000 national election. It was a question of priorities and strategy. If the priority was building workers' power in America, then reining in the highly mobilized Nevada local in exchange for an iffy deal in Florida was absurd. If the priority was using the national union as a base for the leadership to engage in Washington politics, anything that would support a move into Florida was a good deal. And this seemed to be Stern's priority. He had evidently developed a theory that employees' power on the shop floor had been eroded to the point that there was little to be won through direct struggle there with the boss, but that this weakness in the workplace could be made up for in the political arena.

Larry Fox, however, dug in his heels. Though Larry saw the strategic potential in national accords, he also believed that the right of workers to engage in struggle with their boss, up to and including the right to strike, was the foundation upon which everything else in the labor movement was built. He was adamant that the accord needed to cover all five Florida hospitals *and* retain the union's right to organize Mountain View. And that was the deal that was finally signed.

The accord called for the Florida hospital elections to be run immediately. I think we all assumed that HCA would begin to violate the accord the minute the ink was dry. Scott Courtney, a top organizer from the Ohio union, was dispatched to Florida to win the elections. Only, right off the bat, things didn't go well. The first election was a big loss. SEIU cried foul and accused HCA of violating the rules of the accord, which they certainly had. But I felt that the deeper problem was that the disorganized SEIU local in Florida had no accomplishments that would convince workers to form a union with it. This is an inherent weakness in the idea that you can use national accords to air-drop a functional union into a state without doing all the real organizing from the ground up.

Predictably enough, I was soon called to an emergency meeting of our HCA unity council to discuss how to force a renegotiation of the HCA deal based on employer violations of the accord in Florida. When I walked into the meeting I was surprised to find some new players in the room. Judy Scott, the national legal counsel for SEIU, showed up, along with Jim Phillio, a top assistant to Mary Kay Henry, the Stern loyalist who had replaced Larry Fox as head of the hospital division. The moment I walked into the room I knew that something big was going to happen. You just feel this sort of thing, the way animals sense that an earthquake is coming.

Monica Russo kicked off the meeting with a long report about how HCA had violated the accord in Florida. Yawn. This was how you knew a fix was on. We were a small team of sophisticated union leaders and lawyers, and we didn't need to be educated on all these mean things the employer had done. We were persuaded to blow up the national accord altogether and try to force HCA back to the table. We would have to count on lots of workers from one hospital in Florida testifying that their boss had done these bad things, and hope that would persuade the national arbitrator to rule in the national union's favor. Not a great plan, but the best option available. OK, fine. And then it happened.

Almost as an aside, near the end of the discussion, Judy Scott said, "Oh, and Larry Fox will be an adviser, but Jim Phillio will be in charge of this round of negotiations with HCA."

Say what?

Larry looked taken aback, but he said nothing. I grabbed him outside in the hall. "Did you hear what I just heard?" He vaguely acknowledged me but was clearly off in his own head, trying to sort out what had just happened.

The whole thing was classic Andy Stern. In fact, it was a replay of the way Larry had been forced out as director of the hospital division at the national convention. Both were Machiavellian moves, sprung as a surprise, and in a confusing manner that offered a little ledge to cling to, the belief that maybe you weren't really being cut off at the knees.

It didn't take a crystal ball to see what the likely upshot of Jim Phillio replacing Larry would be: Any new accord SEIU would sign with HCA would trade away our right to organize Mountain View. Sure enough, within a couple of weeks the arbitrator ruled that HCA had indeed violated the accord. The union was heading back to the table with HCA, with Jim Phillio as the national negotiator. Fox had been taken out of the process. Scott Courtney, the organizer the national union had sent to Florida, called me to say that since we couldn't win an organizing drive at Mountain View anyway, did I mind if they handed over Mountain View to the boss in the national accord?

I could feel my nostrils flaring before Scott finished laying out how he was about to sell us out.

I called Larry. He was sort of quiet, which was a telling sign. He explained that when he settled the original HCA accord, Andy Stern and those around him were not at all happy that he had refused to give in on Mountain View. I had a renewed rush of that sinking feeling that told me the fix was in. But Larry, ever the optimist, thought Sal Rosselli could be an ally on this. Surely Rosselli would understand why organizing Mountain View was key to the strategy of taking an entire health-care market into the union in Vegas.

I was skeptical. I had a healthy respect for the union Rosselli had built in California, even if some of it resulted from a merger. But still I didn't trust him. I had first met him when I was working with nursing-home workers in New England and had looked around to see what sort of contracts our nursing-home workers had elsewhere. And I had been surprised to learn that nursing-home workers in Sal's jurisdiction, in highly unionized northern California, had contracts that were not as good as the first contracts we were winning for newly organized nursing homes in Connecticut.

Furthermore, I had been rejecting Rosselli's repeated and pointed offers to merge the Nevada local into his, and there was little doubt that by doing so I was pissing him off. By this time, most of the Northeastern hospital locals had merged into one big powerhouse, United Healthcare Workers East, under the leadership of Dennis Rivera in New York City. Rosselli wanted a United Healthcare Workers West, with himself as Rivera's western counterpart. He wanted to bring in Nevada first, then eventually Oregon, Washington, and Arizona. Rosselli had just barely convinced the national union to agree to the merger of the big Los Angeles hospital workers union with his northern California local. The person who had provided him the decisive support in the national union was Larry Fox. But by this point I had seen enough of Rosselli to know that there was nothing atypical about the way he let Larry Fox use every ounce of his influence in the national union to push through the merger of the California locals, and then did not rise to defend Larry when Larry was pushed aside.

By the spring of 2006 I had been wined and dined by Sal several times. He had taken me to a San Francisco 49ers game. He had offered to fly to Vegas anytime I wanted to have dinner to talk about merging Nevada with his union. He offered to make me a top vice president in the big new powerhouse he would build. He explained to me that he needed women who were tough enough to survive in his testosterone-heavy union leadership team. This last point wasn't exactly a successful pickup line. I always responded in a straightforward way, explaining that I simply couldn't see how it would be in the interest of workers in a right-to-work state to merge into a larger union in a union security state. The strategies, priorities, resources, and everything else simply wouldn't mesh. California and Nevada weren't just apples and oranges; they were more like apples and rocks. I certainly could understand how it made sense for Sal's ambitions, but those were his, not mine. I was trying to see things from the point of view of the workers in Nevada. If anything, it made more sense for the locals in the right-to-work states of Nevada, Arizona and Colorado to merge. At any rate, I repeatedly communicated to Sal that I had a ton of respect for his union, but the merger didn't make sense.

I told Larry that I thought he was being naïve about Sal but that I would dearly love to be proven wrong. In any event, if Sal wanted to demonstrate his commitment to workers' power in Nevada he would soon have his chance, as he could have the decisive sway in a unity council decision about Mountain View hospital. So Larry set out to get Rosselli on board.

Instead, Rosselli tried to ingratiate himself with Stern and the national office by agreeing to have an organizer from his local cold-call workers at Mountain View to "sample" their support for the union. This was a maddening, ridiculous exercise. And the fact that Rosselli went along with it was one on a growing list of reasons why in the end I just didn't trust the guy. The Nevada local had charted that hospital, unit by unit and worker by worker. We knew what the workers at Mountain View thought, and we knew the sort of intimidation campaign the boss had run there. And now Rosselli was going to have an unknown organizer from another state randomly cold-call these workers and ask them to share their private opinions on the phone as a test of whether or not they were ready to form a union? I can't imagine what Rosselli would have said if I had agreed to such an obvious setup against his outfit. But the real point of the exercise had nothing to do with the workers at Mountain View and everything to do with Rosselli signaling to Stern that the California local could play ball with headquarters, even if it meant screwing the Nevada union.

Within weeks, the deal was done but no one even told us. Fox was out, and Jim Phillio never felt the need to convene the HCA unity council or even put in a call to the locals once he reached his deal. Instead, he informed us after the fact. And what he had done was even worse than we had imagined. Not only was there no fair election procedure accord for organizing Mountain View, they had actually placed Mountain View on the infamous "no-fly zone" list. The national SEIU had officially *prohibited* the workers at the Mountain View hospital from organizing a union that would affiliate with the SEIU.

I was done with SEIU right there. As far as I was concerned, my journey trying to build that union was over. This was manipulative and just plain idiotic. At one point we had even told the national union, "Look, if you think you need a negotiating chip with HCA, tell them you will give up an organizing agreement at Mountain View, because we are confident we can win an election there without it. Just don't put us on the no-fly zone list." And here they had prohibited us from organizing the only significant nonunion hospital left in Las Vegas, right when our organization was peaking and the market-wide 2006 Las Vegas labor juggernaut was moving ahead at full throttle.

Then things got a whole lot worse, which brings us back to the contract negotiations at Sunrise hospital.

Jeff Bell, HCA's negotiator for Sunrise, was playing hardball. It sure seemed he was talking with Larry Arnold and UHS. There were doubtless employer conversations all over town about how to stop our campaign to force for-profit hospitals in Las Vegas to meet the standards we had set at the Catholic hospitals. But Mr. Bell had also just received a huge shot in the arm. Relations between national labor unions and huge corporations are sort of like international diplomacy: you read every little move of those on the other side. And the national SEIU had just sent HCA a clear and unambiguous message: Florida matters to us; Las Vegas does not. Great. With friends like these, who needs enemies? But of course, we had enemies too. They were sitting across the negotiations table and they weren't giving an inch, secure in the belief that the national union was hanging us out to dry.

From the perspective of the workers there was only one way forward, and that was to escalate. We did sticker-ups, marches on the boss, majority petitions, and more. One day all the workers wore roses, in reference to the local CHW hospitals, named the St. Roses. Our organizers and their new rank-and-file leadership team were rocking the house at Sunrise. We had our highest membership levels ever at Sunrise, and a tight structure throughout the hospital, including in the semi-distinct children's hospital, an area that had never before been organized as well as now. And our strategy of aligning the entire market in one year was paying off in spades. The workers at Sunrise knew what they wanted and had the confidence to win it, because they had seen workers at other hospitals pull it off. Fuck the national union.

Who needs a shitty national accord with the boss? We had a real labor movement.

As we neared the expiration date of the old Sunrise contract, the brinksmanship kicked into high gear. We were heading into that legal "window" in which the union can strike and the corporation can pull shenanigans like not collecting union dues. High stakes stuff. In the bargaining-team caucus we had discussed the strategy of not asking for a contract extension when the expiration hit. It would be far better to make the boss ask us for an extension. This was risky, but would send a clear message: we weren't scared. The workers voted not to ask for the extension, and also that if the boss asked for one, we would respond with a demand for an across-the-board raise, to signal to all the workers at the hospital that their union was winning.

The boss blinked first. Jeff Bell called and asked for an extension, and he was ready with his offer: an across-the-board five-percent pay raise. These workers had never had anything of the sort, and they were ecstatic. We extended the contract for one month, and plastered the hospital with flyers calling the raise a "down payment on our future contract!" This gave our momentum inside the hospital a huge boost. Even the employer started referring to the raise as a down payment. Our membership peaked at 72 percent in a hospital with nearly 2,500 workers.

But as the summer wore on, HCA didn't budge. In fact, their positions were hardening. We stickered-up with "Patients Before Profits," no big move for us at that point. Oddly enough, it was this routine sticker-up that finally got my phone to ring. But the call was not from HCA. It was from Judy Scott, head of legal counsel for the national SEIU.

"Jane, that sticker was a violation of the labor peace accord."

"What? We aren't under a labor peace accord."

"Yes you are, Jane. Don't play games with us. There's a peace accord from last winter and you are obligated under it."

"Huh?"

My mind raced through everything I could remember about the accord Larry Fox had negotiated with HCA, which had been invalidated anyway when the arbitrator ruled that HCA had violated its terms during the Florida organizing. Larry had told Sal Rosselli and me that HCA had wanted a labor peace accord that would tie the hands of the California and Nevada locals when it came time to bargain our next HCA contracts.

Sal and I both vetoed the first draft we saw, which was awful. Then Larry got HCA to agree to an election procedure agreement that included the Mountain View hospital workers, and the deal was on. When he'd reported on this success, he had mentioned in passing, "OK, McAlevey, what they will want in return is a softer version of that labor peace accord they originally demanded. But don't worry, we won't give away your right to strike or anything serious." I'd had no problem with this. It was a good trade—we'd bring the last big non-union hospital into the union, adding even more strength to the workers in the balance of power. And I trusted that Larry Fox would never compromise on the fundamental right of workers to engage in a struggle on their own behalf.

"Judy, are you talking about that thing from the old HCA accord, the one that was torn up?"

"Yes."

"You must be kidding."

"No, Jane, why would I be kidding?"

Well gee whiz, how could I count the reasons? I couldn't believe I was even having this conversation. It was like I was stuck in the twilight zone of the labor movement. This call was going nowhere good. I wanted off it and fast.

"Well, Judy, for one thing, no one discussed this with anyone here. That's just for starters. And then after that, let's see. How about it doesn't make a damn bit of sense? But really, I am heading into a meeting right now. I'll get back to you."

"Actually, Jane, you still have to sign a document called the labor peace accord. It's a rider to the national HCA agreement."

"You must be joking. When was I supposed to have signed it? And whoever said that the workers in Nevada would agree to such a piece of paper?"

OK, now it was really time to hang up.

This was just the first of many calls from lawyers at the national union. I ignored them and instead had a long talk with still-recovering-from-his-on-the-plane-to-Vegas-heart-attack Jerry Brown. Jerry advised me to stick to my guns, saying that I should sign only accords that the worker leaders in Nevada had authorized me to sign. This was true, and I always discussed everything of significance with the workers before acting. Back when Larry Fox was negotiating the original accord, I had discussed it with the leaders and they had decided it made sense. Both HCA and its workers got something in Vegas: the Mountain View workers got the right to a fast election procedure, and HCA got a soft sort of labor peace accord with our local that did not take away any of our key mechanisms of worker power, such as the right to strike. None of us—not the worker leaders, not our organizers, and certainly not me—imagined that our national union would eventually restructure a deal with HCA that was supposed to help the workers at Mountain View unionize into an out-right ban on those workers forming a union, while handing HCA a peace accord covering the rest of their Vegas hospitals. But this was apparently what Jim Phillio had signed.

Andy Stern had stripped Larry Fox of his power and handed the HCA accord to Stern's loyal enforcer, who had turned the terms of the accord Fox had negotiated upside down, completely selling out the workers in Nevada. Fox was gone. And Sal Rosselli, the supposed leftist sitting on top of the big local in California, was playing along with Stern. The bitter truth was that the workers in Las Vegas, who had fought so hard to build their union from one of the weakest locals in the nation to a mini powerhouse in a very short time, had nothing left on their side but their own power. And HCA clearly thought that wouldn't be enough to win them anything, which was why the HCA negotiating team had suddenly become so hard-nosed.

Needless to say, I was not looking forward to breaking this news to the workers, but after a week of phone calls from lawyers in Washington, I had no choice. I asked Jessica Foster, our lead organizer at Sunrise hospital, to invite the top leaders, the leaders of the leaders, to my house that night (about sixteen of them). I laid the whole thing out. I explained that the reason HCA was not moving at the negotiations table was because they now had an agreement with our own national union that prohibited us from taking militant action. Militant action? Hell, HCA had our national union telling us we couldn't even do a sticker-up that said, "Patients Before Profits."

"What about the California union? Won't they help us?"

I had to explain that we had to assume Rosselli was working his own deals and wasn't going to lift a finger on our behalf.

Nothing ever demonstrated the sort of union we were building in Nevada better than the response of the sixteen leaders that night. No one was for any sort of compromise. It wasn't that they didn't understand what they were up against, it was just that they were confident in their ability to win this thing, Andy Stern and Sal Rosselli be damned. We agreed that I would refuse to sign the labor peace accord.

I knew that this "committee of sixteen" would have to be fully brought into the running of the show, if their insurrection against their own union was to have a snowball's chance in hell. When the phone in my office rang at the designated time for the next call from the lawyers in Washington, I had some of the Sunrise hospital worker leaders with me in my office.

"Hi Judy, this is Jane. I am putting you on speakerphone so that the worker leaders at HCA Sunrise who are here with me can hear. I believe they have something to tell you."

A cold war between the national SEIU and its Nevada local had officially begun.

It was August; the Sunrise hospital contract extension was near expiration. I told the worker leaders that I did not expect the boss to call this time, and neither should we call them. It was time to escalate. We would set a deadline and drive toward it. In one month the temperature in Vegas would change to beautiful strike weather. And then the next shoe dropped. HCA Sunrise, taking a page from UHS, announced they would no longer collect our dues and political contributions. We would be losing $50,000 a month.

I called DC to let them know that the Hospital Corporation of America, that scumbag corporation they had such a wonderful "working relationship" with, was trying to bankrupt our union. And that it was the actions of the national union, not of the affected workers, that were creating the space for HCA to do it. Then I called Jerry Brown to fill him in. Jerry said he would call Sal Rosselli and "make sure that he doesn't settle his HCA contract before you guys. That way Nevada and California can stand together against HCA no matter what the national office says." Jerry remained convinced that Rosselli was the sort of union leader he made himself out to be.

Within weeks, Rosselli had settled his HCA contract without us and without consulting us in any way. The workers of the Nevada SEIU were on their own.

The worker leaders decided on informational picketing. They were pissed off in that special way you are when those on your own side betray you.

We set the date for picketing and began to mobilize like crazy. We circulated "I will be there" pledges throughout the hospital. Workers were in motion: people like Kay Bins, a Republican, who worked tirelessly to organize and mobilize the radiology department, and Michael McDonald, a surgical technician who read books about Zen Buddhism during meeting breaks, and the first time we asked for his picture for a union bulletin, to be distributed hospital-wide, had us photograph him in front of his Harley Davidson.

And then my phone rang. It was the national union. This time I was told that if we went ahead with the informational picketing they really would trustee our union, no more messing around.

The committee of sixteen decided to stay out of the way of the DC wrecking ball and called off the picket. But they weren't backing down. On the contrary, they were escalating. The national union said they couldn't picket? Fine. They would call a strike vote instead. The national union had not told us we couldn't do that. And we would hold the vote on the day originally designated for the picket. That gave us just 48 hours.

We brainstormed about how to take a strike vote at the hospital on such short notice. HCA would certainly not let us put up ballot boxes. The workers suggested sharp boxes: the hard plastic containers hospitals use for discarded needles. You shove the used needle through the top, and it's designed so that once you put it in you can't get it back out. Every hospital worker knows what a sharp box is. It was perfect for a mobile sealed ballot, and we could get a lot of them right away. Wonderful.

The workers authorized the strike with a 99.4 percent yes vote. Perfect. By the terms specified on the ballot, the workers had authorized their bargaining team to send a picket notice and a strike notice and, before actually walking out, the bargaining team would bring the boss's best offer before all workers for one last vote.

I couldn't imagine that the national union had any more shoes to drop. I was wrong. The day after the strike vote, when the workers were running a sticker-up at the hospital that simply said "99.4%," my phone rang. It was the top lawyer for the national SEIU hospital division.

"Jane, I want you to know I am dead serious about what I am about to say to you. If you continue with the strike discussion at HCA we will put your local union into trusteeship immediately."

I took a deep breath and said, "Well you just go ahead and make my day. I can't wait to have you explain to the entire world that you are now trusteeing local unions because their members have built a tremendous organization and are trying to exercise their most basic right to strike to win a contract. Go ahead and do it. I'm tired. You come to Las Vegas and take over tomorrow, and I will take a nap."

I halfway meant it. I was so done with SEIU at that point that if I could have walked away, I would have. I had been seriously considering it all summer, thought about it long and hard. I had even discussed it with Larry Fox, but he correctly pointed out that if I quit at that point the whole effort to align the market and win meaningful victories with thousands of workers would collapse. There just seemed no way for me to get out of this outfit before we had settled all of the remaining open contracts. Well, maybe the national union was about to solve the problem for me by trusteeing the local because the workers were exercising their right to call a strike.

Then Larry Fox called, and I could tell it was serious, because he was not acting like himself. Larry informed me that the national union had been spitting knives since I had dared them to put our local into trusteeship.

"Jane, they hate you now. Mary Kay Henry called saying you had lost your mind. They were going to remove you and put the national lawyer at the head of your HCA negotiations, but I persuaded them that I should go to Nevada and work with you to settle the contract. I also informed them that they have completely misjudged you and your relationship with the workers, and that removing you would lead to a total disaster in Vegas."

I sat there listening, thinking about all the hard work we had done. Larry asked me to tell the worker leaders that if they would wait to send the strike notice, he would come to Vegas and so would Bob Waterman, the HCA big shot from Nashville who made all the contract decisions for the national corporation, and Gerry McKay, the arbitrator selected by HCA and SEIU to handle any arbitration covered by the national accord. There would be two days of nonstop negotiations to see if we could reach a great contract. If we did, fantastic. If we didn't, I could tell the workers we were back to deciding if we wanted to strike. Larry was clear that this was the local's best option, given that the national union had sold them out and the company knew it. He suggested we could actually make the rift with the national union work in our favor by privately warning HCA about "that crazy McAlevey who might just take the workers out on strike despite SEIU's best attempts to control her."

I called Jessica and asked her to convene the worker leaders at my house that night for an urgent discussion. I repeated to them every detail of my conversation with Larry, and recommended that they take this one last chance to settle. I also told them that I thought they had HCA scared shitless. This lone local in the desert, working in opposition to their own national union, had the top brass from one of the nation's largest health care corporations flying in from Nashville to try to settle a contract with them. The workers agreed to give it a go.

The heavyweights landed in Vegas and the negotiations began, but in a manner I was neither used to nor comfortable with. Gerald McKay, the famous arbitrator, refused to sit down with the workers. I would have to shuttle back and forth between one room with him and another with them. Great.

The workers wanted to meet this McKay character before being effectively sent to their room, and they also wanted to meet Bob Waterman, the big cheese from HCA headquarters. I had met Waterman on several occasions when I worked at the national union, and I knew him to be a smart, funny, and sensible man. And he was a Jew who was surprised that I could crack time-honored jokes with him in Yiddish. Waterman also knew of my role in the Kansas City fight a couple of years back, so I had earned his respect as someone who could beat the odds against big companies.

McKay walked into the room with the workers and immediately took several uncalled-for jabs at me while carelessly insulting the workers. This guy was supposed to be a mediator, but already he was playing the role of bad boss. Waterman behaved like himself, funny and friendly, and essentially acknowledged the power that the workers had built for themselves.

Now the shuffling between rooms began in earnest: Larry Fox, Jeff Bell, Gerald McKay, Bob Waterman, and Sunrise CEO Brian Robinson all playing musical chairs. This could only work because the workers trusted me, and I in turn trusted Larry Fox. Larry had also met some of our workers back in 2003, and they sensed that he was a principled guy. In fact, Larry is almost uniquely principled at the level he plays in the labor movement.

Not a lot of productive stuff happened on that first day. Nerves were fraying. Fox was getting snippy with me, and I was starting to lose it with him. But the next morning the HCA team arrived and caved on almost every major issue within hours. Apparently Bob Waterman had seen enough. He had heard from his managers about how the union had become so thoroughly mobilized that his employees had made his hospital unmanageable, and then on the first day of bargaining he had seen how tightly organized and militant the members of our team were. Big-shot corporate leaders think their own time is valuable, and he wasn't going to waste his banging his head against the wall our union had become.

For starters, every worker at Sunrise would be immediately placed on the CHW wage scale. This meant huge raises. The average wage increase for the 2,500 workers at Sunrise would be 17.2 percent, effective in the first pay period after contract ratification. Then came fully employer-paid family health care, better call pay, their first weekend pay differential, and improved shift differentials. It was literally everything we had won at the CHW hospitals except for pensions and nurse-to-patient staffing ratios, but the workers had long understood that before we could even hope to win pensions or strong ratios from HCA, our union would have to organize more HCA hospitals.

There was one last issue, one that was very important to Melanie Sisson, the old-guard member of our local's executive board who Jerry Brown had immediately flagged to me as trouble when he had started the HCA negotiations, before his heart attack grounded him. Melanie insisted that we continue to fight for "part-time FMLA," the right of a part-time worker to invoke the Family Medical Leave Act to take off, say, one day per week to care for a sick parent and still get paid. This was unknown in Las Vegas. The full-time workers at Sunrise already had paid FMLA leave, and even that was unusual—in essence, it made the promise of FMLA real for the lower-wage workers. HCA had come into negotiations saying that one of their top bargaining priorities was to eliminate this benefit, which no other workers in Vegas—or in their entire company nationwide—had. To HCA, it was an expensive aberration, but it was really good for the workers, and it was just, so we made a priority of holding onto it and we did. Now Melanie insisted that we actually expand it to include part-time employees. It was important to her personally because she was about to go part-time at Sunrise, enabling her to take more shifts at the CHW hospitals, where workers were flocking to take advantage of our extraordinary CHW contracts. I thought it was a long shot, but long shot seemed to be the game we were playing. And I naïvely hoped that if we pulled a win on "Melanie's issue," it would make her happier with her contract, and with me.

I told Larry we needed to go back and win this one last thing. Larry wasn't interested.

"Fox, come on, let me at least try. Let me into that room with those guys and you play me as a crazy loon and I will say you give us this one last thing and we will all be done here."

Larry was pissed, but he agreed, all the while telling me it was a tremendous overreach, that we had already won more in terms of real money than Sal Rosselli and his much bigger local had in their settlements with HCA, and that I shouldn't insist on this. Down the hall the two of us went.

When I walked in, Fox gave them a look that told them he thought I was out of my mind. McKay, the allegedly neutral arbitrator, immediately blurted out, "We are done, Jane, take it or leave it." I couldn't stand him. I replied slowly and carefully, my eyes trained on Waterman.

"I have one more serious issue before I can get the workers to officially turn down their strike option."

Within a minute, they caved. Fox couldn't believe it. He would later come back to that moment again and again when carrying on about the power the workers in Las Vegas had built and how scared the employer was of them.

CHAPTER TWELVE

Strike! Victory at Universal Health Services, Victory in the Public Sector

While the struggle at Sunrise hospital was unfolding, our local was also fighting to get Chris G elected in the County Commission primary. Her district was a Democratic Party stronghold, where a win in August generally meant a win in November. But according to Nevada election law, if no opposing-party candidate is on the November ballot, the general election becomes a run-off between the two candidates who polled highest in the primary. We calculated that Chris G would place first and that the runner-up would be the incumbent, Myrna Williams, whose opposition to a good contract for county employees was the reason our local had thrown so much into the race. Both the carpenters' and casino workers' unions had endorsed Williams, because she was an incumbent Democrat and hey, carpenters and casino workers didn't have to negotiate contracts for their members with the county.

The only way to avoid this was to ensure that there would be a Republican nominee. If the final day for nominations arrived and no Republican had filed, we had a member who was a Republican ready to go. Then, if Chris G won the primary, she'd face a Republican in the general election who wouldn't campaign. And if she lost the primary, we could actually run our Republican member against Williams. Of course, we would only win if we caught Williams with her hand in the cookie jar or bags of cash in her car trunk—but how hard could that be in Vegas, right? Either way, we figured we had outsmarted a system designed to protect incumbents.

Our revitalized local was, as we would say, "in it to win it." We had members walk Chris G's precincts multiple times a week, all through the summer heat. We put up the money for a huge mail campaign about how Myrna Williams had been working with big developers to carve up neighborhoods to favor her donors. We scanned our member lists for Republicans and launched a blitz to get every Republican SEIU member to switch parties just for the primary. This worked well, because we facilitated their return to their party of choice by having each fill in *two* new voter forms, the first to switch to Democratic for the primary, and we gave them the second form so they could switch back the day after.

Chris G was a great candidate. She had charisma, smarts and tenacity, and she was genuinely pro-union and progressive. In the press, the story line surrounding the election was that Chris G and the new SEIU were the bellwethers of a major change in the political landscape of southern Nevada: this was the second time in two years that our local was backing a potentially successful challenge to a bad democrat in the primary system for the County Commission. The press attention was great for momentum with workers, but it also put us squarely on the radar of the Nevada power elite, who had decidedly mixed feelings about our upstart union. They definitely liked the new money and volunteer hours SEIU was bringing to Nevada Democrats, but they wanted to dictate the sort of candidates these resources would support. Challenging incumbents in Democratic primaries was not what they had in mind.

Then, just before the August primary, the Clark County manager, Tom Reilly, suddenly resigned. This was a big break for us, as Reilly was a smart administrator committed to saving County money by shedding our members and replacing them with a contingency workforce. The commission quickly replaced Reilly with Virginia Valentine, Clark County's first female county manager. Valentine reached out to me right away for dinner and drinks. She couldn't have possibly set a more different tone from her predecessor's, and we went on to enjoy a decent relationship.

Chris G won her primary. So we shifted our entire political operation into another County Commission race, backing Susan Braeger, who was also being supported by the cops' and casino workers' and other unions. The seat was in a district that had long been safe for the Republican incumbent but was slowly trending toward greater parity between the parties. Every single union in Vegas was in that race, backing Braeger.

We convened the master joint negotiations table for the county hospital and civil service twice during this period, but we knew nothing major was going to happen before the general election. After lots of workers spoke and everyone got back in touch with how big and united we were, I told everyone I would see them in November.

Just as we were settling the contract with HCA at Sunrise, Universal Health Services fired a union activist from Desert Springs. That kind of boss-fight escalation is very scary for the workers. They are struggling for better job conditions, and the possibility that they could end up losing their jobs entirely because of those efforts definitely makes them think twice and even three times. But if organizing has been strong, that fear will turn to anger.

Right on the heels of the first firing, UHS sacked another nurse, this time from Valley hospital. Joan Wells was a union rock star from Valley's ICU, among our top worker leaders in Vegas, and a member of our executive board. She had been a nurse for a long time, she was a true expert at her trade, and her coworkers loved her. She was also absolutely fearless, which was one reason why she was increasingly the face of the union at Valley as UHS was ratcheting up the heat. She was a natural at conveying the justice of what the nurses wanted to the broader public, and she had a perfect human resources record, with nothing but star evaluations for years, which made it difficult for the employer to retaliate against her. Until they did.

Just before she was fired, she had appeared at a press conference along with a number of local politicians to announce the launch of a new website our local had created. The site compared all the available statistics about quality of care at local hospitals, and a quick look at the data made it clear as day that if you were sick in Las Vegas, you wanted to go anywhere except one run by UHS. We'd also recently held a press conference to unveil our new enormous "Patients Before Profits" billboard with Joan's picture on it, set up just down the road from Valley Hospital by Interstate 15, Vegas's main traffic artery.

Several days before she was fired, Joan arrived at Valley just as the day shift nurses were being informed by their manager that the hospital was going to "work them short," meaning with high nurse-to-patient ratios, one nurse to three, maybe even four patients in the ICU, where good hospitals keep the nurse-to-patient ratio at one to two and often one to one. That is the whole point of an *intensive care* unit, which is full of patients balancing on the edge of life and death. I have spoken with nurses around the country who simply didn't believe me when I told them the UHS hospitals in Vegas worked one nurse to three patients in their ICUs, even four patients to one nurse on occasion.

This sort of short staffing was a big priority for us in the contract negotiations, and on this particular morning the nurses huddled in a break room and decided to refuse to work under what they considered dangerous conditions. The management had no choice but to call in more nurses. Despite her incredible strength, she was devastated. She had no interest in playing celebrity or martyr. She just wanted to be a good nurse.

UHS had thrown down the gauntlet. When the employer starts firing workers for their union work, either the union steps right up to the plate that very minute, or it immediately starts to die. As Jerry Brown had coached me for a couple of years now, it was time to create a crisis by creating a deadline. We were now well into the fall. We had won every campaign of the year thus far. The public sector workers were in great shape, because we were on track to change the County Commission in November. The time to win at UHS was now, and we didn't waste a minute. With the HCA contracts settled, I was returning to be the closer at UHS. Shortly thereafter, UHS bargaining teams decided that on November 17 the workers would vote to accept or reject the best offer the employer had made. And if the management's final offer was rejected by a majority of the workers, the second question on the ballot would kick in, which was they would vote on whether to authorize a strike. I sent a letter to the employer informing them that we had just three more negotiating sessions planned and that the workers had decided to vote the contracts up or down on November 17. The horse was saddled up. All that was left to do was get on and ride.

After we won the contract we had wanted at HCA Sunrise, a fight the national union had demanded that we give up, our relationship with DC was, um, not an easy one. It didn't help that over the past twelve months I'd been called away to attend national meetings in which we would debate things like Andy Stern's discovery that the word union didn't poll well. The word worker didn't poll well either. I sat through serious discussions about how if we just changed SEIU's name and stopped saying worker and union, we could organize more you-know-whats into a bigger you-know-what. Fortunately we were so crazy busy in Nevada that I escaped the worst of it. I even skipped the big June 2006 kick-off conference for our new national health-care whatever-the-name-finally-was-that-wasn't-"union."*

And now here we were again, our little Nevada local looking down the barrel of a strike. Once more: Whether you actually strike or not, for a strike threat to be credible you have to really be ready to do it. Organization is key, and after organization comes resources. Strike funds are one of the most important things a national union provides to a local, and one of the main reasons every worker contributes a portion of their dues to the national union. I mean at least this was the theory of labor at some point. So I was keeping Washington fully informed of the situation with UHS, the upcoming strike vote, and our looming need for strike funds.

SEIU had two distinct strike funds. The one run by the national union is quite small, a pittance really, reflecting the fact that strikes are simply not part of the Andy Stern playbook. The second, much larger fund was a holdover from the old national hospital workers' union, District 1199, before they merged with SEIU back in 1989. At the time, the District 1199 leaders conditioned the merger on being allowed to retain control over their strike fund. Not every SEIU local had access to this fund. You had to commit to it in advance and pay in a higher contribution per worker per year than was required for the smaller DC fund. Our membership had approved exactly this when they passed the big dues increase in April. In the lead-up to that vote, we held lots of worker dis-cussions on how when you work in the private sector the strike is your ultimate weapon, and to use it, or even threaten to use it, the workers must have access to a real strike fund. The April ballot had included a question about joining the more secure 1199 fund, which our members overwhelmingly approved.

---

* The new name is Healthcare United!

But then the bullshit started all over again. I got a call from Washington informing me that I had to talk to Dennis Rivera, the powerful leader of the huge local based in New York City, before I could access the national union strike fund, and I needed access to both funds to take 1,000 nurses out on strike. What the fuck? There came that feeling in the pit of my stomach again. Something was clearly up. Why did I have to talk to Dennis?

I had enormous respect for Dennis Rivera, a tough, experienced union leader with a long history. He was in New York City and I was in Nevada, so we weren't close, but neither was there any tension between us. He knew something of my work, and most importantly he knew that our local in right-to-work-for-less Nevada was third only to his local in New York City and Rosselli's Oakland-based local (both in union-security states) for having the highest percentage of workers voluntarily contributing to our political funds in the healthcare division. That is the sort of thing that impresses Dennis, and for good reason.

Andy Stern had just created a big position in the national union for Rivera: chair of *Healthcare United!* (first in the contest to name a union without calling it a union, complete with the exclamation point because apparently exclamation points polled well). This was classic Stern. It surely indicated that he was preparing some sort of internal power play that required buttering up Rivera and bringing him closer in. When he needed people, he would invent posts with important-sounding names for them. And when he didn't need them he would boot them out of power so smoothly it took them a while to even notice what had happened. I called it the Andy Stern yo-yo effect.

On the appointed time and day I got the call that had been set up with Dennis, but when I picked up the phone the guy on the other end was Jim Phillio, the one Stern had brought in to cut the deal with HCA that sold out our workers in Nevada for some crumbs in Florida. There goes that stomach feeling again. Soon Rivera joined us on the line and—to sum up—says:

"Oh, Jane. Hi there. So, I hear you are having a hard time getting a contract out there. Listen, here's what you need to do, you need to just think harder about a few compromises and then just settle with the hospitals. OK? I mean, look, strikes are really hard, and I think you are just not working hard enough to find points of agreement with the employer.

We do this in New York City all the time, you know. Like you are doing now. You threaten them, get the workers rallying and such, and then you just settle the contract. Why don't you try that before we talk about accessing the strike fund, OK? Thanks."

I hung up and actually began to cry. I just couldn't believe that a guy who sat on top of a local with 200,000 longtime members who had union security in the powerful unionized bastion of New York had just lectured me on how we were missing an opportunity to settle. And said we couldn't access the strike fund until we had pursued that settlement to his satisfaction. What planet was I on? Our local had been winning groundbreaking contract after groundbreaking contract in right-to-work Nevada and I was being told that now I was to do just what they did in New York City?

I gathered my wits and phoned Eliseo Medina, who as SEIU's executive vice president for the South-Southwest was my immediate superior.

"Medina, it's McAlevey. Listen, I just had a call with Dennis Rivera and, well, I need to fly to wherever you are right away and meet with you. I can fly to Texas, Los Angeles, wherever you are. Where will you be in the next few days where you have a little time?"

"What do we need to talk about?"

"It's time to plan my exit. This is ridiculous. The employer hasn't made an offer that's even close to acceptable. There is no point of compromise. There is no union left in the contract they want us to sign. There is no 'signal to settle' I missed. I am not having some crazy strike fantasy like Washington thinks. I am fighting an employer that just succeeded in busting the union at two California Nurses Association hospitals in California. I want out."

Eliseo agreed that dudes from the highly unionized Northeast don't always understand what we're up against in the Wild West, and promised to meet me in Los Angeles in a couple of weeks. Until then, he advised me, I was not to lose my cool. Actually, I hadn't lost my cool on the call with Rivera. I had been too flabbergasted.

Fortunately, things were moving so fast on the ground in Las Vegas I had no time to sit around fretting about the national union. And it was in our interest to push even faster, because our members at the hospitals were getting worn down. Working at the UHS hospitals was always hard because of the short staffing, but Brent Yessin and his goons made things much, much worse, and they'd been dug in at those hospitals for ten months. Every day Yessin's gang wrote up negative evaluations on good nurses and techs. Pro-union workers were under constant surveillance, and their managers actually followed them around the hospital, inventing reasons to write them up. It is not a pretty situation when you have been a great nurse for twenty years and suddenly a file is created that sets you up to be fired. The nurses were also being denied days off, use of vacation time and even permission to leave the facilities at lunchtime to run whatever errands nurses try to fit in during a 12-hour shift. Their jobs had become so grinding that employees were starting to talk about quitting—not the union but the hospital. This is not the sort of thing that people who are drawn to nursing think they are signing up for. Management had turned Desert Springs and Valley into war zones.

Catholic Healthcare West was about to open their third Las Vegas hospital. And as part of the gold standard contract we had settled earlier in the year, we had won organizing-by-accretion rights in our contract settlement. The terms were that we had to sign up a majority of the workers in the new hospital and it would be covered by the same agreement. We had explained to the workers at the time of settlement that the workers themselves would have to do 100 percent of the work to sign up and build the new union because there wouldn't be any staff available—and because we knew they were more than capable of this. We had won the model new employee orientation language. The worker leaders were averaging 90 percent sign-up at each new employee orientation. The leaders from the existing two hospitals were getting competitive about which one of them could sign up the most new hires. It was rather remarkable, really, but we were so busy with the UHS wars this model worker organizing program practically gets lost in this story. The union at the new hospital was built entirely on nurse-to-nurse, worker-to-worker organizing. And now nurses burned out by the labor wars at UHS facilities—including some of our longtime leaders there—were considering jumping ship to the soon-to-open third CHW hospital, where they would enjoy the best hospital working conditions in Nevada.

Nancy De Jovin, a veteran leader in the ICU at Desert Springs, announced she was doing just that. Nancy's move was particularly telling. She was a tenacious fighter at the core of the battle for a union at the UHS hospitals and she had been a pillar of her ICU. When I'd first met Nancy a few years back, I asked her why she put up with the awful working conditions at UHS. She said what nurses often say when they have a bad employer: "I love my team, Jane. I love everyone I work with, we are like a family, I have been sitting in the break room with this great crew of nurses for so long I don't ever want to leave them." Now, she was outta there.

This, no doubt, was Yessin's goal: to create a sense of futility until people just wanted out. So we urged them to stay. Essentially we were asking them to make a sacrifice for the good of all the hospital workers in the city. The great contracts we had won at other hospitals could not be sustained if those hospitals had to compete with others nearby with significantly lower labor costs. And UHS was the fastest-growing hospital employer in southern Nevada. Eventually they would drag down the rest of the state if we couldn't get them to the market standard. Our ace card was the fact that the workers at Sunrise had just won nearly the same economic package the workers at CHW hospitals enjoyed, and if our tired leaders at the UHS hospitals stayed and fought they could have those same conditions right where they were.

There is no doubt that without our big win at Sunrise we could never have held the supermajority memberships we had at Valley and Desert Springs, but we did. At one point we actually made a deal with a group of key Valley and Desert Springs workers, promising them that the union would support their departure for another hospital after the fight with UHS had been won. It was quite a sacrifice—the kind these hospital workers had been making for months.

During our planning sessions, the workers brought up the purple RV we had borrowed for the campaign against the decert at Desert Springs, and spoke of how powerful they'd felt when we were running the workers' organization 24/7 on the sidewalks just outside the workplace. So I added a purple RV to my list of requests to DC, only this time we would need two, one for each UHS hospital. Access to the RVs proved easier than access to the DC strike fund, and in a few days they appeared.

Our nurses were in the news practically every day with one clever action after the next. We filed thirty-seven complaints of patient abuse with the Nevada Department of Health. The nurses described in detail having to leave UHS patients in their own feces because there was too little staff there to clean them all, and how bedsores were a growing problem because the patients weren't being turned often enough. And then there was our website, comparing quality of care among Nevada hospitals. Each one of these stories was big news in Las Vegas. It never ceased to amaze me that stories of overburdened nurses literally breaking their backs got no attention at all, but the moment a nurse on television said "feces" or "bedsores" there was an outpouring of public sympathy and anger. But we'd take it.

Las Vegas has a rich history of casino strikes, but the city had never once seen a hospital strike. Nurses are not casino workers. Polls consistently show that Americans view nurses and firefighters as the most trustworthy of all professionals. And our nurses were known to the community, having been all over the local news for two years, at pickets and rallies, reporting on the quality of care at area hospitals, and walking precincts for candidates. Of course, hospital strikes also have a particular edge to them because of the kinds of services that are interrupted. As D Taylor of the casino workers once put it, when his union went on strike, people didn't get their cocktails; when our union struck, people didn't get health care. That's an oversimplification, since his members sustain by far the most important industry in Vegas. But in terms of the public's reaction to nurses walking out of hospitals versus cocktail waitresses walking out of casinos, he was absolutely right.

At the UHS negotiations table, nothing was happening. The federal mediators (by now there were more than one) had given up. The area's politicians were getting antsy. The first call I received was from Oscar Goodman, Mayor of Las Vegas.

Goodman was not only the mayor of Las Vegas, he was also the city's most famous mafia lawyer, though he personally preferred the term "mob lawyer." In his early career he had represented more mafia figures, and kept more of them out of jail, than any other attorney. Remember what I have been saying about Las Vegas being the Wild West? And frankly, in a town like this, when a powerful mob lawyer who also happens to be mayor calls to offer his help, the workers are delighted to hear from him. The guy had poll ratings that would make any politician green with envy—approval in the 75 percent range. Most of Vegas had come to the conclusion that they would rather have him than some guy who talks an ethical line while accepting bag money from the trunks of cars. Better to have Mayor Goodman, who puts it all out front and walks around town with a Vegas showgirl on each arm.

Oscar Goodman was a New York Jew and proud of it. He'd never lost his accent, even though he'd been in Vegas since the Rat Pack first showed up. He and I got on famously right off the bat. One time in his presence I referred to a local boss as a schmuck and the mayor raised his eyebrows at me as if to say, "Goyim can't use our words, shiksa." Mayor Goodman has a way of sticking to the facts as he invents them and ignoring those that don't fit his story line, and I mean that in the best way. I remember the first time I went to the Bali Jai, a legendary golf course and club at the south end of the Strip, for the annual fundraiser of the ACLU. (If you use your imagination, you can probably come up with many reasons why the ACLU would have lots of well-heeled patrons in Vegas. You might begin with the right to freely advertise the sex industry.) I had met the mayor maybe twice before. I had just walked into a very large room and from all the way across it came his bellowing voice: "Hey, everyone be quiet! Quiet please! I want you all to meet the new union leader in town. Her name is Jane and she is a NURSE and I hope you all get to know her!"

Schmuck would be one of the kinder Yiddish words for the boss at the ambulance company that had tried to decertify us when I first arrived in Vegas. They had once been called Mercy Ambulance and had a good reputation as a well-run company, but when they were bought by the big conglomerate AMR, the service fell to pieces.

AMR did what all the health-care corporations do in Nevada—milked their Vegas cash cow to feed the parent corporation. When we hit a brick wall in contract negotiations with them, we sent a delegation of EMTs and paramedics to brief the mayor on conditions at the company: old rigs, ambulances that broke down, and, most important, poor response time—according to our research, below federally established norms on something like eight out of every ten calls. If you want to see the mayor of Las Vegas get angry, tell him his constituents are being screwed by a wealthy out-of-state corporation. As soon as the workers left, he was on the phone: "Jane, get to my office." That's how the mayor was, and I appreciated it. No time to chat, get right to the point.

Over at his office I gave him a quick briefing on how the workers had been trying to get a first union contract for well over a year at that point and we couldn't even get the boss to the negotiating table, despite the NLRB ruling them in violation of labor law and ordering them to start negotiations. He replied by asking me for the name and phone number for the head of HR—the top vice president for Human Resources nationally, not the local guy. When I asked him what he planned to say, his response was pure Goodman.

"Jane, how dare you? I am the most successful mob lawyer in the nation and you think you need to brief me for this call? You leave my office and let me know as soon as this vice president calls you. Make sure you report back to me and that's an order."

The next morning, before 9 am even rolled around, AMR's VP for Human Resources called me on his cell phone to say he wanted to get "several negotiation dates right away so we can get a contract done." I would love to know exactly what the fine mayor of Las Vegas said to this guy, but that isn't my realm. The workers won their first contract shortly thereafter.

I had made it a practice to take nurses and other workers with me to whatever social confabs of the Vegas power elite I was invited to. As the UHS fight escalated, the nurse in tow was usually Joan Wells, our union rock star and billboard celebrity fired by UHS from Valley hospital. At one fundraiser, Joan made a particularly nice connection with the mayor's wife, who by the end of the evening was decidedly unhappy that UHS was firing nurses. Soon enough, my cell phone rang, while I was in negotiations.

"Jane, this is the mayor. I want you in my office first thing tomorrow morning. We need to settle this hospital dispute. It's ridiculous. I will not tolerate emergency rooms in my city shut down over a dispute with the nurses. I want you prepared and in my office, and I am summoning the UHS negotiators and top Nevada guys too. Can you be here?"

"Of course I will be there, Mayor, but I want to warn you, this is not going to be easy..."

"Yes, Jane, you told me that the last time we did this. I know what I am doing and I will see you tomorrow morning."

"Well OK, hot shot," I thought to myself, "you go." But I wasn't sure Goodman quite understood whom he was dealing with in UHS. In fact, I was reminded of the phone conversation with Dennis Rivera. In both cases I was talking with a very powerful man who assumed that he could just brush aside obstacles a little girl like me couldn't budge.

I arrived in the lobby of the mayor's office the next morning to find the top UHS guy in Nevada sitting in the lobby with hired guns Larry Arnold and Rick Albert. It was almost as bad as being locked in the elevator with Brent Yessin. I got my next surprise when we were ushered inside to find not only the mayor but also County Commission chair Rory Reid, the son of Senator Harry Reid. The meeting kicked off with lots of small talk, and then the mayor asked why we couldn't reach settlement. I explained that we weren't asking UHS to agree to anything that the other Vegas hospitals hadn't already agreed to. I had even brought those other contracts with me. I said that the entire situation could be resolved if the UHS guys in the room would simply sign their names to the same contract as either the Healthcare Corporation of America or Catholic Healthcare West had signed, their choice. The UHS guys responded by talking about the intimidation charges they had filed against me. Good grief.

After more than half an hour it was clear the meeting was producing nothing but rancor, and the mayor brought it to a close. I lingered, and when the UHS guys were gone I asked Reid and Goodman why they hadn't pressed harder. They both said it was more than clear that UHS didn't have any plans to move. "Aha," I thought to myself. "Maybe you could call my own national union and let them in on that keen observation."

I left the meeting feeling that nothing good had come of it, and maybe even a little bit of damage, as Reid had become defensive when I commented to him afterward that it was past time for powerful people in Vegas to put some pressure on UHS. But I had misread how deeply insulting the two politicians had found the UHS team's behavior. They were not used to being treated the way they had been in that meeting, even by representatives of powerful corporations. By the end of the day, they had their wheels in motion.

D Taylor called me to tell me that the political establishment was abuzz about the meeting at the mayor's office, where the union presented simple solutions that UHS had rebuffed. Taylor is the man most politicians in town call if they want to know what's going on in labor, whether their question deals with the casino workers union or not. That is just how Nevada is. It's a tight club and it takes years to join. I was still a newbie by the norms of insider politics here. Plus, our local wasn't playing by the rules, in that we were running our own people in Democratic primaries. This was November, and both candidates we had backed had just won resounding victories in the County Commission races, changing the southern Nevada political landscape.

The final negotiating session opened with Larry Arnold screaming. "*You, Jane,* will be leading the employees to take a strike vote tomorrow, so why are we even sitting here?"

"Larry, we are waiting for a contract offer, something real, something that in some way resembles the other settlements in Vegas, anything that might show you are willing to treat your nurses and techs with the same respect they get at every other hospital in town."

He was the most exhausting asshole I have ever had to deal with. He said he was ready to offer the same wages as CHW, and tossed his proposals across the fifteen-foot expanse separating our tables so that they scattered all over. We took a caucus to read the papers and quickly saw that he was lying. The wage package was not the same as CHW's, and nothing else in what he called his comprehensive counterproposal had changed. You could feel the chill spreading in the room. This was it. There were no more negotiations. We were taking a strike vote the next day. If the employer was ever going to budge, this would have been the time. And they hadn't moved an inch.

The purple RVs were in position. Ballots were being printed. I was busy preparing summaries of Arnold's final offer. I then paired these with the workers' own proposals and similar sections of the HCA and CHW contracts. All this would be distributed with the ballots so the workers could make the most informed vote possible. Our union hall was in full battle dress. Workers and organizers were everywhere, coming and going, hanging off the rafters. The war room was in chaos. All hands were on deck.

The polls opened for voting at our two RVs at 6 am. We had reassigned staff from HCA so that now Jessica Foster was the lead organizer at Valley Hospital, and Morgan Levi at Desert Springs. We knew we would win the strike vote; the question was how many nurses would turn out for it. We needed overwhelming participation, because this vote was not about presenting the employer with a "credible threat." In all likelihood, these workers were actually going to walk off the job at a hospital for the first time in the history of Vegas.

By the end of the day we had the numbers. Of those voting, 98 percent had rejected the boss's final offer and 95.6 percent had voted to strike. At both hospitals, it was the Filipina leaders who'd delivered the biggest voter turn-out. Two years of work trying to bring them and the white nurses together had paid off. With all the young staff organizers and workers in the room, I declared the vote a tremendous victory. But inside I was sick to my stomach, because I knew the total number of ballots was insufficient. Only 75 percent of the workers had voted. A solid majority, but we needed more than that to sustain a real strike. And we had worked our asses off to get every possible ballot returned. Morgan and Jessica had stayed up all night doing something we call a name-by-name, assessing the status of every worker who hadn't come to one of the strike RVs to vote. By morning they were able to report a real support level of 86 percent. But it was only November 19. Allowing time for the legal notices and other preliminaries, the strike couldn't begin until December 3. The boss would peel off some of our numbers in the meantime, no question about it.

Larry Fox and Jerry Brown had taught me that you wanted to be at 90 percent on strike vote day. Heading into a strike with less than 80 percent was dangerous. I was starting to flip out, but I didn't share any of this with anyone, not even Morgan or Jessica. I told them we would be fine if they could hold the hospitals to a real 80 percent, and confidently told them, "Go make it happen," just as I always did.

For the next week we ran a test every day that produced numbers we could assess. The first test was having the workers sign up for picketing shifts. After that we had workers file strike-pay forms. The 1199 strike fund had sent us a formal letter pledging $15 million toward worker pay, which sounds like an awful lot, but given the number of workers involved and the fact that many were highly skilled nurses, it wasn't. Nurses were holding fundraisers. We set up an internal pledge system, asking our members at other hospitals to "adopt a striker" and pledge a certain amount of money to the person's family. We ordered port–o-potties, food, water. We lined up solidarity pledges from other unions. We sent some nurses to brief local politicians and others to speak on television and radio. Everywhere you looked in Vegas, there were nurses.

But as the days ticked down, we began to fall below 80 percent. Management was on a tear, running captive audience meetings and one-on-ones in which they claimed that every single worker was going to be fired forever. They seemed to be putting out a new leaflet every hour, claiming that the union was planning to get violent and would force its members to go to jail. They were calling in the Filipina nurses and telling them that if they walked out they would lose their work visas and be deported.

I had been talking to Jerry and Larry nearly every day, and we all agreed that we needed a major Plan B. This started to materialize when Mary Kay Henry called from DC to say she was coming to Vegas to try to get D Taylor to engage more in trying to force a settlement. She had as good a relationship with D Taylor as anyone at the national SEIU, though that wasn't saying much. He started every meeting with me by telling me how much he hated absolutely everything about Andy Stern. I would just say, "OK, D, I hear you. I am not Andy Stern. Can you and I get down to the business of our meeting?" My own relationship with Mary Kay had been severely damaged by the HCA sellout just two months before. I didn't trust her and she didn't trust me, which was a big part of why I had flown to Los Angeles to tell Medina I would be leaving the union and that he needed to start making a plan for how the Nevada local would work without me. I didn't know if he had mentioned this to Mary Kay. In the weird leadership scene around Andy Stern, you never knew who told what to whom among the top players. Each had a separate empire and distinct group of confidants. After what the national union had just done to the local at the height of the HCA battle, I had to wonder what Mary Kay was coming to tell me: that we couldn't strike, or that the national union had cut a deal with UHS, or who knows what.

Mary Kay landed and went off to meet with D Taylor. She was different from the endless rows of guys back east who simply hadn't believed that this company wouldn't settle—by the time she landed in Vegas, she knew that UHS was out to kill the union. And, importantly, SEIU had no national agreement with UHS that would complicate our striking. I joined her and D a couple of hours later, and found they'd hatched a smart plan: get the incoming Republican governor to call on both the union and the employer to agree to a thirty-day cooling-off period. This would be a brilliant move if we could pull it off, since our numbers were starting to fall and there was no good way out of an immediate strike otherwise. And if UHS did what we expected them to do and turned the governor down, then technically we would no longer be in a strike but in a lockout, and the rules governing what the boss can and can't do in a lockout are much better. You can win a lockout with 80 percent. And we thought we might actually get the governor to do it, in part because UHS had so badly offended Nevada's political leadership.

Harry Reid, who had just been elected majority leader of the US Senate, had been a big supporter of our nurses all along. He met with us frequently, and we worked together to protect the public hospital, of which he was a leading proponent. Now he was angry because UHS had pissed off his son Rory. Well, if you wanted to write a political to-do list for what *not* to do in Nevada, it would be to piss off US Senator and now Majority Leader Harry Reid, Rory Reid, who was chair of the County Commission, and Oscar Goodman, mayor of Las Vegas. I had been telling all of them, "So, if UHS won't take calls from the newly elected US Senate Majority leader, do you think they have been listening to their nurses?"

The new governor was no friend of unions, and getting him to make common cause with Democrats by laying strictures on a corporation that donated heavily to Republicans was hardly a sure thing. Fortunately, UHS hadn't yet given much money out in Nevada, and the governor had barely squeaked into office. He was also fighting off a major scandal in the press involving an accusation that he had gotten drunk at a local steakhouse and followed a female patron into the parking garage, where he'd tried to force her to have sex with him. Kind of embarrassing for a Mormon politician, even a Nevada one.

Our challenge was to make all of this happen in forty-eight hours. It was now late on Friday. We would need to get the call from the governor by Sunday morning so I could take the offer to the workers for a decision before the strike began. I made it clear to everyone that the workers would make the decision, not me.

I called Jerry at about 7 am his time Saturday to report the plan, which he emphatically supported. But he added a caution:

"You will have the most difficult meeting of your life with the workers. You have spent the past month, and especially the past two weeks, revving the entire place up to be ready to strike, and most people are ready to strike, only not enough—most is not enough. This will be the ultimate test of your leadership. You know what the right decision is, but they have to make it. You will actually have to lead at some point in the mass meeting you need to call."

Late Saturday night Barbara Buckley, the speaker of the Nevada Assembly, phoned to say that I would receive a call first thing in the morning from the governor's chief of staff asking me to agree to the cooling-off period. I explained, to her intense annoyance, that I would be delighted to take the call but that our actual decision would have to be made at an emergency mass meeting of the workers.

I hung up and dialed Morgan and Jessica.

"Listen, you two, don't ask me any questions, and don't call anyone tonight. But be ready to have every organizer in the union working first thing in the morning to convene an emergency meeting of all the nurses and techs at the hall. It has to happen by noon. You can't call them till morning, but make your plan now for how you will get everyone who is not at work to the union hall in time."

Did I sound like Larry or Jerry or what? And Morgan and Jessica answered me as I would have answered my mentors: "Got it."

Just after 9 am I received the promised call. Immediately afterward, I called Morgan.

"Here we go. The governor is proposing a thirty-day cooling off period and has pledged to directly intervene to help us reach settlement. Get every single nurse in here who isn't working. *Go Morgy go!*"

Morgy was what I called her when I was either very happy or very nervous—and at that moment, I was both. Morgan and Jessica were mostly relieved. I didn't have time to tell them how hard I thought the meeting would be. By the time the nurses began arriving, all three major television stations were outside with satellite hookups, and their reporters were trying to grab nurses going into the hall for comment. The parking lot was a full-on scene.

The meeting ran for three hours. I congratulated the workers for bringing the state of Nevada to a standstill, and people began chanting and clapping and cheering. But as soon as I outlined the offer that we call off the strike for thirty days, the activists in the crowd began to chant, "*Strike! Strike! Strike!*" The chant would periodically erupt throughout the meeting. Now someone shouted out, "This is the first bad advice you have ever given us, Jane—you can't really think we should accept this." But I hadn't given any opinion yet. The workers needed to own this decision or nothing would work.

The workers who dominated the first hour all spoke passionately about how we needed to strike. Then some of the real leaders began to speak. They began simply to ask questions: "Well, the truth is, I am hearing from so-and-so that she might not walk out tomorrow. What do we do then?"

After another hour of tense debate, in which the most extreme activists were yelling at the real leaders, someone finally stood up and questioned me.

"OK, we have heard from each other for two hours. Jane, we have not heard from you. I want to know what you think we should do."

The room dropped dead silent. Even the staff didn't know my thoughts.

"So, who here thinks this company is going to accept the governor's request?"

Many voices shouted back, "Not me! Not me!"

"So, how do you think this company will appear to the political elite, and to the press, and to the public if the nurses agree to a cooling-off period out of respect for their patients and the incoming governor, and the boss doesn't?"

At once a whole slew of people stood and shouted a motion to accept the governor's offer, and it overwhelmingly passed. I asked everyone to stay indoors, because the press was swarming outside and I needed to inform the governor, the speaker, and County Commissioner Reid of the decision before we spoke to the media. Fifteen minutes later we held an enormous press conference, with our top nurse leaders on the air in scrubs, accepting the governor's offer. Less than an hour later UHS formally announced they were rejecting it.

The boss is always the best organizer.

That was pretty much the end for UHS politically in Nevada at that point. There simply wasn't anyone else for them to piss off. Democrats and Republicans, the governor and the assembly, local leaders and the people in Washington. Even the Mormons. Everyone who was anyone was lining up to condemn UHS and support the nurses.

But we still had a strike to run. The game plan had changed only slightly. The nurses announced they would all show up ready to work in the morning, though of course we knew that the employer was going to lock them out. The story was breaking nationally by late Monday morning. No one had ever heard of *a hospital locking out its nurses*. We had a delegation of politicians with us that morning, along with D Taylor and a number of labor leaders. As the workers attempted to walk in for work, sure enough, management stopped them. Fences were thrown up. Hospital security was everywhere. Our picketing began. There was no story but the nurse lockout in the Vegas media that day.

The picket lines were like a big celebration, with nurses chanting and dancing and singing. I was on the phone nonstop with politicians who were all denouncing UHS. One real highlight came early, when the TV cameras caught the CEO of Valley on his way into the hospital. When the reporter asked him why he was rejecting a request from the governor and the powerful speaker of the assembly, he replied, "The only person who can call off a strike is the President of the United States, and the last time I looked, Barbara Buckley doesn't live in that zip code." I was standing nearby, and I almost felt sorry for him. You could see that the TV people knew they had just gotten the sound bite that was going to loop all day.

By Tuesday morning the picket lines were already feeling more like work, already not quite as fun. But other workers were joining us: carpenters, cab drivers, all sorts of people were coming down and helping us keep the lines up. I was busy fielding calls from politicians. Rory Reid had taken the lead in challenging the company. And he was doing a hell of a job, really. He phoned to say that he, the mayor, the speaker, the governor, and others were summoning UHS to an emergency meeting. He didn't want or need me there. He assured me he knew that we were the sensible ones. A while later, with the UHS men and the entire political leadership with him in the room, he called to report that if we would accept some terms, UHS would agree to a sixty-day cooling-off period, and the governor would appoint a special emergency mediator, as the Nevada constitution authorized him to do.

I knew right away that we didn't want a sixty-day cooling-off period. I saw it as a signal that the company wanted to keep fighting, wear us down over two grueling months and then crush us. I asked for thirty days instead, with the additional commitment that no one could be fired during that period and that all of the workers would get their normal shifts back. Reid got an agreement to the "cease-firing" clause, but couldn't move UHS off the sixty days. The political leaders had been doing nothing for five straight days but deal with this mess, and I could tell they were sick of it. I reminded them that I couldn't make the actual decision and that they would have to wait for an answer until the workers could vote. This actually really pissed some of them off—the ones who assumed that all my talk about union democracy was just rhetoric and that I actually made the decisions myself. In this case, I quite frankly didn't know what the workers would think.

I hung up and got Morgan and Jessica on the phone. "There's an offer. Get a room and get everyone and move fast."

Soon one team of organizers had everyone from the picket lines at both hospitals loading into buses bound for the big meeting. Another team was on the phone rounding up everyone who wasn't at the pickets that day. I was with Mary Kay Henry in a car, on the phone the entire time en route, brokering the details of the back-to-work order to be sure the no firings and normal shifts provisions were included and insisting that the politicians not announce anything to the press until our workers accepted or rejected the deal. I reminded Reid that the nurses had been the reasonable ones and now deserved the chance to make their own decision. Essentially, I was holding the government and UHS top brass locked in a room, because if they stepped outside they would be swarmed by the press.

As we approached the hall, I called ahead to get a sense of the room. I couldn't reach Jessica or Morgan, so I got hold of Neal Bisno, one of the best organizers I know, who had flown in from Pennsylvania once it was pretty clear we had a strike coming. Neal had plenty of strike experience.

"Neal, it's Jane, how do the workers seem? Are they pissed, do they look angry? What's the tone?"

"It's a little hard to tell, Jane, but I think they are totally up for hearing whatever you have to say."

When we got there, I stood outside for a second just to gather my wits about me. Mary Kay and D were with me, and Neal had joined us. The press were arriving. It was time. I opened the door and walked into a room filled with more than 500 workers chanting my name. It was overwhelming. I walked to the front of the room and shouted at the top of my lungs, "What do we want?" Everyone yelled back, "A contract!"

"An offer to return to work has been brokered with the governor, the speaker, the chair of the County Commission, the mayor …"

I didn't even get to the details before everyone began screaming and clapping. I called for silence and insisted they let me explain the rest, because we needed to call the political leaders right away—they were holding the bosses hostage. Someone made a motion and it was all over. Then D Taylor whispered to me that he wanted to speak. I introduced him with a great deal of affection and acknowledged the crucial role he had been playing. The workers gave him a standing ovation.

"I have run a lot of strikes in Nevada over the past twenty years. A few of them went on for more than one year, one of them lasted seven years, and, never, ever did the governor of the state even call me, let alone broker a settlement. You are nurses, and I hope you understand now that when you choose to exercise it, you have a lot of power."

The house came down.

The next few days were spent assessing which workers had actually crossed and gone to work, and paying out checks from the strike fund to the nurses who had been picketing.

It was the second week of December. Eliseo Medina flew into town and we threw a big dinner for all the workers who had joined the picketing, and their children and spouses—even some grandchildren. Eliseo was a natural with the workers and their families. He gave a moving, rousing speech about what the workers had achieved by standing up to their employer with the ultimate action, a strike. You could see the pride among the workers families in that room.

The UHS contract wasn't the only outstanding contract. It was now time to convene the master joint table negotiations for the county and public hospital workers. The hard work to win this contract had been done in the County Commission elections, which we had won, though our two new pro-union commissioners wouldn't be sworn in until January.

I gave all the staff except the UHS team two paid weeks off, not to be charged as their vacation time. The UHS team and me, just like the workers in the hospitals, wouldn't be getting a break any time soon.

When most staff came back to work the calendar said January 2007, but as far as we were concerned the great Las Vegas labor war of 2006 was not over. We still had contracts to win for 8,000 public-sector workers, and the battle at UHS was unresolved and "cooling off." Right away, UHS refused to negotiate during the period and began harassing workers in ways forbidden by the agreement brokered by the political leaders. So what else was new? It was obvious that UHS intended to wear us down and exhaust the workers over sixty grinding days, and then dare us to strike again. That was their final strategy: They would bleed us to death. We knew we wouldn't be able to sustain a second strike. We were in good shape, but not that good. And they knew we knew that. And we knew they knew we knew that.

We started publishing a weekly "Cooling-off Period Community Report" for journalists and politicians, detailing all the violations of the agreement UHS was committing. Armed with these reports, we began rounding up support among politicians for forcing a governor's appointed mediator on the company. Way behind the scenes, we were putting together a list of potential mediators who would be both acceptable to us and so prestigious that UHS couldn't turn them down. It was tricky. It would be the governor's appointment, and he was an anti-union Republican. We assumed that UHS was busy using their huge financial clout to make up for insulting him so badly. We later discovered they were so arrogant that they hadn't even bothered to.

It was once again the savvy D Taylor who came up with the perfect mediator: Phil Satre, a multimillionaire casino mogul with a lot of power and respect in Nevada. Satre had been CEO of the empire known as Harrah's Casinos. He was on a par with UHS CEO Alan Miller as someone who had run a huge private company. There were rumors Satre might run for governor at some point, and he lived in Reno, the state capital.

D Taylor had known him for years. Satre hadn't wanted his company unionized any more than any other CEO, but he had learned over time how to work with the casino workers union to get himself the best employees in exchange for good contracts. Satre had been to D's union what the CHW hospitals had become to us.

The first task was to get Satre to agree. He had recently retired to enjoy his life (as he would remind me many times) and was off on a hunting trip in Africa. Then we had to get the governor to agree to appoint him. Then we had to get UHS to accept him. After a week of nonstop meetings, phone calls, and escalating threats between the Las Vegas political elite and the corporation, UHS finally caved. But Satre conditioned his own acceptance on the condition that the mediation would be done with just me, a company rep, and himself. No workers in the room. I was going to say no, but first I called Jerry Brown.

"McAlevey, this guy sounds like he's perfect, right? You've got no choice. You explain this to the workers. Be creative. Fly back from Reno every two days and brief them or whatever. Be an organizer. It's fine. It's more than fine. You actually got a good mediator. Be happy. But you are going to need Fox. The company will bring in their brass and their lawyers. You don't need any of that, but you need one more smart person to brainstorm with and to help you so you don't lose perspective in the room. Call headquarters, get Fox, make a plan to keep in touch with the workers, and go win. Time is running out."

It was already the end of the first week of January and the cooling-off period would end the second week of February. We had a lot to do.

I insisted that before mediation began Satre had to come to a private meeting, away from the media, with the nurses and techs to hear them talk about conditions in the hospitals. He agreed. I met with our bargaining team and explained the deal to them, and they approved. Honestly, many were actually relieved that they wouldn't have to sit in a room with Larry Arnold throwing insults at them. I was well aware that I was often more of a stickler for the formalities of union democracy than the workers were, but I also knew that this was a big reason why they trusted me. The trust was crucial; without it, everything would fall apart.

We organized a mass meeting for Satre and the workers. We set up two panels of nurses and techs, who told Satre stories from their working lives. This meeting was hugely important for them, and in the end even more for Satre. Later on, when he was locked in a room in Reno with a company rep who insisted day after day that I was an outside manipulator duping naïve workers, Satre could fall back on his memory of the hundreds of nurses he had talked to.

Larry Fox flew into town, and he and I met with Satre together. We liked him instantly. Satre cared about the world, he was smart, nonideological, cared about environmental issues, understood that a good union could be an asset, not a liability, and on top of it all, he was a former college football star who was part of the Raider Nation. I have been a hardcore Oakland Raiders fan since I was a little girl. Given that I was from New York and not one of my six brothers cared about football, this was as far-fetched as the fact that I had been partly raised a Jew, and wore cowboy boots, but all of it was true. It was the end of football season and the Super Bowl was approaching. You should have seen the look on Phil Satre's face when in response to some comment he made about the Raiders, the girl from the union mentioned her love for Jim Plunkett, a former Raiders quarterback who, she happened to know, was the first Latino to play that position, and the only quarterback to have won two Superbowls, and yet had never been inducted into the NFL's Hall of Fame. Well, who knew that Satre had actually played for Stanford with Plunkett—in two Rose Bowls? I replied that he and I should start a campaign to get our hero into the Hall of Fame. We could shame the league, make the players' union an ally… It was clear Satre and I could talk football all day long. And he was an avid skier. Larry Fox was just cracking up watching the man who had until recently been the most powerful casino CEO in the nation and the woman who headed the local he was supposedly there to mentor lock in on each other. Soon I would be telling Satre that if he ran for governor I would be his first volunteer.

The contrast couldn't have been greater a few days later, when the mediation began in Reno and Satre got to meet Larry Arnold. We were in a basement office at Harrah's Casino. After Satre had introduced us to the office staff and showed us around to the photocopier and restrooms, Arnold handed Satre some proposals and said, "Can you copy that for me?" I just about fell off my chair. "Copy this?" I kept a poker face and did my own photocopying.

After three days locked in that room from nine in the morning until six at night, Larry Arnold hadn't moved an inch. Satre called the governor's people to report on our lack of progress. Since the union had already expressed willingness to move on certain things, and UHS kept refusing on every point, I imagine he had to be telling them about the reasonable union and the unreasonable boss. In our private sessions with him (each side had many), I would explain that I was not in the least surprised, that this was who these guys were and what this company was, and that unless something changed, we were headed straight back into an ugly strike.

At the outset of the mediation, Satre had told everyone that if we could get a contract wrapped up by Sunday, he would take us to his home in the Sierras to watch the Super Bowl together. Good luck. Come Super Bowl Sunday there were Satre and I, locked in mediation with Larry Arnold, missing the Super Bowl for the first time in years. Satre had brought us some of those long casino-style betting sheets that let you put money on all sorts of weird statistical minutiae of the game. Of course I took him up on it, and after filling out our sheets, we discovered we had made some of the exact same bets. Another good bonding moment for me, but Satre was getting grumpy. Very grumpy. This was not a guy who accepted failure. He had agreed to take on the mediation as a major assignment from the entire political elite of Nevada and had assumed it would be an opportunity to demonstrate his own incredible political skills.

When the five straight days Satre had allocated in his schedule for his volunteer mediation were up, we had gone nowhere. Fox and I knew that Satre had been working his ass off and that once again UHS had been working their true colors. Satre declared that he was done, and would report back to the governor that he couldn't get an agreement. It was pretty grim. I returned to Vegas and asked Fox to stick around. The press was all over it in that frantic way they have, with count-down banners and tabloid-style headlines and the whole bit. The day after the talks broke down, and with Satre getting ready to board a plane for Australia, UHS agreed to one more day of talks. I never knew exactly what behind-the-scenes arm twisting got that done.

When we walked back into mediation, this time at the Harrah's Casino in Vegas, everything suddenly starting to move. I knew we had a real chance now, but there were still key issues that UHS had said they would "never, ever" move on. Then came another full day of behind-the-scenes threats and posturing, and then we won. I mean, we really won. I was in shock. I called Morgan and Jessica and said, "Get the workers together, fast." The press had been covering this thing nonstop for three months, and by now they were doing our communications work for us. Half the workers knew they had to get to the union hall for a mass meeting to discuss a possible settlement before our own phone tree could even find them.

Everyone crowded in and the meeting began. The atmosphere was electric. People had no idea what I was bringing before them to vote on. You really can't start telling people stuff individually while hundreds of others are entering the room. I had made a slide show that laid out how we had won everything in the pattern we had developed over the year, and that the contract was comparable to the HCA settlement down to a decimal point. I didn't even make it through the slide show before I was interrupted by shouting.

"Did we get 100 percent retroactivity?"[†]

"Yes, 100 percent retroactivity for every worker."

The room exploded.

"Did we win the new wage scale for just the nurses or did we also win it for the techs?"

"What do you think?"

And the room exploded again. People were crying; I was smiling from ear to ear. I was so lost in the process I didn't even fully understand that it was really over.

Before the week was out, pushing through sheer exhaustion because there was no other choice, I convened the master joint table and the public-sector workers in Clark County won a terrific contract. It contained every key benefit we had sought, gave us organizing rights for the part-timers, and established a committee to examine new rules for subcontracting, which the new pro-union County Commission had agreed we should move on right away.

And with that we called 2006 a total victory. It was February 14, 2007.

---

† Retroactivity means that the workers will be compensated on the terms of the new contract backward to the date on which the old contract expired. This is often difficult to win, and can result in workers receiving large individual checks at the time of the implementation of a new contract.

CHAPTER THIRTEEN

Things Fall Apart: How National and Local Labor Leaders Undermined the Workers of Nevada

Our long 2006 campaign was finally done, and it was time for me to leave Las Vegas and the SEIU. According to the calendar I had imagined when I arrived in the desert, it was past time. I had no ambition to become the Sal Rosselli or Dennis Rivera of Nevada. That just isn't something I am cut out for. I thrive on movement. Challenging power structures is what fascinates me, not administering a power structure of my own.

I had been straightforward about this with the local executive board. When I arrived in 2004 they wanted me to sign a multiyear contract. The local had never done a real search for an executive director, and of course there had been no search for me. I'd wanted to end this shoddiness right away and insisted on a one-year contract, after which I insisted on a full performance evaluation. Amazingly, the local had never done a job performance evaluation either, and I had to train them so they could evaluate me.

At the end of that first year, in the spring of 2005, the board evaluated my performance and again offered me a five-year contract and a $20,000 raise. I explained that money wasn't the issue and I just couldn't imagine myself lasting five years, and anyway I didn't think it would take that long to get the local into shape. I was suggesting a three-year contract. Eric Taylor, a board member from CHW, spoke up. Eric was a compelling guy. His legs had been crushed in a tractor accident when he was a kid, and his current hobby was driving racing cars, crushed legs and all.

Eric had been resolutely anti-union during the organizing drive at CHW, a problem for us because he was a real leader. At the first meeting to discuss the campaign to win the contract at CHW, Eric pushed his wheelchair right up to the front of the room and parked directly in front of me, pen and paper in hand. Morgan had shot me one of those "Jane-that's-the-strongly-anti-union-worker-leader-so-please-do-something" looks. As soon as the meeting began, Eric put his hand up and said, "My name is Eric Taylor, I campaigned against the union, but now you are here, so I am here to learn what this means." And now he was a brand new member of the executive board of the local. And he put his hand up and said, "OK, this is silly, Jane, please just sign the five-year contract. This is a right-to-work state, so you can quit whenever you want. No one is going to force you to stay." I couldn't argue with that.

But all of this was just my personal stuff. When I arrived in Vegas, I still thought the SEIU was a national union I actually wanted to work for when I was done in Nevada. This was no longer the case. I had gone to Nevada at the urging of Larry Fox, who had a vision of building a national hospital workers union market by market. In Larry's grand plan, the key was strong worker organization on the ground, focused not on one hospital but on entire markets. This approach dovetailed perfectly with the power structure analysis approach I had been developing for years. Larry also saw that national accords with corporations that had hospitals in multiple markets could be valuable, but only when added to ground-level worker organization that could credibly threaten an employer. The chance to actually realize this vision inspired me to move to that most unlikely city, Las Vegas.

Just three months after I landed in Sin City, the wheels came off the bus, when Andy Stern removed Larry Fox from leadership. And he did it in that special Andy Stern way, in which it wasn't clear how the decision had been made or even what it meant, with the cover that Larry was just being given a new title. The real consequences of the change only became clear two years later, during the pitched battle between the Hospital Corporation of America and their unionized employees at Sunrise Hospital.

The national hospital division had no strategy for the next several years and lurched from one nonsensical plan to the next. The division meetings featured elaborate slide shows that had us winning imaginary big agreements with national employers yielding the exact number of workers per hospital owner that we needed in order to tell the 2008 convention we had met the goals of our 2004 convention. Only none of it happened. And after two years of nothing much happening for SEIU in hospitals outside of Nevada and California, Stern announced that he was anointing Dennis Rivera as head of something called Healthcare United!. Now the slide shows at national division meetings had us achieving new far-reaching goals, because under Rivera's New York model we would trade our political power for deals with hospital executives who wanted increases in Medicare and Medicaid payments. I was from New York, and I knew that the New York model entailed the union harnessing every available dollar of public money at the expense of, oh, education, affordable housing, environmental cleanup, or just about anything else that the members of the mighty SEIU might also need when they left their badly run hospitals to return to their underfunded communities. It was eerily reminiscent of mistakes the UAW had made in its heyday: focusing so narrowly on pay and benefits that they forgot to notice what a bad industry they were facilitating. Moreover, since most states don't have a power equation between unions and the state lawmakers anything like New York's, that model just doesn't add up in the rest of the country, even on its own terms.

By the beginning of 2007 I knew that I couldn't sit through any more presentations on "Exporting the New York Model" or "growth strategies" that involved everyone but workers. My views were hardly a secret. I had discussed them at length with the national leadership. And I had discussed my intention to leave the SEIU with both Mary Kay Henry, the new head of the hospital division, and Eliseo Medina, who now headed the South-Southwestern region of SEIU. I was ready to pack up my bags in the next five seconds.

Yet as bad as things were in DC, Nevada made it tempting to stay. The national Democratic Party had just decided to move up the presidential primaries in Nevada and South Carolina, putting them on an equal footing with Iowa's and New Hampshire's. The Republicans followed suit by bumping up their Nevada timeline as well. There hadn't been an inkling of this in 2003, when Fox and Medina persuaded me to go to Vegas.

The synergy of political developments with the development of our

Nevada local couldn't have been more striking. Once we'd wrapped up the hospital market in Las Vegas, the obvious next step was to take our whole-market strategy to Reno and Elko up north. In fact, we had already won the first nurses' election in Elko in late 2005, and their first contract in 2006. Elko was not just any new market; it's the third most important town in Nevada, right after Vegas and Reno. It's considered the symbolic heart of Nevada's rural communities—and it's also the site of the third-largest gold mine in the world. Mining industries still have a lot of sway in Nevada politics and policymaking. An indication of Elko's role in Nevada politics is how many candidates for statewide office kick off their campaigns there. After the Elko nurses' victory, the rest of the hospital workers in town had patiently waited for us to win the big Las Vegas labor war of 2006 so that we could send an organizer to help them win their own election and organize the whole Elko hospital into one big union. In 2007, we did just that. In Reno, the nurses at the big Washoe Medical Center (now called Renown) had also been waiting for 2006 to end so that we could help them form a new union there.* And we had just played a role in winning three County Commission elections, so our electoral clout had been duly noted.

Both national political parties could see that rapidly shifting demographics had turned the "new west" into critical swing states. Anyone familiar with the Nevada electoral map knew that the crucial battleground in the 2008 presidential election would be northern Nevada in general and Reno in particular. Reno and the northern counties were to Nevada what Florida was to the nation. And Reno was a town with weak unions. A win at the Washoe hospital would make us the biggest union in town overnight.

Well, one plus one plus one equals three. When you put all the pieces of this puzzle together, the picture that jumped out was that if we could do in Reno and Elko in 2007 what we had done in Las Vegas in 2006, not

---

* Both the Washoe Medical Center and Elko RNs were previously members of the Operating Engineers. They were sold to SEIU at the time I arrived in Nevada. In practice, all that really meant was we got an employee list—there was no union in either hospital. Both units of RNs had a dues-paying membership in the *single* digits. And practically speaking, the NLRB rejected our attempts to find a legal way to simply transfer the workers from one union to the next. In the end, we had to run full NLRB elections at both facilities, with boss fights, fear, personal intimidation, futility and the rest of the kitchen sink management throws at workers.

only would we improve health care for a quarter of a million people, we could have a say in who the Democratic presidential nominee would be, and ultimately play a role in turning Nevada from red to blue.

And we were ready to roll. We had one of the hottest local union organizing teams in the national SEIU. We had nurses who were filled with evangelical fire about their union, and whose contracts gave them the right to take some leave if, for example, they wanted to spend a little time explaining to nurses in Reno what the nurses in Vegas had done.

Yeah, the national SEIU sucked. But as bad as headquarters had been, they still hadn't managed to derail the little juggernaut we had put together in Vegas. And it wasn't as if there were some other, much better national organization I could join where I could have a hand in helping to improve the future direction of the world's remaining super power.

We decided the entire UHS organizing team minus Morgan would head north to Reno. It was March; the Nevada presidential primary was set for the following January. What was another nine months? I decided that if I could make it through 2006 promising myself I would leave in early 2007, I could make it through 2007 telling myself I would leave in early 2008. That was the exact timeline I had given to the executive board in 2005. I mean, the bullshit from the national union couldn't really get any worse than it had already been.

Looking back, I can see now that this assessment of the situation was naïve. My relationship with Andy Stern and his lieutenants had changed forever during the HCA fight of 2006, and the moment it did can be pinpointed: when Judy Scott, head of the national legal team, called to browbeat me into capitulating to HCA and I put some top worker leaders on speakerphone to explain why they were going to do no such thing. The basic assumption that has guided my organizing is that you can stay principled in all kinds of messy situations if you just keep winning. I knew my version of union democracy and worker leadership develop-ment drove the Stern people berserk, but I also knew their number one priority was growing the size of the union, and there were few locals in the country doing that more successfully than ours. Just keep winning and it will be okay.

And that was probably true before the HCA disagreement, but not after. There is exactly one reason a huge corporation would bother to talk to a national union about a labor accord: because they think the union can actually deliver the labor peace they so greatly desire. But if the union people the corporate leadership are talking to can't actually deliver their locals, that train comes to a screeching halt. The speakerphone call made the national SEIU realize that the labor movement emerging in Nevada really was democratic, and that they couldn't turn the members off like a light switch. After that DC didn't care how many new members we were organizing in Nevada, because these members couldn't be used as poker chips in their national game. Certainly the HCA was not the only health care corporation that noticed that the national SEIU had failed to force its Nevada local to comply with a deal it had cut. I kick myself for not seeing this at the time, but I didn't. This was supposed to be New Labor, after all, and by every metric new labor used to measure success— organizing wins, political gains, first contract wins, member participation —we were all-stars. From Washington's perspective, however, the situation in Nevada was that at some point soon I had to go. The only questions were when and how to do it, and how many more wins they could get out of us before push came to shove.

The national union was not the only cloud on the horizon. Others were piling up that I similarly misjudged. One was Rose Ann DeMoro and her California Nurses Association. Paradoxically, DeMoro is seen by progressives outside the labor movement—in other words, by people who don't actually have to try to work with her—as the left wing of the labor movement. Another was the ruthless presidential primary campaign. But the first challenge in what eventually became the great unraveling of 2007 came not from any of these power players, but from a quarter I had nearly forgotten about.

In late April I got a call from Molly Gibbons, one of the hundreds of new leaders who had emerged from our 2006 campaigns. She was now the chief nursing steward at Sunrise Hospital and a new member of the executive board. She was really upset about something, so upset she couldn't talk about it on the phone. When we got together, she told me that Melanie Sisson, our other board member from Sunrise, and a long-time one at that, had approached her to say that she and Vicky Hedderman were looking to our upcoming executive board elections as a way to "get rid of Jane."

How bizarre, I thought. These old-guard people really are crazy. We had just won great contracts across the board, contracts that Sisson and Hedderman were now benefiting from, and in the process Sisson had gained more access to and participation in the real workings of both the national union and HCA than she had ever had before. I shrugged it off and kept my focus on organizing the nearly 900 nurses in Reno. A couple of weeks later another worker, Craig McNair, pulled me aside to tell me that Hedderman had asked him to promise that if he ran against her for president of the local and won, he would fire me. McNair was not part of the old guard, though he was a county civil servant. He had good looks and he came from a powerful political family in Vegas, and most of the members thought he was using the union to launch a future political career. They didn't take him seriously as a candidate; he had no real base among the workers. I thought he was trying to suss out if he could win me over by sharing this secret with me. Ugh. Clearly some chatter was happening somewhere that I needed to pay attention to.

The local's executive board elections were coming up in June. The last elections had taken place in 2004, just after I had arrived. I had ignored them entirely; from the minute I'd got off the plane I'd been putting out contract fires. This turned out to be OK, as every time we won a new hospital election we added seats to the board that were filled by the best leaders to emerge from the struggle. In the meantime some old-guard board members from the public sector had left, because they had been promoted into management or else had retired or quit. Furthermore, after a very rocky start Hedderman and I had developed a workable relationship. I consulted her on all major decisions and didn't threaten the perks she and her crowd enjoyed, and she pretty much stayed out of my way. In fact, she told me several times that she didn't intend to run for reelection. I was pleased to hear it but didn't really care that much. The local was in great shape. By the terms of its constitution, the post of rank-and-file president didn't carry much weight. The real power was with the executive board and the executive director. I would soon be leaving that position, but as long as our wonderful cohort of new leaders was in control of the board, the local would be just fine. And in my grand plan, Morgan or Jessica would become the executive director.

When Vicky Hedderman told me she was running again, I told her I thought she should pick one of the newly organized private sector nurses to be her executive vice president. All the top posts in the union in terms of title were from the public sector. But just before the deadline for candidate filing, Hedderman announced she was going to keep her current vice president, an old-guard public-sector buddy of hers. I then sat down with Shauna Hamel, the star leader at the CHW hospitals and one of the smartest nurses I had ever met, and told her that I thought she should run for executive vice president. Shauna agreed.

Over at HCA Sunrise, there was a charming and gregarious nurse named Fredo Serrano who referred to himself as "the Queer Mexican." During the final Sunrise negotiations, I had relied on Fredo's wit to bring positive energy into the caucus room to counter Melanie Sisson's negative vibe. Molly Gibbons and Fredo and I agreed that Fredo would run against Sisson for the other Sunrise Board seat.

Craig McNair finally announced he was challenging Hedderman. His motivations seemed to me to be of the most boring self-interested kind. Whenever the topic of McNair came up, members simply shrugged their shoulders. People imagined him to be like so many politicians in the post-Clinton era, who make their opinions known only after dozens of field-tested opinion-research firms have led them to their "position."

Voter turnout in the local's previous elections had been low. And some races had resulted in Department of Labor election violation findings and monitored do-overs, including the election that made Hedderman president. But we were building a labor movement and we wanted the workers to own their union. I was more concerned about how of many them turned out than about who voted for whom. In the past, the local had met the minimum constitutional requirement of a formal notification of the election, in small fonts, with even smaller margins—the kind of notice you recycle without reading because it's painful to the eyes. Now, for the first time, we did colorful and exciting mailers, worksite leaflets and a candidate forum, and generally talked the process up. We even planned to extend voting from one to two days: the first at polling places geographically spread across the county to facilitate greater participation and the second at the union hall. I was up in Reno the entire week leading into the election, staying focused on the nurses' organizing campaign. At the end of the first day of voting, I got a call from Morgan. "Big problem down here, Jane." A worker who was also a candidate running for a position in his shop named Mike Elgas had come to the union hall to complain that the final and formal election notification mailing he had received did not match the one a colleague of his at another job site had received. Not unreasonably, he wanted to know which was correct. Morgan looked into it and discovered that some election mailers had incorrectly stated that the members could vote at their worksites on either of the two voting days. This was wrong. Really wrong. And it was not a problem that would be easy to solve. I jumped on the next flight from Reno down and asked the staff and the election committee to be ready to meet that night to try to find a solution.

Suddenly accusations were flying. This guy Mike Elgas was saying he was going to file a formal protest and inform the press about the rigged elections that Hedderman had arranged to protect a long-time ally at the convention center where he worked. Elgas had been around a long time, and was neither in Hedderman's inner circle nor among the new generation of militants. Tensions were exploding. I proposed that we keep voting open at all locations the second day—the union hall and the worksites. That way, both mailers would be correct. The election committee agreed and our attorneys approved it, but they noted that if a member filed a protest about the discrepant mailings, the Department of Labor would likely force a new election.

Well, Mike Elgas lost his election, and a little after 7 am the following morning he was screaming over the phone at me, using language so foul that it actually offended me, and that takes some pretty bad language. He said he was going to file a protest immediately. Wonderful. I was dead tired from having been up all night observing ballot counting, which was necessary because the person in charge of borrowing Clark County's touch-screen machines, which we had been using for interim elections and contract ratifications, had somehow dropped the ball, so we had to use paper ballots. I tried to calm Elgas down and persuade him not to go to the media, as he was threatening. For a moment I began to think maybe this guy had something, that maybe there were too many strange things happening—the different mailings, the machines not arriving, the rumors I had started to hear that I was running McNair's campaign (a guy I didn't like or even know very well). But in the end it didn't seem to amount to much more than the usual background bullshit.

I called Larry and Jerry for advice. They were dumbfounded. "Jesus, Jane, you were supposed to run a slate. You should have kicked out those old-guard folks once and for all. What were you thinking?" I explained that only a handful of out of more than forty were in contention, and that the old guard would not control the board no matter what the election outcome. They didn't care. In their view, consolidating political control in the hands of the best workers was a central part of building a strong local.

Elgas filed his protest with both the union and the Department of Labor. According to our lawyers, it was only a matter of time until the Department of Labor called for a new election. With our legal counsel guiding them, our election committee decided to hold the voting again with the same ballot, which would not be opened up for new nominations. This was the remedy the legal team assured us the Department of Labor would order if we didn't remedy the situation first ourselves.

Suddenly the union was full of tension, anger, and rumors. Molly Gibbons was convinced that the Sunrise management had illegally given unacknowledged support to the hospital's Hedderman candidates, and she filed charges of her own. Hedderman was telling anyone who would listen that I had run Craig McNair's campaign and then rigged the election so I could overturn it when he lost. This was absurd. First, if I had run someone for president it would have been one of the many militant worker leaders who had emerged from our battles of the previous year, not an apolitical anomaly from the county unit who probably wanted to become a career politician. Second, the person who was in charge of the elections was Hedderman's closest ally on the staff, hardly someone who would conspire with me to rig an election. And third, if I had run someone for president, we would have won.

At the July executive board meeting, the tension broke out, with open accusations of vote rigging and more hurled across the room. The board split on the election committee's recommendation to revote the same ballot. As president, Hedderman had no voting power except to break a tie, and now she cast the deciding vote, rejecting the re-running of the election and sealing her own reelection. Elgas appealed the decision to the national union the following day. And all the while the Department of Labor was sitting on the original Elgas complaint, waiting to see if SEIU could remedy the situation on its own before they stepped in. What a mess.

Now the national union's attorneys began to investigate the appeal. Their conclusion mirrored that of our local's attorney: Something as clear-cut as mailings that gave conflicting information about time and place of voting would lead the Department of Labor to overturn the election if SEIU did not, and the correct remedy was to vote again using the same ballot as before. This was profoundly disappointing to me, because after watching this whole train wreck I was thoroughly convinced of my error in not running a slate of my own that would have knocked the old guard from their last perch of power once and for all. If nominations had been reopened, I'd have had a second chance to do that. But that was not to be.

It wasn't as if I didn't have other things to do. On July 25 we filed for the election of the 900-nurse unit at Washoe Medical Center. Reno was a complex town, but we were well on track to turning it union and, hopefully, blue. But any hope I had of keeping my eyes on the prize in Reno was dashed when Andy Stern decided that if there was going to be a re-run of the ballot in Vegas, he wanted it done quickly. I couldn't disagree.

It was hard to get excited about the re-run, because we couldn't nominate anyone new, especially for president, and the Reno vote was coming up in a few weeks. To my mind, the Reno election was real work, this other thing was… well, I didn't know what it was. It had nothing to do with organizing workers. But OK, I thought. Fine. Let's make sure good people take every seat they can, and just get past this moment.

I sat down with Shauna Hamel and Fredo Serrano and two wonderful Black women, Rhonda Jackson-Pullens and Venita Smith, who had been the real leaders at the City Housing Authority but had lost their races to a pair of awful old-guard white men backed by Hedderman. Whites were in the minority at the predominantly black CHA, and all the time I'd been in Vegas, racial tensions had racked that chapter. One of the first meetings I had back in 2004 was one Maryanne Salm had set up with Rhonda and Ms. Venita. They came to me with years of paperwork showing how Hedderman had defended with these very same guys who had been taking preferential shifts and more. Now Rhonda and Ms. Venita were furious, and felt that Hedderman had fomented racial divisions in their chapter in order to defeat them.

Shauna, Fredo, Rhonda, and Venita became the core of our slate. Not one of them trusted McNair, so we left Hedderman uncontested for president. Then there was a nurse from the public hospital named Martin

Gallagher who had been nominated for secretary almost as a joke. He'd been standing around in the union hall during the nominations meeting, and after only one person was proposed for that position, some worker yelled out, "Let's nominate Gallagher, he'd be good, would you accept, Gallagher?" And he'd sort of laughed and said yes. He didn't really want the job and had not campaigned at all, but we all thought he was a great guy. In fact, Martin had become the single biggest rank-and-file donor to the entire *national* union's voluntary political elections campaign fund: $55 per paycheck. He was Scottish, with an endearing accent, and had brought a more resolute form of working-class politics with him to Las Vegas. Over two months had passed since Martin had laughingly allowed his name to be placed on the ballot, but in the interim Hedderman's plan for undoing much of what we had built had been exposed, and Martin was a true believer in the new union. So Martin was added to our core group. Looking further through the candidate list, we found Rosita Behn and Steve Spindell, not real leaders during the battles of 2006 but decent enough people who were not Hedderman allies. This rounded out our little slate at seven. It was now late July in Vegas, and I thought the heat was going to melt my brain.

For the first time in nine years in the labor movement I was now being counseled in what was legal and illegal in internal union elections. It had never been my ambition to consolidate power in a union. I knew chapter and verse about labor laws that related to beating multinational corporations. And I could tell you all about real-world election laws and obscure things like independent expenditures in County Commission races. But internal union election law was all news to me.

There were three real guidelines: only members of the union could be involved in union elections; money spent in an election could come only from union members, but not from their dues; and no election activities could be conducted during regular work hours. The basic idea was that no union resources could be used to favor one candidate over another. And "union" in this case meant the whole SEIU, not just the Nevada local. It all seemed pretty reasonable on paper, but there was a problem. Morgan and I had both grown up in the 1199 tradition, from locals where staff were members of the union along with the rank and file. But we had left these locals a few years earlier. And none of the other staff in Nevada were union members, since they had been recruited directly into our local, which had a constitution in which staff was not members. Great. So much for our last-minute slate.

Thankfully, at that moment I got to escape the late July heat to attend a meeting of the national SEIU public sector division in Colorado. Andy Stern was there, and sitting in the lobby after hours one night he asked me for an update on the election squabble. It was an awkward moment. We were not accustomed to spending time chatting, and this was not a pleasant subject. I told him I thought that the new-guard folks could win their races, but we couldn't challenge Hedderman for rank-and-file president, because new nominations were not allowed. Echoing the words of Larry Fox and Jerry Brown, Stern replied, "Jane, go win the damn election." I told him I had no money for union-wide mailings, which would surely be needed, and no staff who could do the work, so it was actually a long shot that on such a short timeline we could overcome the Hedderman voting base, built on fifteen years of ramming through grievances. Stern replied, "Someone will figure out the union membership issue, and let me worry about getting you some money—you will probably need twenty or thirty thousand dollars for multiple mailings. I'll take care of that; you go win the elections."

I'd hardly been in the habit of following the advice of Andy Stern. To the contrary, I had enraged him and his lieutenants by refusing to follow their orders in matters of utmost importance to the national union. So why did I listen to him then? It is a painful question I have often asked myself. I think the first part of the answer is that Stern was giving me the same advice as both Larry Fox and Jerry Brown. This had rarely if ever happened, and I assured myself that he was just telling me how to implement the course of action that my two respected mentors had already said was the right one. And beyond that, I can only say I was seriously off my game. I was on my way out of the SEIU, and this election thing seemed so small compared to the whole movement we had built in Nevada.

In the final analysis, I think my single-minded focus on organizing, to the detriment of organization-building, was wrong. I have a fundamental mistrust of empire builders—the Andy Sterns, Sal Rossellis, and Rose Ann DeMoros of the world. In many ways this has served me well. But when I took this to the point of believing that fighting the boss is "real" union work, and consolidating the power of the most militant and democratically minded workers within the union is not, I made a costly error. And that's an understatement.

Time was of the essence, as the re-run was only a month away—just enough time to meet the legal standards for notifying the membership. When I returned to Nevada the next day I purchased a new cell phone with my own money so I could use it before 9 am and after 5 pm to talk about elections. I told Morgan to call her old union and get her dues current. I called up 1199 New England to get my own union card and pay some back dues. The following day, Sheila Velasco, Eliseo Medina's super human assistant in the Southwest, called my personal phone from her personal phone to say that she had consulted the Arizona local and they would be happy to let our staff pay dues to their union. This might seem bizarre—indeed, it is bizarre—but in the union world, it's not unusual.

Winning the rerun election was not going to be easy. Hedderman had a well-oiled election machine; and we had was a slate of folks with no internal union election experience. Looking at the numbers, I figured that the only way to pull it off would be to double the voter turnout. We knew that the new members would never vote for the old guard and what it represented, so we had to get lots of them to the polls. In the past there had been internal union elections in which only two votes were cast from the private-sector hospitals, and those were from candidates voting for themselves.

For my part, I was determined to return to Reno. I put Jessica Foster in charge of the election campaign, gave her the keys to my house for use as election headquarters, and headed north. Jessica's team included several of our best young organizers, among them the incredibly talented Kristin Warner, trained first as an organizer, then a lead organizer, in the UHS wars. Kristin came from Vermont, where she was a rank-and-file union member at the Vermont Worker Center. In a fundamental way, both she and Jessica appreciated the importance of the internal election more than I did. They got right to work, but the only money that arrived from back east was two $5,000 checks each from two locals there. This was legal, because the checks were from the locals' personal campaign funds, raised outside their dues, but it was obvious that the only reason the money was sent was because Stern had in one way or another told them to. The leader of one of these locals was at the opposite end of the spectrum from me in terms of union politics. This was not the way I was used to operating. I couldn't wait for the election to be over. More than that, I couldn't wait to be outside the SEIU altogether. And even more than that, I couldn't wait for the rest of the money Stern had promised when he had urged me to fight this campaign, because our slate was accumulating a large unpaid bill with the printer. Finally, I called Stern from my elections-only phone on his non-SEIU cell phone.

"Jane, I am telling you not to worry about the money. I am sure some local union leaders from across the country will call to offer your slate money. This is all legal. This is how it's done. Stop your worrying and go win."

Jessica and our slate ran a high-road campaign that was a reflection of the vision we had been driving in the new union all along. The old guard? One of their mailings had the word STRIKE in giant capital letters across the top. And underneath some verbiage along the lines of: "We must remove Jane McAlevey and her puppets because she wants to get famous in Nevada and run a BIG STRIKE across the valley in 2009." The text, which was long, got even crazier. It was the sort of flyer one would expect from a boss fight. They were running on division and fear, we were running on raising expectations.

When the votes were tallied up we found that the turnout had indeed nearly doubled—an all-time record. Everyone on our slate won except Rosita Behn. I was already in Reno. The day after the election I'd got a call from a young organizer named Peter Hasagawa that had me on the next airplane north.

"Jane! The California Nurses Association has five people in the hospital cafeteria and more outside for shift change. They are trying to intervene in the election. What should we do?"

The sudden appearance of the California Nurses Association in Reno requires some explanation. The CNA, though based in California, had strong national ambitions.† Everything about it—its union politics, organizing approach, alliances, and general political tenor—was (and still is) tightly controlled by its longtime executive director, Rose Ann

† Subsequent to the Nevada raids, the CNA would go on to form National Nurses United (NNU)—a national union of nurses formed primarily of affiliations with and mergers of existing groups—not the same thing as organizing the unorganized.

DeMoro. DeMoro and the CNA are popular among progressives because they talk a very progressive line, and in California they have played a key role in several progressive political campaigns. Early in DeMoro's tenure as executive director, she aligned with a respected labor radical named Tony Mazocchi and called for the formation of a Labor Party. And she did not flinch from advocating single-payer health care. These two positions alone were so at odds with the rest of the nation's unions that many progressives gave DeMoro their unconditional support. A generation of academic Marxists, student radicals, and others on the margins of unions placed DeMoro at the center of their hopes for a more left-wing unionism in America. Her willingness to take radical positions on issues outside the union has shielded her from the kind of public accountability most other labor leaders endure.

Since SEIU is the other large union representing nurses in the United States, it's not surprising that the relationship between the CNA and SEIU has often been tense.‡ In California, the relationship has run hot and cold (even boiling or freezing) depending on the ever-shifting political ambitions of DeMoro, California SEIU leader Sal Rosselli, and SEIU's national leadership. Rosselli and DeMoro have been the closest of allies and the bitterest of enemies, a history that has less to do with any fundamental differences about union politics than with the outsized ambitions of each.

What makes DeMoro's support among nonunion progressives so paradoxical is that despite her progressive stance in the electoral arena, her approach to labor is completely retrogressive. The CNA is for nurses only, which in my view is a profound mistake. Nothing could be worse for a movement aimed at improving the quality of health care while empowering health-care workers than splitting the workers at the top of the industry off into their own union. In every hospital, nurses are the most powerful employees.§ Ultimately, the only way to force a hospital boss to reckon with the workers is for the nurses—not the technicians or dieticians or housekeepers or cooks—to credibly threaten to withhold

---

‡ After the period under discussion, SEIU cut a deal with DeMoro and the CNA that would allow the CNA to organize RNs alongside SEIU members as part of jointly brokered national agreements—the very kind of agreements that DeMoro loudly criticized before joining SEIU in the deal making.

§ Obviously, doctors have power, but they are mostly considered management and not union eligible.

their labor. Separating these structurally powerful workers from the rest of the hospital staff condemns that staff to an extremely subordinate position and encourages an attitude of elitism rather than solidarity.

This harks all the way back to the 1930s, when the militant CIO organized entire factories into one industrial union while the conservative craft unions of the AFL tried to break up the most skilled workers into locals that would look out only for their own. The debate goes to the core of what should be the mission of any progressive working in a union context: *building solidarity*. No matter how many times DeMoro assures progressive nonunion audiences that the CNA stands with the rest of the workers in the hospitals, it doesn't add up. Contract battles in the US right now are *hard*. When and if the boss finally makes a good offer, you accept and settle. All the statements about solidarity go out the window right about then. Sure, it's nice when an elite worker union prints flyers proclaiming its support for workers lower on the food chain, but the result is nothing remotely like what happens when settling a contract requires agreement from all of the workers together. Even on the rare occasion where the CNA has done more than flyers in support of the rest of the hospital workers, it's not sufficient.

Now that heavy industry has largely fled this country, hospitals are one of the few remaining institutions employing large numbers of workers When you look at the demographics, you find Blacks in the kitchens, Latinos doing the cleaning, an ethnic mix in the middle-range jobs, and mostly white RNs. Pedagogically speaking, there's no excuse for missing the deep and radical education of forming one big union among one of the largest workforces in the service economy. The fundamental issues here have not changed since the 1930s, and craft unionism CNA-style undermines our ability to construct solidarity across race and class. And it has to be constructed; it doesn't just happen. A core mission of any good organizer is to help humans feel deep and meaningful solidarity with one another, the kind that makes you willing to give up something of your own for the sake of the greater good.

Take the airline unions, for example. There's a powerful pilots' union. Then there's a flight attendants' union, condemned to an extremely weak position by being separate from the pilots. Between those are the organized mechanics, less able to ground a plane than the pilots but much more able than the flight attendants, and so on. DeMoro promises nurses that if they just split off into their own union, they can have more. And she's right. If the nurses are just out for themselves, and implicitly willing to screw every other worker in the hospital, they can win better wages. In every single hospital contract negotiation I have been involved in that included other staff, the boss tried to play divide-and-conquer by offering more to the nurses than to everyone else. Every time.

In the union we built in Nevada, our nurse leaders understood that the cost of living in Vegas hadn't increased only for them; it had gone up for everyone. They stood with their coworkers to ensure that everyone got an equal across-the-board wage increase, equal shift differentials, and equal access to the same health-care plans. The only fair way to differentiate the pay of nurses from cafeteria workers' is to construct a sophisticated wage scale like the one we won in Nevada. In our scale, the nurses are compensated based on skill, training, and education in what they do—and so is everyone else. That's where the fairness comes in.

Beyond wages, there is no reason a nurse should have a different pension or health-care plan than a dietary worker, or that an operating room nurse should have the right to be late more often than an anesthesia tech. And there is no reason that any worker should have less pregnancy or family leave than a nurse. As we demonstrated in Nevada, you don't have to split the nurses off to build a strong union. On the contrary, when all the workers in the hospital stand together, the nurses end up members of a more powerful union than they would have had on their own. In 2006, the techs and licensed practical nurses in Vegas beat Brent Yessin and UHS, but next door in California Yessin got the CNA decertified in UHS's two hospitals there.

The same holds true for quality of patient care. The best patient outcomes require a seamless health-care team, and the best way to get there is to have all the workers in one organization where they can sit side by side and bargain for new and better work systems as well as fair pay. Here is a concrete example that goes straight to the heart of the difference between the CNA approach and what we were doing in Nevada. In 2004, California became the only state in the nation to implement legally guaranteed minimum nurse-to-patient ratios.[§] That victory is one of the CNA's main claims to fame. And they deserve plenty of credit—it took

---

[§] The law was originally passed in 1999 but it would take several more years of campaigning to formulate the actual ratios.

a huge political fight to win, which the CNA is capable of waging. And, it's an incredibly important law. Years later, they successfully defended the ratios when Governor Arnold Schwarzenegger made a concerted attempt to roll the law back. In 2006, our local also won minimum nurse-to-patient ratios in our contract with the CHW hospitals in Las Vegas—it had been one of our top demands. But in our CHW contracts, we also won language prohibiting management, as they implemented our new nurse-to-patient ratios, from cutting non-nurse positions. This difference is crucial. Because the CNA was only fighting for the elite workers, the intent of the California law, when it took effect, was grossly undermined by hospital bosses, who gutted their ancillary staffs to pay for the additional nurses they were required to hire. Nurses in California now have many additional tasks that were formerly performed by aids, housekeepers, techs, phlebotomists, and others. In Nevada, when the CHW hospitals began to implement the new nurse-patient ratios stipulated in our contracts, they had to keep all existing positions on the ancillary staff.

In Reno, our local had been organizing the Washoe Medical Center hospital for six long months and was finally at the tail end of a nasty boss fight with just three weeks to go before the big NLRB election. Under US labor law, a union has to have the support of at least 30 percent of the workers in a facility in order to file for an election. But once the workers have filed, any competing union can get itself added to the ballot as a third alternative with the support of only 10 percent of the workers. Often employers facing a worker vote for a militant union use this law to invite in a weak one.

Most hospitals in this country have no union at all. If you want to bring a union to unorganized nurses, our nation offers a cornucopia of possibilities. So why would the California Nurses Association suddenly show up at a Nevada hospital we were already organizing just weeks before the voting? In labor movement shoptalk, the CNA was conducting a raid. Raids are one of the sleaziest things one union can do to another, and they leave animosities that last for many years. But there was much more to it than that: The CNA was launching their first frontal attack in a war they had declared on the Nevada SEIU, a war that had nothing to do with empowering the workers of Nevada and everything to do with Rose Ann DeMoro's ambitions for power in the national labor movement.

All of this was loaded into the subtext of that brief call I got from our young Reno organizer Peter Hasagawa. I told him to find every single nurse leader who was about to go off day shift, get them to the cafeteria, and get the doors and parking lots covered too. A few hours later, our best nurse leaders were in the cafeteria in a standoff with the CNA organizers, saying they wouldn't go home until the CNA went back to California.

The next day the CNA was back. And the next. And the next. Our wonderful leaders in Reno were now doing double duty: holding on to their majorities for the upcoming NLRB election and keeping these jerks from California at bay. Tactically, it wasn't that hard. All our nurses had to say, over and over, was "We have been fighting this ruthless boss here for more than half a year. Where were you then?" But we were nervous; the CNA had a reputation for winning elections against the SEIU. In part, this was because it is relatively easy to play to the self-interest of the most elite workers. And if anyone doubts the messaging of elitism in the CNA, go spend some time looking at their materials in these contested inter-union wars. In addition, our substantive differences on issues like hospital-wide staffing ratios couldn't be fully explained in the brief text on a flyer. But this was Nevada, where for three years we had been left to ourselves to grow a health-care workers union in a right-to-work state, and we knew what we were doing. Despite all the resources that the CNA spent in Reno, in the end they couldn't get the support even of the 10 percent of workers required to get their name on the ballot.

In three days of voting in late September, the nurses at Washoe Medical Center voted 491 to 213 to form a union; the turnout was nearly 80 percent. Nurses had packed the vote count room and burst into tears and high fives when the results were clear. For a brief moment, it felt like 2006 again, with the militant new movement of health-care workers in Nevada kicking things up to a new level.

Back in Las Vegas, the brouhaha over the election rerun was getting worse. Now it was Hedderman's crowd that had lost and it was her turn to file charges. Great. I jokingly asked myself if an award was being offered to whoever could be the pettiest, not realizing that in a real sense, there was.

Hedderman's official complaint was that the staff had been involved in campaigning. This was indeed a technical violation of the *local's* constitution, which was absurd, because that provision made the *local*'s constitution *invalid* under both the constitution of the national SEIU and the rules of the US Department of Labor. The charge was just as absurd substantively as it was legally, since our staff had been openly involved in *every* single union election since I had arrived in Nevada, from interim elections to bargaining team elections to dues votes to contract ratifications. What made it even more ridiculous was that in the 2004 elections Hedderman herself had pleaded with staffer Maryanne Salm to design her campaign. Essentially, Hedderman's beef was that the staff was running the union; well, according to the local's constitution that was our job. And because we were doing it right, the rank-and-file *members* were making decisions about the direction of their union for the first time ever. The executive board was real and functioning, worker leaders were actually running their shops every day, finances were transparent, negotiations were done by huge teams of elected workers and were open to everyone else to observe. Not least of all, members had just voted in significant numbers in an internal election for the first time in the history of the local—and they had voted against Hedderman's slate. Hedderman's complaints were farcical, and would have spelled the final demise of her cadre had not, at that very moment, a very powerful outside force decided to use them as the figurehead for an assault on Nevada. That force was the CNA.

By now the CNA's initial foray at Washoe had escalated into a frontal attack on the Nevada SEIU, and they were coordinating it with the help of the old-guard nurses among the leadership inside the local. This really was special: the CNA, which presents itself as the self-styled left wing of the labor movement, in cahoots with the dinosaur leaders of a Las Vegas local that under their regime had all but fallen to pieces.

By the October executive board meeting, the last twenty or so holdouts of the Hedderman years suddenly had a name, Movement for Union Democracy (MUD); a glossy newsletter; and a sophisticated media strategy. The main item on the agenda was Hedderman's complaint against the second elections. The charges had already been heard by the local's elections committee, the same committee that had sustained the complaint against the first elections based on the discrepancy in the mailers. But the committee had found no merit in Hedderman's charges, and was set to report this to the executive board. But before the board could accept the report, a small group of angry people busted into the room shouting "*Sieg heil!*" at the top of their lungs. "Jane McAlevey! You stole the election! You stole $50,000 in dues money! You rigged it! You...." At the time this simply seemed absurd to me, an attempt to shut down the meeting and stop the board from voting to accept the committee's report. The whole thing eerily reminded me of my experience in Florida in 2000, when a small mob of Republican staffers busted into the recount room and disrupted the recount. Only now I was the one being naïve, just like Gore and his forces, believing that the process worked and the truth would prevail. As I said, I was off my game.

A few days later, however, the real purpose of the disruption became clear, when a slickly edited video of the whole incident was posted on YouTube, loaded with shots of angry "workers" screaming at me and complete with running type:

MOVEMENT FOR UNION DEMOCRACY MEMBERS CHARGE JANE MCALEVEY, EXECUTIVE DIRECTOR, SEIU LOCAL 1107, WITH ILLEGALLY OUSTING RANK-AND-FILE MEMBERS OF M.U.D.

AFTER THEY WON THEIR EXECUTIVE BOARD ELECTIONS FAIR AND SQUARE.

BECAUSE THEY DID NOT SHARE HER AGENDA OF "QUIET COMPLIANCE" INSTEAD OF AGGRESSIVE CONTRACT ENFORCEMENT AND GRIEVANCES.

Interestingly, there was never any effort to get any workers to watch this video, though it would have been simple enough to circulate flyers in the name of MUD throughout the union. The target audience was not workers but the local media, and on them the strategy worked brilliantly. Within a couple of weeks, in November, "Split in the SEIU" was headline news in Las Vegas.

The bit about how I favored "compliance" instead of "aggressive contract enforcement and grievances" was a particularly low blow, taking a complex issue and reducing it to a sound bite. We had put years of effort into trying to create an alternative to grievance-based unionism. The bosses had to be amused that our Wobbly-style direct-action approach to shop floor issues was being called quietly compliant.

It was right about this time that all the heavyweight political maneuvering surrounding Nevada's new role as an early presidential primary state kicked into high gear. As if things weren't already complex enough. And Andy Stern multiplied that complexity by some very large number when he led the national executive board to allow each local union to make its own endorsement from among the Democratic candidates. I argued as forcefully as I could that this would be a disaster for locals in key states, and it was. In Nevada, a swing state, the presidential campaigns were suddenly pressing for things like access to union rosters linking the names of SEIU members to their voter turnout lists. All of the campaigns were pulling nasty maneuvers. National candidates vying to replace Bush were lining up all kinds of state and local political figures. Had the national union officially endorsed a single candidate or made a binding decision to keep SEIU neutral nationwide, a local union leader pressed by local and state politicians representing national candidates could simply have said, "Sorry, hands tied by the national union." Instead, they were forced into the ring for a hard-knuckle bout of presidential politics, and that produced major internal schisms in SEIU locals in the key swing states of Iowa, New Hampshire and, of course, Nevada. The Clinton, Obama and Edwards campaigns couldn't have cared less about what impact their actions had on a local in any given state—all they cared about was winning the state's delegates. In Nevada, where in a very short time we had built the union into a powerful political player, the timing of these cutthroat races couldn't have been worse, locked as we were in a defensive battle with a rival union raiding from out of state.

Even within the very top echelon of the national SEIU there was division. Anna Burger, second only to Stern in the national hierarchy, was all Edwards all the time. I liked Edwards, but my impulse was toward Obama. I thought there was nothing special enough about any of the candidates that could trump breaking the race barrier in the White House. And I was super impressed by the campaign team Obama had put together. Publicly, Stern was leaning toward Edwards, though not nearly so outspokenly as Burger. Privately he told me that SEIU "needed some locals in important states to go for Obama in case he is the winner of the primary—so sure, Jane, go ahead."

No one around SEIU was seriously interested in Clinton, who had appointed Mark Penn, a notorious union buster, as her top campaign strategist. But the Democratic Party power structure in Nevada was going for Clinton big-time. Rory Reid was heading Clinton's Nevada campaign and putting heavy pressure on me, reminding me of all he had done for our nurses in the UHS fight and at the County Commission. Everything he said was true, but what he had done there was what I though any good politician should do: the right thing. And then there was Brian Greenspun, a Las Vegas media mogul who owned a TV station and several magazines and published one of the city's two newspapers, the *Las Vegas Sun*. And, as he told everyone who would listen, he had been Bill Clinton's college roommate, and he was fiercely intent on being recognized as one of the key players that would deliver Nevada's Democratic Convention delegates to Hillary Clinton.

With the old guard now suddenly appearing in the *Sun* as the "Movement for Union Democracy," I was hardly surprised when in November the Reid-Clinton team presented MUD members to the press to announce that Las Vegas nurses were actually for Hillary, but Jane McAlevey wouldn't "let the members make the decision." The *Sun* ran hard with this, reporting it not only as fact but as if it were the major news of the campaign.

Great. Now the birther-esque MUD crazies were getting wind in their sails from the CNA, Rory Reid, the newspaper, and the Clinton campaign. And the ugliness just escalated from there. For two straight months, our members in large numbers participated in forums and events with the actual presidential candidates. There was little question that we were trending toward Obama. In January, the local executive board voted nearly unanimously to back him, but magically the headlines in the *Sun* were all about a split union fighting over the endorsement. Remarkably, someone had allowed the *Sun* reporter to listen to our confidential executive board endorsement call. Since the reporter came from the paper that was cheerleading Clinton, I imagine that had we endorsed her, there would have been no mention of a split, but instead something like "In Total Unity, Nation's Largest Union's Nevada Chapter Backs Clinton."

In February 2008 the "window period" opened on our contracts at the three Vegas hospitals owned by Catholic Healthcare West. This time, though, it wasn't the boss but the CNA that was suddenly mounting a full-throttle campaign to get the union decertified. And the union they were targeting was the very same union that had won these workers contracts that were so good it had taken a year-long bare-knuckled labor war to bring the rest of the hospitals in the city up to that high standard.

When I say the CNA launched a full-throttle decert campaign, I am not exaggerating. Rose Ann DeMoro sent forty raiders to town, including her top national organizing staff and a bunch of California nurses. Never in all the victories our union had won in Nevada over the previous three years had we had those kind of resources. The total number of nurses at all the CHW hospitals in Las Vegas was roughly equal to the number we'd just organized at the huge Washoe Medical Center in Reno, and just ten of our people had run that campaign until the last few days, when we threw in absolutely everything we had, which brought our team up to thirty.

Not by any standard set by any union was there a problem with how the workers at these hospitals felt about their local. We had over 70 percent membership in those hospitals, in a right-to-work state, when the CNA launched its war against us. And by the way, I could walk into *any* CNA hospital in California on *any* day and easily find some nurses pissed off at their union, but that wouldn't make it right for me to launch a jihad against the CNA when the vast majority of nurses in the United States have no union at all. There are twenty-two right-to-work states where just about every hospital is unorganized.** Why did the CNA choose to raid a hospital where the RNs had great contracts and a great union instead of focusing their attention on nurses who had nothing?

Their campaign had all the features of a boss fight, relying on fear and distortions to divide the workers. They promised the nurses that they could win even better contracts than SEIU's if they jumped ship. They handed out thousands of copies of the CNA's best contract, from the CNA's San Francisco hospitals, and told the nurses over and over that they, too, could win those wages if they joined the CNA. This was ridiculous. The hospital market in San Francisco couldn't have been more different from the one in Las Vegas. There was a long history of unions in San Francisco, a liberal political power structure, and the list could go on and on. The CNA hadn't been able to match their own San Francisco contracts elsewhere in California. Hell, the CNA had hospitals in their union-friendly state where the nurses were making less than their counterparts in Vegas.

** Indiana joined this infamous roster in 2012—making it now twenty-three states.

The CNA's campaign talking points were lifted directly from MUD's YouTube video. (Or was it that the text in the MUD video had been taken from the CNA's talking points?) They always led with the line that Jane McAlevey was "soft on the bosses" or even "in bed with the bosses," and the evidence they provided, just as in the YouTube video, was that in the CHW hospitals we didn't file grievances.

Our local had deliberately developed a critique of the grievance-based model of job conflict resolution and had put enormous efforts into pioneering what we named the "Fast and Fair" alternative in the CHW hospitals that would move boss-worker disputes out of the grievance labyrinth and into the open, where they could be quickly resolved based on the collective input and power of the workers on the unit. Our fast and fair model was designed to give the workers an actual say not only in the resolution of on-the-job conflict but also in weeding out workers who were performing poorly or were simply lazy from those that had legitimate complaints against management. And this system was being applied equally to managers and workers. I have never seen a workplace, before or since, where a union had forced the boss to accept a system in which job-site conflicts were settled every two weeks by teams that were half management personnel and half workers, and where workers and management used the same system to hold each other account-able to the contract. We had been experimenting with the details of this for a full year and had been preparing to formalize it during the 2008 hospital-wide contract negotiations, when the CNA launched their decert blitzkrieg, arguing we were "in bed with the boss" because we weren't filing grievances. The system wasn't perfect in the experimental phase, but it was already working considerably better than a traditional grievance arbitration system.

Yet of everything we did in Las Vegas, this work was in a sense the most radical, as we were seriously attempting to develop a new model of unionism. Besides designing a more effective way of handling shop floor issues in these three hospitals, we were designing better workflow and work systems. Instead of functioning as alienated and powerless labor, nurses were pulling up a seat at the table to actually engage in reform-ing hospital practices—alongside other hospital workers in the CHW facilities. But there was no easy way to condense all of this work into a simple sound bite or flyer headline like "Jane McAlevey has never filed a grievance at a CHW hospital!" DeMoro was promising to file lots of grievances, a process that enmeshes the union in defending a handful of individual workers and essentially puts the decision-making power over worker issues into the hands of the boss.

All of this was piled on top of the CNA's usual elitist come-on, telling nurses they'd be better off without the service workers in tow. So much for leftist rhetoric. To make matters worse, the CHW corporate leadership in San Francisco had ordered their Las Vegas hospitals to give the forty CNA raiders full building access. Remember back to the earlier chapters in this book about UHS goons chasing me through hospitals and pinning me down in elevators, and hospital security men photographing workers who dared to approach the RV we had parked out front because we couldn't get in the hospital door? Well, CHW had told the CNA people to walk right in and stay a while, make themselves comfortable. CHW headquarters claimed they were obligated to do so because of an organizing accord they had signed with the CNA, but that was disingenuous: the accord they were referring to covered only California.

What was really going on, it seemed to me at the time, was that the CHW corporation had decided that it was not in their interest to have to deal with yet another militant union in Nevada when they already had to deal with Rose Ann DeMoro and Sal Rosselli in California. DeMoro and Rosselli were working well together in those days and CHW could deal with them as a sort of de facto team, but this Nevada local was a maverick that not even their own national union could rope in. What's more, our Nevada outfit was pushing hard for a new form of conflict resolution that seemed to take a lot of power out of the hands of management. To this day, I believe that Rod Davis, the local head of CHW whom we had engaged in the "Fast and Fair" pilot program, actually was committed to the vision we had launched, but not to the point where he would challenge his national corporate headquarters in defense of a union.

Just two weeks before the decert vote, the Department of Labor issued a letter that poured a can of kerosene on the open fire. The letter announced that the department had opened a *preliminary* investigation into Vicky Hedderman's complaints about the local's election proceedings. This was bizarre. The DOL typically only releases letters once charges have been ruled on. Our local's attorney, who had been doing labor law since he first started working with the United Farm Workers, thirty-five years before, had never heard of the department sending a letter announcing a preliminary investigation. Jennifer Bergschneider, the DOL functionary who had signed the letter, would later personally apologize to our lawyer, saying that she had no idea when she wrote the letter that our local was in a dispute with another union. Vicky Hedderman and Rose Ann DeMoro's immediately made thousands of copies and handed them to everyone at the CHW hospitals in Las Vegas in the critical hours before the election.

When the votes were finally counted, we had fought the CNA to a near draw. There were actually three check boxes on the ballot: SEIU, CNA, and "no union." In addition, there were challenges to some of the ballots that totaled a number greater than the thirteen-vote margin CNA had claimed. For us, this was a victory. Around the country, the SEIU had very rarely fought the CNA to a tie in a head-to-head vote. And because the nurses already had a union and the decert was not decisive, the nurses would remain in SEIU for a long and drawn out legal battle.

Our local's lawyer explained to us that the easiest way to handle the charges that had been filed over our internal elections would be to simply forestall their resolution until the next regularly scheduled elections made them moot. That way, no side gets to ultimately "win" the disputed election, and eventually more clearly recognized victors emerge from a new election everyone acknowledges as fair. He also explained that this is actually common, as complaints of one sort or another crop up in internal union elections with some degree of regularity. But even this way out of the morass was soon closed off by yet another self-interested deal. Not surprisingly, the self who was interested was Andy Stern.

Among the allegations concerning the elections listed in the Department of Labor letter, most were ridiculous but two were not completely bogus. They didn't involve any subversion of the democratic process of the union, and our lawyer was confident that we would beat them when given a chance (a chance we would never get), but Hedderman had her facts right. Our slate in the election had in fact run up a large printer's bill, still unpaid because the money that Stern had told me repeatedly to stop worrying about had never come. Even worse, one of the two donations that Stern had brokered from other locals turned out—and this was news to all of us—to be money that technically could not be used for elections. Not surprisingly, it was the donation from the politically unsympathetic leader, the Stern loyalist who was just following orders. He had raised it independently of dues, so substantively it was kosher, but he had then had a staff person manage the account on union time. It was a technicality, but enough to make it illegal. Thanks, Mr. Andy Stern. This was the only time in seven years in the SEIU I had taken his advice, and I got stuck with an unpaid bill and a check for illegal funds. But none of this was very important to Stern. What really mattered to him—and I mean *really* mattered—was that the man who had sent the illegal check wasn't just any old local leader, he was Dave Regan.

Stern was busy preparing for the 2008 SEIU convention, which would consolidate the national union's power. Stern was also, clearly, lining up the union against Sal Rosselli. The gloves had come off between those two. And Stern was running Regan for a brand new leadership post in the national outfit, executive vice president of something-or-other. And now, before Regan even made it to his first national convention in his new clothes, he had been busted for sending illegal money to the local election in Nevada. No one knew that it was Stern himself who had brokered the money or that it was he who had promised to get our printer's bill paid. With his showdown with Rosselli looming, Stern's people called our lawyer and ordered him to stop contesting the complaints.

That was the end for me. I had wanted out for over a year, but each time I had tried to quit I got played to stay for just one more fight. And now I had stayed so long that the only way out was to take the fall for Andy Stern.

I did my best to negotiate my departure from Nevada so as to leave the local in the hands of the best of the new leaders. I suggested that Stern could broker an agreement in which Vicky Hedderman and I would resign at the same time, and he did so. My hope was that this would finally break the hold of the old guard on the union. And the executive vice president, who according to the union's constitution would now be elevated to rank-and-file president, was Shauna Hamel.

No sooner was I gone than Stern turned around and did the opposite of what I felt he had committed to. He sent some national staff to Las

Vegas who immediately pushed aside Hamel and just about the whole generation of worker leaders and staff organizers who had won the victories of the past few years. I imagine that Stern's team cut a deal with the non-nurse faction of MUD in an effort to defeat the CNA. The national staffers then divided and conquered the MUD gang, with some of them taking deals for staff and leadership positions in Vegas and in the national union.[††] Then the national gang threw themselves into defeating the CNA in the next round of voting at the CHW hospitals. And they went about it by systematically trying to undo all of our most innovative work.

First they split the CHW hospital workers into two totally separate teams—nurses over here, everyone else over there. But if the SEIU is going to split the nurses off from everyone else, why not just bring in the CNA and give the nurses their own damn union? And these were the nurses who had just won contracts that set standards for the entire market by organizing together with everyone else. Next, without consulting a single elected worker leader in the CHW hospitals (there were seven), who for three years had led the effort to create a better, radical alternative and not filed a traditional grievance in favor of "Fast & Fair" problem solving, the national SEIU staff gathered up and filed dozens of grievances from workers. Then, just days after the grievances were filed, the lead DC staffer stood up in front of a room full of worker leaders during a bargaining caucus and announced, "You can stop recruiting more members, you guys are at over 70 percent. That's great, you are fine, you don't need any more members, stop worrying about growing your union." The least sophisticated worker leader could see that this person didn't understand the first thing about organizing in a right-to-work state. It was as if someone had let the air out of a balloon in that room.

After six months of this "campaign" and enormous expenditure of money and staff time from the national SEIU, the run-off vote at CHW ended in the exact same dead heat as the first election. Which meant the nurses continued to be in SEIU. In the meantime, the national team had taken a wrecking ball to the local union. None of the organizers or worker leaders who had been the core of that local had bought into the shrill criticisms of me, and they did not appreciate the national team's

---

†† In fact, the staff person responsible for screwing up the original election ballots was made chief of staff of the local.

strong-arm style after having participated in the hyperdemocratic union we had built together. Now all of those top organizers we had hired and developed were either forced out or reassigned to do-nothing jobs, or they simply quit in shock at what was taking place around them. Our militant new worker leaders were harassed, ignored, and essentially told they weren't in charge anymore.

While his team unraveled the Nevada local, Stern consolidated his hold on the national SEIU and moved it sharply to the right, away from the organizing that was supposed to have been what was new in New Labor and back into the corporatist model of top-down unionism, with members and political donations used as props for deals cut in private between corporate behemoths and the national union. Organizing, the systematic engagement of workers individually and collectively with a deliberate leadership development strategy, had been replaced by growth, Stern's new word for the focus of his leadership of SEIU. Appropriately enough, he borrowed it from the lexicon of Wall Street. And he meant it. Stern was no longer interested in organizing, which was costly, slow, messy, and hard to control from an office in Washington. He wanted to grow in almost exactly the same sense that CEOs want their corporations to grow.

This turnabout was the subject of intense debate during the year and a half leading up to the national SEIU convention in 2008. Progressive leaders of locals around the country began to talk with each other about the direction Stern was taking the union. In private one-on-ones and confidential conference calls, there were quiet conversations on strategy. We knew it would be a mistake to challenge Stern personally. He was powerful and popular. Nevertheless, the agenda he was pushing had aroused broad concern throughout the SEIU. By focusing on the issues rather than on the man, we thought we could modify the worst aspects of Stern's program in the short term, and lay the basis for a broader challenge in the long term. I could not help noticing that, in a movement dominated by men, most of those involved in this discussion were women.

Unfortunately, the moderate course they planned was preempted by a frontal assault on Stern's leadership by Sal Rosselli. Rosselli's challenge was the opposite of ours: loud, even bombastic, and geared to make the battle between Stern and himself the main issue. Rosselli presented himself as the progressive alternative to Stern, but in fact his campaign had the effect of short-circuiting rational discussion of the real issues, as personal acrimony crowded out substance. Rosselli didn't have a snowball's chance in hell of actually winning in a head-on collision with Stern. The national war between them did have an effect on Nevada in tangible ways—notably, Rosselli was courting DeMoro in the long buildup to the 2008 SEIU national convention. He wanted more cards in the hand he would play against Stern, and wanted to keep DeMoro. Rosselli and DeMoro had a long history of all-out war one moment, and truce a minute later. I knew that the reason our local's contracts with the three CHW hospitals in Nevada expired in 2008 was because Rosselli had convinced me that instead of aligning these contracts with the rest of the Las Vegas market, so that all the hospital workers in Vegas could stand shoulder to shoulder in bargaining, it would be preferable to align them with the CHW contracts his local had in California, so the Vegas local could confront the boss aligned with his much bigger Oakland-based local. But when the moment came, instead of resources and solidarity from Rosselli for CHW negotiations California sent Nevada forty union raiders from Rosselli's friends in the CNA.

So what about Rose Ann DeMoro? Twice I sent private emissaries to her, people who knew both of us well enough to have our mutual trust. They personally assured DeMoro that I was a principled and militant union leader building a real labor movement in Nevada, and that far from being in Andy Stern's pocket I was working to build opposition to his policies in the SEIU. The reports back from all essentially said that DeMoro needed to force Stern to make a deal with her and she thought she could advance that cause by putting an end to the successful run of nurse organizing in Nevada. The Nevada nurses were cannon fodder in this national war.

Rosselli's challenge to Stern at the 2008 convention fizzled. Not long after, Stern placed Rosselli's huge California local in trusteeship on corruption charges. This move was so heavy-handed, it took even the most cynical observers' breath away. It would have been one thing if Stern had followed through on this threat to trustee the comparatively small Nevada local. But trusteeing a local that encompassed the entire state of California, was headed by Sal Rosselli, and was actually not corrupt in any way as far as I am concerned was another thing entirely. Stern sent an occupying army of five hundred (yes, you read that right, 500) staff into California to literally seize the union. Rosselli, of course, didn't take this sitting down, and the resulting war between the two of them tore yet another great SEIU local to shreds. The stooge that Stern sent to California to run the whole dirty operation was none other than Dave Regan. That would be the same Dave Regan whose political fund Stern had tapped for a down payment on the money he had promised me for the union election in Nevada—the down payment that turned out to be technically illegal.

Rosselli was out of the SEIU local in California, but he still had a large base of loyal staff and workers who were not yet ready to accept defeat. Obviously, Stern's big worry would be that Rosselli would form a breakaway union that would ally with DeMoro and the CNA, an alliance that might be strong enough to raid SEIU nationwide. And Rosselli had potential access to the money to make it happen: financial backing from the many labor leaders whose toes Stern had stepped on. This, finally, was enough to send Stern to DeMoro looking for a deal. Stern and DeMoro then stunned the labor movement by announcing that SEIU was immediately giving all the nurses in Nevada who worked at CHW to the CNA, even though the CNA had been unable to get them in an open election.

So Stern and DeMoro set up an election to be held five days later, which could only be called a sham, with the understanding that SEIU wouldn't campaign against the CNA. For the NLRB in America in 2008 to sign off on a timeline like that, there had to be a deal between every power player involved. It meant the CEOs had agreed, the corporation had agreed, the leadership of the two unions had agreed—and forget whatever the nurses thought. The short timeline also forestalled the possibility of putting a third union on the ballot—my guess is, that option would have had real traction when the nurses realized the two unions were using them as bargaining chips. In fact, it forestalled any independent action by the nurses—exactly the kind of deal that DeMoro had criticized our national union for making, time and again. Union democracy only has meaning when it's working for you—and in this case, DeMoro was just as dirty as Stern.

In his ambition to grow beyond his home state, Rosselli careened from an alliance with Andy Stern to an alliance with Rose Ann DeMoro, and then DeMoro and Stern simply threw him under a bus. But the story isn't over yet. Who knows what will happen when DeMoro's deal with SEIU expires at the end of 2012? Will she realign with Rosselli? Or just use the threat of realigning with him to extract more deals from SEIU? In the meantime, Rosselli does indeed appear to have gained financial backing from the many trade unionists who would like to see SEIU toppled. And Rosselli's new National Union of Healthcare Workers has been winning elections. Most amazing to me is how much the takeover of Rosselli's union in California resembles the US operation in Afghanistan—it's an endless conflict that has wasted in excess of $100 million on one union's civil war—money that could have been used to fight the bosses at a time of despair for the working class.

The fact is, this story never ends. Each round of these brutal turf wars provokes a new one. Only the alliances change. Union strife is a life form that survives through a bizarre process of cell division and recombination, all the while feeding on itself. And labor truly is eating itself alive, in the sense that its turf wars have become so intense that there is very little organizing taking place at all. Anywhere. We've got turf wars and defensive fights, not a revitalized labor movement. Rose Ann DeMoro was handed the nurses in Nevada without having to organize them. All she had to do was engineer the shakedown. No boss fights, no systematic leader ID, no majority petitions, nothing.

The results of all of this can been seen most clearly at those three CHW hospitals in Las Vegas, where the new SEIU local won contracts that set a gold standard for the entire Las Vegas market; where the workers were working together to establish an alternative to the decrepit old grievance system and to create all-new work systems through worker-led initiatives; where a CIO-inspired goal of building one big union and then negotiating one big contract using big, representative bargaining had produced a hyper-democratic, wall-to-wall union, nurses and service workers marching together as one.

And today? When I wrote these words, in November of 2009, the nurses were working without a contract. Not only was the CNA unable to deliver the California-level contract they promised, they hadn't been able to deliver a contract at all after almost a year in charge. And the reason was obvious: At that point, the nurses told me, less than 15 percent of the 1,100 nurses in those hospitals were union members. CNA had only managed to hold on to a minority of them. Of course they didn't have a contract. They didn't have a union anymore. What employer is going to bargain with a union that represents 15 percent of its employees? CNA has never had to file an official report on their Nevada numbers, but the nurses who are still working in those hospitals today claim the percentage has never broken out of the twenties.

Two progressive unions doing radical work were destroyed—the UHW in California and the SEIU in Nevada. One story fits the narrative of some left labor factions; one does not. Both were modern tragedies in a labor movement that desperately needs the kind of militant, hyper-democratic unions we had built.

Afterword: San Francisco, February 2014

One of the most painful experiences of my life was the undoing of the militant, powerful, creative union I spent four years helping to build. Following my tradition, when I left Nevada I boarded an airplane, first to spend a month in Sweden catching up with family and then four months exploring Vietnam, Laos, Cambodia and Thailand. These long, unscheduled solo adventures to faraway places have always cleared my head, reset my dangerously bad sleep habits, and left me recharged and raring to go, ready for the next big battle. Not this time. Upon my return from Southeast Asia I learned that my test for the BRCA1 cancer gene had come back positive. And the first operation at Sloan Kettering to remove my ovaries and fallopian tubes—what we thought was preventative surgery—turned up early-stage ovarian cancer, the deadliest of female malignancies; the death rate is 95 percent. I was in and out of surgery for a year, and there were long periods when I was incapable of much movement at all.

I withdrew from just about everything. My doctors made it clear that I urgently needed to focus on my body. All through that year, and even into 2010, I had literally dozens, if not hundreds, of conversations that began just like this:

FRIEND: Wow, Jane, I heard all about the bad news, how are you feeling? When do you think you will be better?

ME: It's been hell, really devastating; I don't know how long it will take to really recover.

FRIEND: Aren't the doctors able to give you a prognosis and timeline?

JANE: Oh, you're asking about the cancer? They are cutting everything out. I thought you were asking about SEIU.

This book is the result of a year of being forced to lie down. And even though writing about the role of the organizer violates the organizers' creed, as long as I was laid up, writing my own story was the only way that I could tell this one.

The wonderful organizing team we had assembled in Las Vegas has been scattered. All of the good organizers who were still in Nevada with me at the end of our fight were forced out by the national union. Some are now winning campaigns for other unions, some have left unions (they say, for good), and several have left the country, for Australia, Ireland and Mexico. Hedderman immediately took a position with management, in human resources no less, at her old hospital. In 2010, Andy Stern left his top post at SEIU for other pursuits and Mary Kay Henry took his place.

In some limited ways this has been an improvement. Henry spent years as an organizer, and a good one. She is the first acknowledged lesbian to lead a big national union, which is a huge deal, given the culture wars within unions as well as outside them. And I think she actually likes workers. I know that sounds strange, but plenty of labor leaders don't really care for them. Henry can sit in a room full of them for hours on end and enjoy herself. On taking over the reins at SEIU, she set to work cleaning up the major mess Stern had created by his attempt to raid a decades-long ally, the hotel and restaurant workers union (UNITE-HERE). Henry put an end to this costly internal labor war; she hardly had a choice, for SEIU was losing the battle shop by shop and its image was getting badly bruised in the broader social change movement.

But Henry was Stern's loyal protégé for more than two decades, and she was deeply influenced by his philosophy, broad strategy, and tactics. Driving the morally and ethically bankrupt trusteeship of SEIU's second-largest local union, she has pushed the throttle full-thrust forward. Under her leadership, more than $140 million has been spent to date to keep Dave Regan's boot on United Healthcare Workers West, SEIU's California Local. That's not a typo. In the middle of the biggest economic crisis since the 1930s, with unemployment high, home mortgages being foreclosed everywhere, the dignity and savings of the working and middle classes being trashed, the largest labor union in the country devoted its most skilled organizers and more than $140 million to an internal turf war that has nothing to do with advancing the welfare of the embattled working class. While the Birthers and Tea Party were effectively mobilizing all across the nation to destroy health care–reform town halls, SEIU's health-care organizers were busy blowing up one of their best local unions.

Henry's support of Regan has been unswerving, and I believe that will forever shadow her positive achievements. Regan, a union staffer who rose to the top post of WOC, the West Virginia–Ohio-Kentucky local, and made national headlines when staff he had bused to a Labor Notes conference started fist fights with the forces of RoseAnn DeMoro, head of National Nurses United, has all but destroyed SEIU's reputation in California. It's hard for me to find anyone who has anything good to say about Dave Regan's rule over the California local, which leaves the field pretty clear for Sal Rosselli and his new rival union, the National Union of Healthcare Workers (NUHW).

Rosselli and NUHW have shifted between several unions to finance what appears to be endless war against SEIU. Meanwhile, DeMoro maintains a borderline-abusive relationship with Rosselli, alternately turning the spigot of resources on, then off, and then on again depending on her success or failure at what appears to me to be her great SEIU extortion game. Few people understand DeMoro is engaged in a semi-parasitic relationship with SEIU in their national corporate growth deals, making for what can appear to be semi-schizophrenia as she toggles between growing the California Nurses Association off of SEIU's deals while simultaneously attempting to kill her host organism.

While some of our most competent labor leaders perpetrate health care–union fratricide, the health-care system has been failing patients, communities, and workers and the Tea Party has emerged as the dominant voice in health-care policy making. Health-care advocates simply cannot challenge or change profit-driven health care as long as all the health-care unions are killing each other. Divided we fall, again.

SEIU has all but forsaken actual worker organizing in the health-care sector despite the fact that the union's gains in the years under discussion in this book were largest among health-care workers. The multistate assault by the right wing against the public sector has left SEIU fighting a primarily defensive action there. And in the third wing of the union, known most commonly as "Justice for Janitors" and officially as the Property Services sector, Henry forced out longtime organizer Steven Lerner because of his insistence that the union needed to take on the financial and banking industries. Hmm.

"Rudderless" would be my polite description for SEIU today. The union has all but jettisoned the two foundational concepts of unionism: building strong worksite-based worker organizations and collective bargaining. The SEIU we have now more closely resembles a foundation or Nader-type advocacy group than it does a union. Polling workers has replaced talking to them. And the two biggest programs of the union are not organizing and bargaining but immigration reform and fast-food workers' rights, campaigns that could just as easily be financed and orchestrated by a foundation. That said, the immigration fight is essential and should be a core mission for a union with millions of immigrant workers, but the fast-food campaign is off the mark.

Fast Food Forward, or FF15, the effort to boost wages for the lowest-paid food workers, is the only substantial effort for workers being attempted by the union of health-care and government employees and big-city security guards and janitors. But the motivation behind it, often described in SEIU meetings as *easier turf with angrier workers,* and the end goals, *narrative change* and *increasing the minimum wage,* aren't building real power for US labor. Once upon a time, unions—including SEIU—understood that their core mission was to build power: the kind of power that could challenge capital for a seat at the governing table; a level of power that could check the unrelenting stampede of "market forces" that has left hoofmark scars on 90 percent of the United States.

Narrative change and policy fights are precisely what foundations and foundation-funded efforts are good for. Marx got at least one thing right: the unique relationship between workers and the employer leads large numbers of ordinary people to more quickly understand who holds power over whom and how and why. When workers who are taking it in the neck see executive compensation skyrocket, they don't need much political education to figure out why they have no health care or retirement funds, why they haven't had a raise in how long, or why they've got some schmuck messing with their schedules so that they can't get their kids home from the school bus stop or to grandma's in time to get to their second job.

But blaming Stern and Henry for all of the ills of America's unions is ridiculous, even though it's fashionable in some corners. Long before they rose to leadership, most unions had surrendered their core function of helping unorganized workers form strong worksite organizations in favor of negotiating a decent contract for *current* union members, that is, those who vote in union elections. Or, worse, in favor of a steady paycheck for the union brass. But the reason SEIU is under a critical microscope in my book is precisely because it is one of only a handful of entities in this country capable of deciding to launch and then execute a big project. Its direction toward shallow advocacy instead of deep organizing is ass-backward. Abandoning collective bargaining and strong worksite organization hurts the entire movement, not just SEIU.

The Fast Food Forward campaign is targeting a sector of the workforce that simply doesn't have the power to actually change the standard of living for workers and the poor. This doesn't mean union strategy should ignore the lowest-wage workers or the poor (cf. this entire book). But every decision we make should be guided by an understanding of the power required to win, and every strategy we choose should reflect insights about how to build more power. When unions significantly raised living standards in this country, they did so by forming strong worksite organizations that included a mix of easily replaceable and not easily replaceable workers—and then striking until capital surrendered real gains.

So-called strikes in the fast food and Walmart campaigns aren't strikes just because someone spelled them *s-t-r-i-k-e-s*; they are press events and opportunities for liberals to wash away their guilt at this country's disgusting levels of inequality. They are excuses for editorials in the paper of record. They are places where liberal religious leaders take congregants to pray for poverty alleviation. Feel-good narrative change really is good, by the way, but it's utterly insufficient to actually rebalance wealth and power in America. A strike, to refresh our memory, means a majority of workers have walked off the job in a collective and defiant action and crippled production (cf. the Chicago teachers' strike of 2012). A press event is one or two workers who took jobs at an exploitative workplace for a few weeks and have walked off in coordination with other largely powerless groups who show up to cheer them on. Hooray. And the evidence for the success of these strategies? In November 2013, one year after the declaration of low-wage-retail "strikes" by America's big service-worker unions, the retail industry decided on an unprecedented move: they opened stores on Thanksgiving Day. More successes like that and soon we will repeal child labor laws.

With the fast-food campaign getting all the public attention, two key leaders in SEIU are fighting to emerge from the shadows with what they call bold new strategies—and, coincidentally, a path to replace Henry at some future convention. Regan, in occupied California, continues to experiment with perfecting worker-free unionization deals. He's polling the public for winnable words on important initiatives such as limiting executive pay in health-care corporations and demanding more transparency in health-care billing. He uses the favorable polling numbers he gathers as leverage for cutting union-growth deals with CEOs—but does nothing to actually achieve the initiatives. And now he's rolled this strategy into Oregon. It's a brilliant one—for his purposes—and it puts a devastating new spin on the concept of transactional labor politics.

Running in the same direction is David Rolf, another Stern protégé, who shares with Dave Regan a penchant for a mobilizing model that puts a handful of really smart staff in charge of thinking and acting "on behalf of" workers. Rolf is peddling something called the Innovation Center or the Incubation Center, depending on the document. The substance and language of the center's written materials are suspiciously like those of Stern's uninspiring book *A Country That Works*. For example, "Unfortunately, as it stands, collective bargaining is inaccessible to most of today's largely disaggregated and unorganized workforce and work stoppages are no longer a viable threat." And, "But even full-time permanent workers in traditional workplace settings have virtually no chance of successfully organizing and bargaining when their industries are virtually union-free and characterized by low wages, job insecurity, and universal opposition from employers." Rolf's strategy, like Stern's, is appealing to liberals, and for the same reason: liberals are never comfortable talking about power. "Ending poverty" sounds good, and so does "raising wages"—these are safe sound bites. They simply ignore the actual history of how any meaningful progress has been won in America or anywhere else—victories that required organization and power, ah, and another crucial ingredient: moral authority. Mandela didn't change South Africa by being nice, despite the whitewashing of his story after his death. Mandela embraced armed struggle: his analysis of the power context of apartheid demanded it. Each power analysis is contextual, and no, please don't interpret that statement as a suggestion that armed struggle will work here. In the American progressive movement, including unions, there's virtually no discussion of power, the power required per fight, or the relationship between power and strategy.

Meanwhile, the right wing has precision instruments drilling to tap advantages from the biggest problem facing today's unions: the lack of relationship between the union base—meaning the members—and union leaders. Two recent examples measure the success of this strategy: 38 percent of union households in Wisconsin voted to retain Scott Walker, who is pretty nearly the most antiworker, antiunion governor in the state's history, and Michigan voters defeated a measure that would have enshrined the right to collective bargaining in the state's constitution. Michigan governor Rick Snyder, emboldened by the defeat of the initiative, changed Michigan law to make this former bastion of unionization into a right-to-work state. Then, as if that weren't enough, Snyder upended the concept of democracy itself by trusteeing—er, removing and replacing—an elected mayor of Detroit, putting in his own appointee, whose primary mission is to use an African-American city as testing ground zero for the elimination of once sacred public-sector pensions. Power is so skewed today that bosses are reaching into the *past* earnings of workers and stealing them. All this, under a Black Democratic president who bailed out Detroit's CEOs but has failed to bail out the workers who made Motor City work. It's a good thing unions have figured out how to hold "our politicians" accountable.

Heading into 2014, leaders at SEIU and other unions were preoccupied by the Supreme Court. In 2013, the court accepted two cases critically important to what's left of today's unions. The first, called Mulhall (*UNITE HERE local 535 v. Martin Mulhall et al.*), would have examined the legality of the organizing-rights agreements that are often called neutrality deals and are discussed in detail in this book. Labor dodged the bullet, at least temporarily: in December 2013, the court dismissed the case on procedural grounds. But you can bet the farm that the Koch Brothers and their ilk are busy lining up another case to challenge neutrality agreements, and this one won't have procedural flaws.

The second case, *Harris v. Quinn*, could finish off what the 2010 election cycle did not, making "compulsory union dues" illegal across all states, for some workers. When you road-test worker-free union strategies against a national right-to-work scenario, you realize how empty and dangerous SEIU's growth without worksite organizing becomes. For several decades union dues in places like California and New York provided the only funds that came even remotely close to challenging corporations in state and national elections. *Harris v. Quinn*, or another case not far off, will wipe away "advantage blue-state union."

What should SEIU and the handful of other unions that still have the money and brains to mount large-scale efforts to win be doing? They should proceed as if this were entirely a right-to-work country again: they should return to the central task of building powerful worksite organizations. By doing so, they could defeat the intended outcome of a right-wing activist court decision or well-financed right-wing ballot initiatives. The reason collective bargaining is under attack is because it works. Not "worked"—*works*. This entire book describes the building of a strong worksite organization and the power of collective bargaining in the new millennium, accomplished by primarily female service workers in growth sectors of the economy, in a right-to-work state.

The only innovation unions need is a return to knowing how to run and win NLRB elections and how to organize and carry out real—not press-event—strikes. This involves teaching workers the craft of organizing, predicated on the wall-to-wall organization of actually existing big workplaces. Places like hospitals and schools, where we still can build solidarity that crosses the boundaries of class, race, ethnicity, and skill.

And on the crucial question of where should unions look for the additional power sources they need to mobilize against the employer in order to win? At SEIU, and at all the unions still trying to do this, they are looking in the wrong places. The house of labor continues to see the boss as its most important constituency in 2014. It has developed an apparatus called the corporate campaign to weaken employers' resistance until the union can force a deal that allows what the law has long failed to guarantee: a free and fair election—one where the workers can choose unionization. But these deals are often weak and have hurt unions more than helped them, with trade-offs that are too high. Even if they win a vote, workers seldom go on to form strong worksite-based unions, precisely because the rules of the these agreements prevent them from doing so. And though the Supreme Court missed banning such deals altogether for the 2014 cycle, they will be made illegal soon enough, because they have sometimes worked, and "sometimes" is intolerable to today's business class.

The "corporate campaign"—devised by mostly white, educated men— has put everyone but workers in command of the struggle against the employer. Instead, it relies on opposition researchers, lawyers, lawsuits, pension-fund investors, lobbyists, consumers, business partners, pollsters, communication specialists, student radicals, and other nonworker agents deploying "gotcha politics" and a pressure campaign. Workers themselves are not involved, nor do the campaigns rely on workers' knowledge or networks. They do not develop worker leadership. We have forgotten the crucial need to trust workers, to educate them about power and how it works, to educate them in the heat of a fight—which is where most adults learn best, when the stakes are high, not low. Identifying and developing organic worker leadership and teaching these leaders how to construct solidarity would give us back the most important weapons in the labor arsenal.

The fastest route to a powerful labor movement in this country is a straightforward one. Unions need to massively invest in their most important relationship, the one they have with workers, and forget the damn employers. And when more power is needed to win a tough fight— which is inevitable today—unions also need to sincerely invest in their next-most-important relationship, with the workers' families and broader community. How? By asking the workers in the workplace what issues matter to them outside it; by breaking down the walls between workplace and non-workplace issues, by teaching the workers themselves to chart their community connections; by enabling the workers to mobilize their own community.

I offer one method to achieve this, which I call whole-worker organizing. The cadre organizing of the 1930s and '40s, driven by radical political parties, was another model of skilled organizers teaching and mentoring organic leaders. And, by the way, genuine community-based organizations, not labor front groups, need to adopt similar methods of making hard assessments of their claims to leadership development by constantly running leaders in local elections. We win when we create hard assessments and accountability for our efforts, not when we declare a few workers walking out of their shift a "strike."

Every strategy available to our side relies upon sustaining high participation. And high participation is created and sustained only when workers feel deeply engaged in developing the plan to win. Everything that SEIU and other unions do should be measured against three hard tests: Is this strategy actually expanding our base of organic worker leaders? Is this strategy deepening working-class solidarity? And is this strategy building measureable power?

People serious about changing the conditions of inequality in this country have to stop focusing on wealth inequality and start focusing on the inequality of power. When we reset the balance of power by having some all-out, truly mass fights, we can reset the balance of wealth. Only then, and not until.

The good news is that our broadest global problem—saving the planet from climate change—can go hand in hand with rebuilding a bold movement using every strategy in this book. In my decades of talking to workers, and in my decade of bargaining contracts, I discovered that what workers want most are not wage increases but a safe place to live and to raise their families; meaningful work under respectful managers; control over their out-of-control lives. Male decision makers in our movement tend to drive the discussion toward wages, material gain, and putting more money in the hands of workers so workers can shop the capitalists out of this crisis they created. But this trajectory will quite simply burn the planet faster, and it ignores the real desires of most workers. Most workers want a quality-of-life standard more than a simple wage standard. Quality-of-life standards start with basic, inexpensive but profound things like predictable schedules, more time off, clean water and clean air. There is no innovation that will win these things that is more effective than worksite strategies and collective bargaining, by the workers themselves, on workplace issues tethered to broader community issues. That's how we'll win a just, healthy, and safe economy, and an environment guaranteed to support a good life, for all of us.

Acknowledgments

This book is the result of an unusual collaboration between two close comrades who share a common political vision but have very different skill sets. I have known Bob Ostertag for more than twenty-five years, and during that time we have confided in each other and sought each other's advice on every major political endeavor each of us has engaged in.

The story that is told here is mine, but the book you have in your hands is very much a team effort. It's my decade of fighting bosses (and often the labor movement leadership) that's narrated here, but it's our shared belief—no, stone-cold conviction, based on ten years of proof—that workers can win that is the basis of this book. I could not have completed this book without Bob.

In naming just a few of the many people I have to thank for a lifetime of learning, please hold them harmless for any of my mistakes—those are mine alone.

This story has many other "co-conspirators," some 15,000 workers in Nevada alone. Obviously, I cannot thank everyone who deserves to be thanked, and in mentioning just a few I risk slighting those whom I don't mention. So with sincere apologies in advance to those whose names are not included here but deserve to be, I would like to thank a number of beloved and invaluable labor mentors: Larry Fox, Jerry Brown, Merrilee Milstein (presente), Kirk Adams, and David Pickus; and also some of the brilliant staff that played key roles in my teams, without which none of this work would have succeeded: Myrna Melgar, John Stamm, Kate Andreas, Sara Rothstein, Morgan Levi, Jessica Foster, Maryanne Salm,

Chris Salm, Mark Stotik, Hillary Haycock, Jonah McGreevy, Kristin Warner and Cheryl Burch. Thanking worker leaders by name is almost absurd as a complete list would fill pages, but an even partial list would include Shauna Hamel, Bev Phares (presente), Cass McFerron, Nancy DeJovin, Barb Rusigno, Noreen Roberts, April Marsh, June Carter, Regi Werner, Michelle Clouthier, Rah Abdullah, Donna West, Aurora De La Cruz, Joan Wells, Becky Estrella, Fredo Serrano, Tim Kearny (presente), Mary Johnson, Rhonda Jackson-Pullens, Ms. Venita Smith (presente), Courtni Errington, Eric Taylor, Martin Gallagher, and Molly Gibbons. A heartfelt thanks to a few religious leaders who offered their extra special support and faith, Rev. Tommie Jackson, Rev. Winton Hill, Rev. Johnny Bush, Rev. Robert Perry, and Rev. Sam Mann. And while we are on the Rev. Sam Mann, who became one of my key allies while living in Kansas City, that entire effort would have been a failure without Lenny Zeskind and also Rhonda Perry of the Missouri Rural Crisis Center.

My understanding of the world and how to change it began long before the labor movement, and comes as much from these mentors as from the organizations I have been privileged to work for. I have always been very conscious of the role mentors play in developing one's abilities, and I would deliberately seek them out. Either I would spot them or they would spot me, but once I found them, I wouldn't let go until I had sat with them for days or weeks or years learning everything I could. In my student years, Jackie Kendall and Steve Max from the Midwest Academy were a huge influence on me. At Earth Island Institute, Dave Henson, Florence Gardner, and Josh Karliner inducted me into left environmentalism. At the Highlander Center, everyone helped me learn but in particular, John Gaventa who would repeat over and over, "Dogs get trained, Jane, people get educated," and Susan Williams, Paul de Leon, Richard Grossman (presente) and other mentors there. A very particular kind of appreciation goes to Anthony Thigpenn, who first showed me his power structure analysis model while we were on a delegation of progressive organizers touring Central Europe as the Velvet Revolution was happening, and we began to work together at the National Toxics Campaign. Gary Delgado invited me onto the board of the Applied Research Center, and it was invaluable to be on the board of a group focused on race as I was entering the class-focused movement. And in the foundation world, I was fortunate to work with Barbara Dudly,

Margie Fine, Harriet Barlow, Seth Borgos, Victor Quintana, and Andrea Kydd (presente), all of whom I had known first as funders who backed the organizations I worked for and then as colleagues in progressive philanthropy (and life!).

Attempting to add "author" to my skill set has been hard work, and like organizing, requires practice. With the same conviction with which I believe people can learn to be organizers, I have set out to overcome a life where school was a bore, where I learned little to nothing about writing (or math), and yet I have been encouraged by a new round of mentors who believe I can write, and have taught me that each good piece takes many drafts. These include Frances Piven, Jim Jasper, Don Hazen, and Betsy Reed. A big thanks to Andy Hsiao and Verso Books for making the decision to publish this—and for all the great help along the way. Thanks also to Jane Halsey for her excellent copyedit, Mark Martin for driving the process, Jessica Turner for helping to expand the readership, and Matt Gavan for making it all work on the page!

Bob and I would also would like to thank friends and comrades who read the first or second draft of the manuscript, or various parts of the manuscript, and offered invaluable advice that made the book better in every way: Kristin Warner, Jessica Forster, Janice Fine, Harriet Barlow, David Morris, Fran Piven, Patty Goodwin, Seth Borgos, Gary Delgado, Bill Kornblum, Myrna Melgar, Bill Fletcher, and Larry Fox.

Thank you also to the Blue Mountain Center for providing the time and space to focus on this book in a way that otherwise would not have been possible.

Index